Lee Hall

Plays: 1

Cooking With Elvis, Bollocks, Spoonface Steinberg, I Love You, Jimmy Spud, Wittgenstein on Tyne, Genie, Two's Company, Children of the Rain, Child of Snow

'What is it about Hall's work that makes it jump into the lives of strangers? . . . He is a funny writer who puts his characters into the dark and leaves them to find their way home. They do, but it's so scary that you have to laugh.' *Daily Telegraph*

Cooking With Elvis: 'The script is so sharp it could cut itself as it piles on the humour.' *Guardian*

'A work of wonderful bad taste – gut-wrenchingly funny, Hall is a real down-to-earth talent with an impressive ear for both the everyday and the fantastical.'
The Times

Spoonface Steinberg: 'a hard, sad beautiful play' *Sunday Times*

'funny, intense, poetic' *Daily Telegraph*

'it would be a stone heart that could not squeeze a tear, if not for Spoonface, then for ourselves . . .' *Guardian*

'This is a sharp, funny, bittersweet and convincing story, as the dying girl recalls her short life with razor-sharp observation. It confirms Hall as probably our best writer for radio.' *Evening Standard*

Lee Hall was born in Newcastle-upon-Tyne and studied English Literature at Cambridge University. His stage plays include *Cooking with Elvis*, *Bollocks*, *Wittgenstein on Tyne* and *Two's Company* (Live Theatre Newcastle), *Genie* (Paines Plough). He has written extensively for radio, including *I Love You, Jimmy Spud* (Sony Award 1996) and *Spoonface Steinberg*, which was filmed for BBC2 and performed as a play by Kathryn Hunter at the Ambassador's Theatre in January 2000. The award-winning *Child of Our Time* plays were produced by Radio 4 in 2000. He has also written adaptations of Brecht's *Mr Puntila and His Man Matti* (The Right Size/Almeida, Traverse and West End), *Mother Courage and Her Children* (Shared Experience), Goldoni's *A Servant to Two Masters* (RSC and Young Vic) and his adaptation of Herman Heijermans' *The Good Hope* premiered at the Royal National Theatre, London in autumn 2001. His screenplay for *Billy Elliott* was nominated for an Oscar.

LEE HALL

Plays: 1

Cooking With Elvis
Bollocks
Spoonface Steinberg
I Love You, Jimmy Spud
Wittgenstein on Tyne
Genie
Two's Company
Children of the Rain
Child of the Snow

introduced by the author

METHUEN CONTEMPORARY DRAMATISTS

Published by Methuen 2002

1 3 5 7 9 10 8 6 4 2

First published in 2002 by
Methuen Publishing Limited
215 Vauxhall Bridge Road,
London SW1V 1EJ

Introduction and collection copyright © Lee Hall 2002

Lee Hall has asserted his rights under the Copyright, Designs and
Patents Act, 1988, to be identified as the author of this work

Methuen Publishing Limited Reg. No. 3543167

A CIP catalogue record is available from the British Library

ISBN 0 413 77191 1

Typeset by SX Composing DTP, Rayleigh, Essex
Printed and bound in Great Britain by
Cox & Wyman Ltd, Reading, Berkshire

Contents

Lee Hall:
A Chronology

1992 *Bartleby* (adaptation from Hermann Melville) first performed at Dance City, Newcastle as part of Dance Umbrella season

1995 *I Love You, Jimmy Spud* first broadcast on Radio 4

1996 *Blood Sugar* broadcast on Radio 4

Adaptation of *Aunt Julia and the Scriptwriter* by Mario Vargas Llosa broadcast on Radio 4

Bollocks broadcast on Radio 4

January 1997 *Gristle, The Love Letters of Ragie Patel, The Sorrows of Sandra Saint* and *Spoonface Steinberg* broadcast on Radio 4

May 1997 *Wittgenstein on Tyne* first performed at Live Theatre, Newcastle

November 1997 *The Student Prince* broadcast on BBC1

December 1997 *Leonce and Lena* translated from Buchner premiered at The Gate Theatre, London

February 1998 *I Love You, Jimmy Spud* screenplay first read and *Bollocks* first performed at Live Theatre, Newcastle

June 1998 *Spoonface Steinberg* screened on BBC2

August 1998 *Mr Puntila and His Man Matti* (translated from Brecht) first performed by The Right Size opened at the Traverse Theatre before transferring to the West End

October 1998 *Cooking With Elvis* first performed at Live Theatre, Newcastle

March 1999 *Genie* first performed at Live Theatre, Newcastle as a co-production with Paines Plough

December 1999 *The Servant of Two Masters* (adapted from Goldoni) first performed by the Royal Shakespeare Company at Stratford before trasferring to the Young Vic

January 2000 *Spoonface Steinberg* first performed at the Ambassador's Theatre

2000 *Mother Courage and Her Children* (translation from Brecht) first performed by Shared Experience Theatre Company and played at The Ambassadors Theatre, London

June 2000 *Children of the Rain* broadcast on Radio 4 as part of the *Child of Our Time* series

Child of the Snow broadcast on Radio 4 as part of the *Child of Our Time* series

October 2000 *Billy Elliott* directed by Stephen Daldry opens in London

November 2000 *The Adventures of Pinocchio* (adapted from Collodi) first performed at the Lyric Theatre, Hammersmith

Two's Company performed at Live Theatre, Newcastle

November 2001 *Gabriel and me* directed by Udayan Prasad opens in London

The Good Hope (adaptation from Herman Heijermans) opened at the Royal National Theatre

Introduction

This is a strange anthology not least because many of these plays did not start out in the theatre. *Cooking with Elvis*, *Spoonface* and *Jimmy Spud* all started out on the radio, and the *Child of Our Time* plays have in fact never yet appeared on the stage. What connects them all is Live Theatre in Newcastle where each of these pieces was performed or recorded in some shape or form. Live Theatre sprung up in the early 1970s as part of the explosion of theatrical activity informed by the politics of the generation of 1968 which did so much to radically alter the nation's perceptions of theatre. The particular flavour of Live's work has always been to represent local working-class life to local working-class people. As an impressionable teenager, the plays of Tom Haddaway, CP Taylor, Phil Woods and many others helped me realise you did not have to look very far to find real dramatic material. The tone of these plays was important – they were rough, funny, melancholic, and heterodox enough to include songs and dances when necessary, but always with a political understanding that lurked not far beneath the surface. All were very obviously inspired by Joan Littlewood's Theatre Workshop amongst others. At the same time I was watching work by Potter, Bleasdale and Trevor Griffiths on TV and I would like to think my work, in its modest way, stylistically and thematically draws on this tradition.

The other thing that links most of these pieces is their obsession with childhood and I think in many ways this collection, which represents my first five years as a writer, was a working-through of many of the themes and contradictions about growing up in a Northern town whose heritage and industrial base was changing in front of my very eyes. A future under Thatcher was a dour prospect if you were from one of the industrial regions of the country. A yuppie was only something we had heard of on the telly. Anyone who has seen my film *Billy Elliot* will recognise the constellation of themes and relationships. So, as you might have guessed, although they aren't strictly autobiographical these plays are very much about my childhood and finding a voice for it.

Another connection between almost all of these plays was BBC Radio drama and in particular Kate Rowland, a producer who commissioned *Spoonface*, *Bollocks*, the *Child of Our Time* plays and the original pieces that *Cooking With Elvis* and *Jimmy Spud* were based upon. Her guidance and encouragement was invaluable to me during this formative time. Radio drama is bizarrely, an unfashionable medium with young dramatists. But I was interested in developing a broad and demotic voice that would speak to large numbers of people and radio presented an ideal forum for a writer finding their feet. While I was paying the rent I was allowed to play with form and explore things in a much more intimate and prolific way than a straightforward theatre writer. As you will see from the production notes I have been blessed with working with some very talented and sympathetic people again and again – both actors and production people. Although writing is inevitably a solitary exercise I have never done it completely alone or in isolation and I think it is important I acknowledge that here.

The tension in all these plays is my attempt to find a popular voice without, as an avid reader and viewer of plays, losing my natural interest in exploring the possibilities of the form. Most of these plays had their genesis in New York where I went to live when I was starting to write. I think being away from home focussed the mind on where I had come from, but also allowed me to absorb the influences of the theatre that was going on around me in an unselfconscious way. *Genie* bears the stamp of 90s New York performance theatre quite clearly, but I think although most of the pieces are in a recognisable form there is something that undercuts them, an awareness and a slight sending-up of the traditions from which they originate that was an attempt to integrate the various influences.

Cooking With Elvis started life as a radio play, *Blood Sugar*. As radio, it was considerably less smutty, without the Elvis/Dad figure. But as I had failed to deliver a new play for Live Theatre we decided to fill the gap by theatricalising one of my old radio plays. It was done in a matter of weeks and I stole many of the funniest lines from the cast in rehearsal and we managed to scrape together a show. It started off as the tiniest studio piece and graduated to playing 1500 seat theatres which was a strange journey as I see its tone as very intimate.

Bollocks started out life as an adaptation for Radio 3 of Ernst Toller's *Hinkemann*. The Toller estate then withdrew the rights for some reason so I radically updated the play. Radio 3 was rather offended by the title so it was broadcast as *Gristle* but I rejigged the play for a rehearsed reading at Live and a subsequent production at the RSC Fringe. Toller's political concerns, his interest in 'ordinary lives 'under extraordinary pressures and his interest in illness and disability both as a dramatic subject and a provocative metaphor all connected with my own preoccupations. I feel it is a clunky, awkward piece that might bear too much of the Toller model, but the point of the exercise was to explore a harsh and raw subject in a harsh and raw way.

Spoonface Steinberg came from a conversation I had with Andre Gregory, the doyen of New York theatre of the 1960s. Bizarrely I went on a weekend white water rafting with Mr Gregory who was a friend of my girlfriend in New York. He told me over a bowl of porridge about Martin Buber's books on Hasidism . I was immediately hooked. I read the Buber books and wrote the play in two days of almost automatic writing. It seemed a little provocative to send the BBC an hour-long monologue spoken by a seven-year-old, but Kate Rowland bravely followed the play to the letter in her production and it went out to some acclaim. The play is very much a comedy, a parody of the 'ill child' genre, but also deeply serious about the philosophical questions it asks, in a way that I hope is true to the Hasidic sense of play and wonder.

I Love You, Jimmy Spud was my first piece of professional writing. Originally a radio play it was then commissioned as a film. This version is one I wrote early on in the five year process of trying to get it made. I had three or four directors attatched, four or five producers and did about twenty drafts. In the end I was effectively fired and the script was rewritten by Udayan Prasad and filmed as *Gabriel and Me*. It was a typically botched job ruined by its total lack of humour. In my book, the piece works as a comedy or not at all and here you can glimpse what the film might have been. It was important to include a screenplay in this collection because I think the piece thematically makes sense of all the other plays. It was also the sample script which then allowed me to write the eight screenplays I was working on in parallel to the work in this volume. The first fruits of which, was *Billy Elliott*.

The shorter pieces were all performed at Live Theatre as part of communal projects where groups of writers worked together to create evenings of work. *Wittgenstein on Tyne* was written as part of a project *Twelve Tales of Tyneside* where twelve writers wrote about the history of Tyneside. I discovered Ludwig Wittgenstein had lodged in Newcastle during the war and worked as a hospital porter which seemed too good to ignore. Everything in the play is true. *Genie* was originally conceived as a piece for a small play festival in New York. I was writing it at the same time as I was working on *Jimmy Spud* and you will notice one scene is cannibalised from that piece. The Americans smelt the parodic elements of the New York avant-garde a mile off and refused to mount it, so it was first presented at Live Theatre by Paines Plough as part of *Black and White*, a season of new short plays. *Two's Company* was one of twelve monologues that all emerged from a strange karaoke evening of drama entitled *NE1*. The monologue is spoken by the master of ceremonies at the end of an evening of triumphantly bad Karaoke where both members of the audience and characters with songs and monologues have participated in the proceedings.

The last two pieces in this collection were my contribution to a radio series combining documentary and drama to explore the theme of childhood on the eve of the millenium. It included pieces about kids from Sierra Leone, Korea and Brazil. I have always been fascinated by the Sami and had a secret childhood fantasy of living out in the tundra so the chance to go anywhere I wanted to interview a child for *Child of Snow* was a fantastic opportunity to relive this fantasy. What I was most surprised about was the fact that the modernity of much of their lives was mixed with the ancient. And I think

Matti's story which was loosely based on Ole who I met way up in the artic circle seemed to embody many of the huge currents of our history all in this tiny and modest life.

It was always my intention to write a companion piece about a British child and their feelings about their place in the world. But I was increasingly frustrated as everybody I interviewed had a compelling and interesting story and so no one story was representative. What did amaze me about the children was their consistent ignorance about the world in general, their lack of knowledge about the bare facts, never mind the lives and living conditions of anyone outside their back yard. But conversely, combined with this lack of interest in world affairs, I also sensed a real indignation about injustice in general and a tangible concern about morality and being good. It was an impulse that was very striking for me, a some-what cynical and over-informed adult. So, *Children of the Rain* is a collage of my impressions of talking to kids about the world, in the form of a school test. Like everything else in this collection it tries to have its cake and eat it, to take the piss but also keep the seriousness of its message. And after my first five years as a writer that's as far has I have got in terms of a dramatic strategy.

Lee Hall
April, 2002

For Max Roberts and Kate Rowland

Cooking With Elvis

Cooking With Elvis was originally performed as the Radio 4 play *Blood Sugar* on 11 January 1995. The cast was as follows:

Grandma	Elizabeth Kelly
Mam	Charlie Hardwick
Jill	Sharon Percy
Billy	Trevor Fox

Director Kate Rowland

The stage play *Cooking With Elvis* was first performed at Live Theatre, Newcastle-upon-Tyne, on 14 October 1998. The same production opened at the Assembly Rooms, Edinburgh, on 6 August 1999. The cast was as follows:

Dad	Joe Caffrey
Stuart	Trevor Fox
Mam	Charlie Hardwick
Jill	Sharon Percy

Director Max Roberts
Designer Liz Cooke

Scene One

*Theatre in darkness. 'Thus Spake Zarathustra' by Strauss gets louder and louder. A match lights a gas hob which lights **Jill**'s face.*

Jill Scene One. The Prologue. I was standing there with a spatula when they said you were dead.

Lights up. **Jill** *is standing with a wok. She adds oil.*

There was some linguine and a jar full of capers and some nice marinaded olives and they were going on about tubes and intensive care and what a terrible shame it was et cetera. And then they brought in Mam and we went downstairs and all her mascara had run and she was moaning on and everything and I said she better hurry up or the pasta would be boiled to a glue. And then she started shaking and that, and I was in my apron, and then she told me, that in fact there'd been a miracle, and in fact you weren't dead and somehow you'd pulled through. And thought sod the linguine and started to cry.

She has been cooking furiously throughout the speech. She adds more ingredients. And towards the end of the speech she flambés the contents of the wok.

And there at that point something changed deep inside me. Something changed that was good. You see, in my whole life up until that point, in my whole life, I was the one who was always left out, I was the one stuck in my bedroom, I was the one nobody fancied, I was the one they always called fatty, I was the one with the hideous hairband, I was the one who couldn't stop burping, always in her shadow, always the one without a clue. But suddenly, in that special moment, everything became clear and I saw a reason, a purpose, a mission, like a beacon in the darkness, a guiding star in the night, and I just looked at them through the pain and the tears and the anguish and I said: 'Take me back to domestic science.'

She pours the contents of the wok into a pie crust, pops on the top and puts it in the oven.

And they did.

Sampled intro to 'Jailhouse Rock'. Lights snap out. A hand reaches into the room from the doorway and switches on the light. It is the living room and the lighting this time is 'late-night seduction' from a standard lamp. **Mam** *comes in dressed to kill (maybe herself) and* **Stuart** *comes in, in specs. He seems nervously out of his depth.*

Scene Two

Jill   Scene Two. The Living Room.

Stuart   Mind, you've got a lovely house.

Mam   Shh.

Stuart   What's that smell?

Mam   Watch where you're walking.

Stuart   Bloody hell. What's that?

Stuart *sees the tortoise and picks it up.*

Mam   That's Stanley. Do you fancy a drink?

Stuart   Cush.

Mam   I've got a dry white in the fridge.

Stuart   I beg your pardon?

Mam   Dry white.

Stuart   Haven't you got beer.

Mam   I might have some lager.

Stuart   I divvint like wine, me. Here, I thought these were banned.

Mam   It's only a tortoise.

Stuart I know. I thought there was a crisis on *Blue Peter*. Cheers. How much did you pay for this?

Mam I don't know. I got it from Safeway's.

Stuart My brother-in-law goes down to Dieppe, you know. He could save you thirty pee a can.

Mam Stuart. Why don't you put the tortoise down.

Stuart Pernod. Metaxax. The whack.

Mam You seem very interested in food and drink, Stuart.

Stuart What do you mean, like?

Mam Well, ever since we got in the taxi, it's all you've talked about.

Stuart Sorry. I tend to go on a bit. Especially about tarts. It's a professional interest. Cakes and stuff.

Mam You're a baker?

Stuart Not exactly. I'm a supervisor.

Mam Of bakers.

Stuart Of cakes. We make a load of stuff for Marks and Sparks.

Mam Really.

Stuart You know them Christmas puddings? We start making them in July. June sometimes.

Mam Don't they go off?

Stuart No. They're Christmas puddings. Aren't they?

Mam Why did you come here, Stuart?

Stuart Here?

Mam No. Tynemouth Priory.

Stuart I divvint knaa. For a drink and that.

Mam For a drink?

Stuart   Well, you know.

Mam   Do you think I'm attractive, Stuart?

Stuart   Well, you're very nice-looking. I suppose.

Mam   How old do you think I am, Stuart?

Stuart   I don't know. I'm terrible at ages, me.

Mam   Have a guess.

Stuart   I don't know. You seem very mature.

Mam   Mature!

Stuart   Sophisticated, I mean. Wey most lasses don't know their arse from their elbow. Where as you seem, you know, very knowledgeable.

Mam   Would you like another drink, Stuart?

Stuart   I'm OK with this one. I try and keep an interest in things myself, like. You know, expand me horizons.

Mam   What sort of horizons, Stuart?

Stuart   I don't know. Like them programmes about frogs and stuff.

Mam   Have you ever tried tantric sex?

Stuart   I beg your pardon?

Mam   It's like sexual yoga. You bond together and make love without moving. Sting does it for ten hours at a time.

Stuart   You'd be lucky to get ten minutes out of me.

Mam   I don't know.

Stuart   I get winded running for the bus. It was a joke.

Mam   Stuart. Do you think I'm attractive?

Stuart   Yes.

Mam   You know you have a lovely physique, Stuart.

Stuart   Have I?

Mam   You have the body of an athlete. Do you train?

Stuart   I like to have a knock around every so often.

Mam   You know, Stuart, you really turn me on.

Stuart   Thanks very much.

Stuart *stares at* **Mam**. *Knocks back his drink and lunges to kiss her.*

Mam   What you doing?

Stuart   I don't know. I thought I'd give you a kiss.

Mam   Stand over there.

Stuart   Eh?

Mam   I want to look at you.

Stuart   Go on then.

Mam   Take your shirt off, Stuart.

Stuart   What?

Mam   Take it off. Now.

Stuart   Like this?

Mam   Over there. I want to see all of you, Stuart.

Stuart   I feel embarrassed.

Mam   Believe me, Stuart. You have nothing to be embarrassed about. The trousers.

Stuart   Are you sure about this?

Mam   For Christ's sake just shut up for five minutes, Stuart. I want you to touch yourself.

Stuart   What do you mean?

Mam   I want you to caress yourself, Stuart.

Stuart   What do you mean, like? Have a wank?

Mam   For God's sake, just take off your Y-fronts, will you.

Stuart   All right. Calm down.

Stuart *hesitates.*

Mam   Now!

Stuart *gets them halfway down, baring his arse to the audience, when there is a banging at the door.* **Jill** *comes in.*

Stuart   Fucking hell.

Jill   Mam, he's doing it again.

Mam   Go away, darling.

Jill   Mam. He's having a fit.

Stuart   Who the hell are you?

Jill   I'm the daughter.

Stuart   But you must be fifteen!

Jill *wheels in* **Dad**. *He is having a fit.*

Mam   Jesus Christ, Jill. Can't you sort him out for yourself?

Jill   Mam. He's your husband.

Stuart   Frigging hell.

Mam   Watch your language. Did you give him his medicine?

Jill   Of course I gave him his medicine.

Stuart   What's the matter with him?

Jill   What's it look like. He's paralysed, you stupid idiot.

Stuart   Hey, don't call me a stupid idiot.

Mam   Shut it, you.

Jill   He gets these fits sometimes, there's nothing we can do about it.

Stuart Maybe we should call an ambulance.

Jill Look, just help to get him sitting up.

Mam *is pouring herself another drink.*

Jill Mam. What are you doing?

Mam Getting another drink. What does it look like?

Jill Put that down at once. Please help me, Mam. Look at him.

Stuart Look. Here.

Stuart *tries to move* **Dad** *but as he does so* **Dad** *pisses on* **Stuart** *and* **Dad** *falls to the floor.*

Jill What are you doing?

Stuart He's pissed himself.

Jill You've dropped him.

Stuart Oh no.

Jill Oh Christ, man. It's all right, Dad.

Stuart Look, it's all over iz.

Jill Well, it's a good job you're not wearing any clothes then.

Mam This is bloody typical. You haven't got any consideration, have you?

Jill It's not my fault he's having a fit.

Stuart *struggles with* **Dad**.

Stuart How long has he been like this?

Jill Two years. He had an accident.

Stuart You never said anything to me about a crippled husband.

Mam You never asked, sweetheart.

Jill   He can't speak or anything. We think he's a bit depressed.

Stuart   I'm not surprised.

Mam   He's not depressed, Jilly. It's that bloody medication.

Stuart   I think he's nodding off now.

Mam   You just did this to embarrass me. Didn't you?

Jill   Of course I didn't.

Mam   You're perverse. You know that.

Jill   Mam. I am not perverse.

Mam   Just because you're jealous.

Jill   Jealous. Of him.

Stuart   What's wrong with me, like?

Mam   Nobody's asking your opinion. It's pathological this, Jill. Every bloody time I try and enjoy myself. You're a fucking embarrassment.

Stuart   Look, it's not embarrassing. Not really.

Mam   Of course it's embarrassing.

Stuart   No, honest. This sort of thing probably happens every day.

Mam   Don't be ridiculous.

Jill   I think you should put some pants on.

Stuart   There's nothing to be ashamed about.

Mam   Who said I'm ashamed? You're the one standing about covered in piss.

Jill   Mam, he's trying to be nice.

Stuart   It's all right. I think she's just had too much to drink.

Mam   You cheeky bastard.

Stuart   I was only saying.

Jill   I think you'd better go.

Stuart   Well, it's very nice to meet you both.

Mam   Get out will you. And mind that bloody tortoise.

Stuart *picks up his clothes and leaves sheepishly.* **Jill** *stares at* **Mam** *who is pouring another glass.*

Mam   What are you looking at?

Blackout.

Scene Three

Jill   Scene Three. Breakfast. I am not fat.

Mam   I'm not saying you're fat. All I said was you should watch those chocolate puddings.

Jill   Shut up, will you. There's nothing wrong with chocolate puddings.

Mam   You'll end up looking like a chocolate pudding if you're not careful. I've got nothing against chocolate puddings per se. It's just not right eating them for breakfast. Have you any idea what's in a chocolate pudding?

Jill   Three hundred and fifty calories.

Mam   Three hundred and fifty-eight calories, darling.

Jill   What were you doing last night?

Mam   It's your funeral. And don't change the subject.

Jill   Who was that man?

Mam   That was not a man, darling. That was Stuart.

Jill   Jesus Christ.

Mam   Don't Jesus Christ me, young lady. Didn't you like him?

Jill   Well, he wasn't exactly Mr Intellectual.

Mam   He was quite good-looking.

Jill   Mam, he was a complete divvy.

Mam   You don't understand anything, do you. I thought he was quite sensitive considering.

Jill   Considering you made him strip off and Dad pissed all over him.

Mam   Don't start blaming me for your father's bodily functions.

Jill   Mam. I don't see why you have to keep bringing them back.

Mam   Where else am I going to go? I've got you and your dad to think of.

Jill   Mam, can't you do an evening class or something?

Mam   Listen, Jill. I am thirty-eight years of age and my life isn't going to stop just because your dad's a vegetable.

Jill   Mam. Dad is not a vegetable. He says things.

Mam   Jill. He does not say things.

Jill   He understands. He understands everything.

Mam   Jill. You have got to stop denying the facts, darling. Dad is a cabbage and that's that. End of story.

Jill   But Mam, what'll people think?

Mam   What do you mean, what will people think?

Jill   The other week someone at school saw you getting off with Helen Storey's brother.

Mam   What were they doing down the Bigg Market?

Jill   Mam, he only just went to university.

Mam Jill. He told me he was twenty-seven.

Jill Mam. It's just not natural.

Mam What's natural. Sitting in your bedroom stuffing barrel-loads of custard creams down your neck till you blow up like a balloon.

Jill Mam. I am not a balloon.

Mam You want to look at yourself in the mirror, young lady.

Jill Mam. You're not supposed to behave like this. You're an English teacher.

Mam What's that got to do with anything?

Jill It's ridiculous. Going round like one of Pan's People.

Mam I do not look like one of Pan's People. Anyway, just because I'm an English teacher does not mean I have to lock myself up like Mother Teresa.

Jill Mam. Mother Teresa is dead.

Mam It's been two years, Jill. What do you expect me to do. I'm in the prime of life, Jilly.

Jill You are not in the prime of life, Mam. Anyway, there's no need to be picking fellas up. There are other things you can do.

Mam I suppose you'd have me down the whist drive with Auntie Irene.

Jill Mam. There are other ways of achieving satisfaction you know.

Mam I don't know why I bother listening to you.

Jill Mam. You could masturbate.

Mam I don't believe I'm hearing this.

Jill It's perfectly natural.

Mam   Listen, if you think I'm going to sit round here wanking my fingers to the bone for your benefit you've got another thing coming.

Jill   It's not for my benefit. It was just a suggestion. So you wouldn't have to go round like a dog's dinner.

Mam   At least I try to look attractive.

Jill   Who are you trying to impress, like? The cake man?

Mam   You're jealous, aren't you. That's what's going on here.

Jill   Mam. I am not getting jealous. All I'm saying is you won't admit to the fact that you're getting old.

Mam   I am not getting old. I think I look rather glamorous.

Jill   You do look glamorous. You just don't look like a mam. Have you ever thought of him stuck in his chair?

Mam   All I ever do is think about him stuck in his bloody chair.

Jill   Mam. That man was virtually naked.

Mam   The trouble is I treat you too much like an adult and you have no real understanding.

Jill   Mam, I do understand.

Mam   No you don't, lover. How could you. Look, just leave me alone to my life and I'll leave you alone to your cooking.

Jill   Does that mean I can have the birthday party?

Mam   I don't think that's a good idea.

Jill   It might stimulate him.

Mam   It won't stimulate him.

Jill   It might jolt his memory.

Mam   Please, darling.

Jill   Just because he's a vegetable doesn't mean he can't have a birthday party.

Mam   OK, please your Bessie. But for God's sake, no chocolate puddings.

Blackout.

Scene Four

Jill *lights a match and then the thirty-nine candles on the huge birthday cake, which lights her up. Dad is next to her but in darkness.*

Jill   Scene Four. Birthday Preparations. Sometimes I think about why we are here. If there's a purpose, to what it all means in the long-term. I mean it's weird, on the one hand, that some people are like beautiful and happy and all that, like Cherie Blair or that bloke off the telly. And then there are some people that are fat or crippled or just miserable like Mam. And I wonder why is it some people get all this misery and suffering and others are just happy all the time. But then probably Cherie Blair isn't all that happy underneath and the fella on the telly is probably on drugs or sleeps with children and that. So maybe nobody's happy – not fundamentally – not deep down. Maybe everybody has a longing – a longing things were different – a longing that people'd get better, longing that she'd shut up, or just longing for a nice piece of pie, or a rhubarb crumble, or a tandooried mackerel or something. Longing for something to fill you up. And maybe it'll be a torte, Dad, or a cabbage or a slice of quiche. It might be something continental or something from the Pacific rim; a steak-and-kidney pudding or just one of them things from Marks and Spencer's. But one day it'll wake you up, Dad. Like a resurrection, and you'll jump up, shake your hips again, and you'll kiss Mam and hold me, and we'll all be back together again.

There is a murmur from **Dad**. *'E . . . e . . . e . . .'*

Dad?

Another murmur. 'E . . . e . . . e.'

What was that, Dad. What were you trying to say?

Murmur. 'E . . .'

What was it, Dad? Elvis?

The lights go up fully and we see **Dad** *is dressed in his Elvis costume.* **Jill** *places a paper crown on his head from a cracker and blows a twizzle thing.*

Scene Five

Jill   Scene Five. The Party. Happy birthday. Come on, Mam.

Mam   Happy birthday. For God's sake take that hat of him.

Jill   It's his birthday.

Mam   It's macabre.

Jill   No it isn't.

Mam   For God's sake, Jilly.

Jill   For once in your life try to have a meal without complaining.

Mam   I just don't think it's very appropriate to dress him like this any more.

Jill   It's completely appropriate. It's like Elvis the King.

Mam   Jill, your dad is crippled.

Jill   But that's what he likes, Elvis Presley.

Mam   He doesn't like Elvis Presley. He doesn't like anything. What on earth is this, Jilly?

Jill   Chitterlings.

Mam   And what are chitterlings, darling?

Jill   Pigs' intestines.

Mam   For God's sake.

Jill   They're nice, Mam. It's what Elvis ate. This is a gumbo and this is a poke salad.

Mam   This is bloody ridiculous. Your dad doesn't want chitterlings or poke salad. He can barely even chew.

Jill   Well, I can liquidise it.

Mam   I'll bloody well liquidise you in a minute, Jilly. I want you to stop cooking these meals.

Jill   What are you on about?

Mam   All this weight you're putting on. Look at you, you're becoming obese.

Jill   Just because you never eat anything doesn't mean I'm becoming obese. Anyway, it's better than being an alcoholic.

Mam   Jilly, I am not an alcoholic.

Mam *takes a drink of wine.*

Jill   You drink all the time.

Mam   Don't be so stupid.

Jill   You want to watch it or you'll rot your liver. Look, you're doing it again.

Mam   Jill, it's the one bit of relaxation I get in this house. Anyway, it wouldn't surprise me if I had become an alcoholic living with him.

Jill   What's that supposed to mean?

Mam   You know quite nicely, Jill.

Jill   Are you referring to Dad?

Mam   I think we should just have a nice meal and then put him in his room.

Jill   I don't know what you are referring to, Mam?

Mam   Just forget it. It's his birthday.

Jill   At least he was nice to me. At least he wasn't pissed all the time.

Mam   Shut it or I'll clip you.

Jill   See, that's all you can think of, isn't it. Resorting to physical violence. I wish it was you who'd had the accident.

Mam   Jill, you have no idea what you are talking about. You seem to forget what I had to put up with with him. You seem to forget certain black eyes, certain trips to the RVI.

Jill   You probably deserved it.

Mam   Don't you dare talk to me like that.

Jill   I think you wanted him to be a disabled.

Mam   Are you out of your mind, Jill? Do you really think I want to be saddled with this for the rest of my life? Do you really think I'm enjoying myself? Jesus Christ.

Jill   Well, you seem to have plenty fun with your boyfriends.

Mam   Jill, I don't have any fun with my boyfriends.

Jill   That's ridiculous.

Mam   Look, all I want is some adult company once in a while.

Jill   You've got me.

Mam   Jill, you are a child.

Jill   No I'm not.

Mam   Gillian, you are a fat child. You should lose some weight and get yourself out from under my feet.

Jill   Mam, I'm not under your feet. I do everything. The cleaning. I do all the cooking, Mam.

Mam   I don't want your bloody cooking. Look, I'm just worried about you, that's all.

Jill   Why do you hate me, Mam?

Mam   I don't hate you. I don't hate him. I don't hate anyone. I hate myself. I'm going upstairs.

Jill   But you haven't eaten anything.

Mam   I've had quite sufficient, thank you very much.

Jill   Mam, it took ages.

Mam   I've told you, Gillian.

Jill   But Mam.

Mam   That's enough.

Mam *leaves.* **Jill** *starts to feed* **Dad**. *The gumbo dribbles down his chin.*

Jill   Great birthday party this has been.

Jill *kisses him.*

Lighting change so only the door is lit. **Dad** *is in darkness.*

Scene Six

Spot up on **Dad**. *He gets up and sings 'Burning Love'.*

Dad   'Oh, oh, oh. I feel my temperature rising.'

This is 'pissy' Elvis. It is like a bad club act. Perhaps there is taped applause at the end of the number. **Dad** *sits back in his chair and adopts his 'vegetable' position.* **Jill** *wheels him off.*

Scene Seven

Jill   Scene Seven. Some Days Later.

Jill *is sitting with a cookery book. The door opens.* **Stuart** *comes in with* **Mam**.

Mam   I'm glad you turned up. For a minute I didn't think you were going to show.

Stuart   Sorry. I had a bit of a problem with the Bakewell tarts.

Mam   You remember Gillian, don't you.

Stuart   Hiya.

Jill   Hello.

Mam   Jill was just off to do her homework.

Jill   No, I wasn't.

Mam   Yes you were, darling.

Jill *glares at* **Mam**, *then harrumphs out – giving them a hacky look.*

Mam   So, how are you?

Stuart   Well, I've been a bit busy, like. We've got a new line of lemon slices, so mostly I've been working nights.

Mam   Look, I just wanted to say that, well, I'm sorry, you know, about last time.

Stuart   Oh, there's no need to apologise.

Mam   I was just a little emotional.

Stuart   Really, it was nothing. I'm used to that sort of thing.

Mam   Really?

Stuart   Oh, yes. Epilepsy, that sort of thing. I've got a first-aid certificate as part of the training.

Mam   Well, you were very good about it.

Stuart   Divvint worry about it. I mean, I'm sorry about your husband being a cabbage and everything. You should have telt is.

Mam   It's not the kind of thing you like to talk about.

Stuart   Oh, it doesn't bother me. Is he here?

Mam   He's in the back. We had it built on with the insurance.

Stuart   Look. I brought you this.

Stuart *produces a small box*.

Mam   You shouldn't have. What is it?

Stuart   It's nothing really. Go on, open it.

Mam   Oh. Lovely. A cake.

Stuart   It's only a Victoria sponge.

Mam   Thanks anyway.

Stuart   It's the most popular line we do.

Mam   Really.

Stuart   Would you like to try some?

Mam   Maybe later. I'm watching my weight.

Stuart   I don't know why. You look fine to me.

Mam   That's because I watch my weight. Do you fancy a drink or something?

Stuart   I dunno. I suppose so.

Mam   Whisky all right?

Enter **Jill**.

Jill   Are you drinking already?

Mam   I thought you were doing your homework.

Jill   I'm finished.

Mam   You can't possibly be finished. You were only gone three minutes.

Jill   You can look at it if you want.

Mam   What about your project?

Jill   I can't do any more until I get the books I need.

Mam   She's doing a project. On food.

Jill   Gastronomy actually.

Mam   She's obsessed with food.

Jill   I am not obsessed.

Stuart   Well, I like a bit of food myself.

Jill   The project is on the philosophy of cooking.

Stuart   Philosophy.

Jill   Did you know in the eighteenth century people thought that meat would taste better if you tortured the animals before they were eaten?

Mam   Here's your Scotch.

Jill   They used to whip pigs to death with knotted ropes. And stamp on chickens.

Stuart   And they teach you that at school.

Jill   What?

Stuart   Chicken abuse.

Jill   No. You pick the subject yourself.

Stuart   I hated school, me.

Jill   Didn't you need GCSEs to be a supervisor?

Stuart   No, me uncle Harry sorted it out for me. I was crap at everything except games.

Mam   Stuart. I think it would be nice to go out and have a drink. Don't you think?

Stuart   I'm all right here. Honest.

Jill   He hasn't even finished his drink yet.

Mam   I'll just go and get smartened up and we'll leave you to it, dear. I'll not be a minute.

Jill *glowers at* **Mam** *as she goes out.*

Jill   Mam's a teacher, you know.

Stuart   A teacher. I thought she worked somewhere part-time.

Jill   That's right, a school.

Stuart   She's not like a normal teacher.

Jill   Perhaps you haven't met many normal teachers.

Stuart   I mean, if there'd been more teachers like your mam at our school I might have paid more interest.

Jill   So you didn't stay on, I take it.

Stuart   There wasn't much point. Anyway, I don't think exams can tell you much. There's some managers at our place with degrees from university and they're as thick as pig shit.

Jill   Mam went to university.

Stuart   Well, I'm not saying everyone's as thick as pig shit.

Jill   Do you think she's good-looking?

Stuart   Who, your mam?

Jill   Yeah.

Stuart   She's a very attractive woman. For her age.

Jill   She's an alcoholic, you know.

Stuart   What do you mean?

Jill   And an anorexic.

Stuart   A what?

Jill   You know. Throws her food up and that.

Stuart   You'd never think to look at her.

Jill   So you don't think it's weird or anything.

Stuart   How do you mean?

Jill   Coming round here when Dad's a quadriplegic with head trauma.

Stuart   Well, it's quite weird.

Jill   So why have you come?

Stuart   I don't know. I wasn't going to. But your mam persuaded iz.

Jill   Maybe you haven't got much self-esteem.

Stuart   So your dad. Is he totally crippled?

Jill   Virtually. Though he does get erections.

Stuart   How do you know?

Jill   You can see them in his trousers. He gets them all the time. It got so embarrassing we stopped taking him into Safeway's.

Stuart   He got an erection in Safeway's.

Jill   I think he fancied the woman on Fruit and Veg.

Stuart   But how does he . . . you know . . . ?

Jill   What?

Stuart   Relieve himself?

Jill   He can't, can he. He's a cripple.

Stuart   What a shame.

Pause.

Jill   Stuart. Do you masturbate?

Stuart   I beg your pardon.

Jill   How often do you masturbate?

Stuart   I don't know. I've never kept count.

Jill   Apparently, the average British man masturbates four times a day.

Stuart   Well, I've never done it that much.

Jill   I thought you'd be at it all the time. Being a single man and everything.

Stuart   Look, this isn't really something I want to get into. Although I once caught a fella messing round in the almond slices.

Jill   What happened?

Stuart   He got promoted.

Jill   After masturbating in the almond slices.

Stuart   Well, it's not the type of thing you want getting out. We just kept him away from the batter.

Jill   So you're not married then?

Stuart   Me? No. I live with me mam, but she's moving into sheltered accommodation.

Jill   You want to be careful. Mam'll have you moving in here.

Stuart   What, with your dad and everything.

Jill   I told you she's mental.

Mam *comes back.* **Stuart** *looks worried.*

Mam   Well, I see you two are getting on like a house on fire.

Jill   We were just talking about my project.

Mam   Well, that's enough to put anybody off.

Scene Eight

Jill   Scene Eight. Elvis the Pelvis.

Spot comes up on **Dad**. *Glitterball*. **Dad** *sings*.

Dad   You know, it ain't easy being King. I mean, things can sure get lonesome down here in old Graceland, there's all the pills I have to take, and all the records I have to do, and there's Pricilla going on and on, Jeez that girl's as uptight as a polecat's arse. Yes, sir. It sure can get lonesome. But say it's the afternoon, and I've been hard at it with my kung fu, or maybe I've been asleep, or maybe I've been lying down or maybe I'm just a bit blue. All I have to do is call Hamburger Joe. I just call him up and I say – Hamburger Joe, I say, boy, you better fix me some burgers and you better be a-gittin them quick. And before you can holler Poke Salad Annie that boy is outta that door and he's a-gittin me my burgers. Then they give me some pills or a little injection and they sit me up ready for the burgers. And then in come the burgers on the burger tray. Then first I take a burger and some dill pickle and then I eat them and then I have a Coke. Then I get another burger and I eat it and have a Coke. Then I eat another burger and some corn relish and then I have me a Doctor Pepper, and then I eat the mash potato and then I have a burger and then I have a Coke. Then sometimes I pass out. And then sometimes I have ice cream. It ain't always easy. But, I tell ya, it sure beats working for a living. Yes, suree.

Dad *gets back into his chair. A lighting change.* **Mam** *is beside him, a glass of Scotch in her hand.*

Scene Nine

Mam   Look, all I want you to know, Davey, is that I don't love him. I know we've . . . you know . . . had sex . . . a few times, but you understand that, don't you. I mean, I'm still a young woman, Davey, I still have needs, and I say we've

had sex, but I mean he's just a young lad, Davey, he might
go like the clappers but it's not what we had, Davey. I
mean, I've never even sucked him off, except that once
when we were watching *Neighbours*, but all I'm saying,
Davey, it's just a way for me to stop losing those feelings for
you. I mean, you wouldn't just want me to be barren, would
you, Davey? You don't want me to become sour. But
sometimes I need it, Davey, to just be held, so I forget, you
know, just so I can remember what it's like, Davey. I look at
us, and we're what? Thirty-eight years of age. What
happened? I know we didn't always see eye to eye. But who
would have expected this when you used to hold me so tight
I could burst, when we had all those plans, Davey, of
growing old together, of fixing things up, of being in love,
Davey. So many things. What happened? Sometimes I just
feel alone. You know, I'm still a young woman, Davey. I still
want to laugh till it hurts and drink till I'm stupid and fuck
till I'm numb and cry till I'm happy again, Davey, and be
alive, I want to be alive.

Pause.

But it's the silence. The silence.

Jill *slowly comes in at the door.*

Jill   Mam.

Mam   I'm just talking to Dad.

Jill   What are you doing with the lights off?

Mam   Nothing.

Jill   Mam. Are you OK?

Mam   I'm drunk.

Jill   Mam.

Mam   And I don't give a shit.

Jill   Perhaps you should go to bed.

Mam   Why?

Jill   You've got school in the morning.

Mam   I'm not going to school in the morning.

Jill   Mam, you've got to. You're the teacher.

Mam   What's the point?

Jill   You know what the point is.

Mam   I am not going. The whole thing is fucking pointless, Jilly.

Jill   Mam. You have to stop this drinking.

Mam   Thirty-eight years of age and on the scrap heap.

They sit in silence.

Jill   I think it's time for his tablets.

Scene Ten

Breakfast. **Jill** *is eating a grapefriut.* **Mam** *takes a Diet Coke out of the fridge.*

Jill   Scene Ten. 'I can't believe you're drinking that.' I can't believe you're drinking that.

Mam   What's wrong with this?

Jill   Diet Coke. For breakfast?

Mam   There's nothing wrong with that.

Jill   Mam, it's not good for you. It can make you fat.

Mam   Diet Coke? It hasn't got any calories.

Jill   Mam, it's the chemicals. Aspartame and that. There are all these people in America who've swollen up like balloons.

Mam   Jill, in case you hadn't noticed. I am not fat.

Jill   Well, why are you drinking Diet Coke then?

Mam   Jill, this food business is getting out of hand.

Jill   Don't talk to me about things getting out of hand.

Mam   It's obsessive. It isn't healthy.

Jill   It's not healthy to throw your food up but I'm not complaining.

Mam   Jill, you have a problem.

Jill   You're the one with the problem. You're the one who's moved your stupid boyfriend in, when Dad is just next door.

Mam   Jill. He is not my boyfriend.

Jill   Well, what's he doing living here then?

Mam   He had nowhere to stay, Jilly. We've been through this.

Jill   Well, what are you screwing him for if he's not your boyfriend?

Mam   Don't start.

Jill   You should only sleep with people if you really love them.

Mam   It's not that simple, sweetheart.

Jill   Well, what's the point of sleeping with him if you don't love him?

Mam   Jilly, there are things I need.

Jill   Have you thought about what Dad thinks?

Mam   He doesn't think anything. He doesn't know what's going on.

Jill   He might.

Mam   With the medication he's on he doesn't know whether he's coming or going.

Jill   But what if he does know?

Mam   What if he does? What difference would it make?

Jill   Mam, what you need is to stop being horrible.

Mam   What you need is to get yourself out more. Get yourself a boyfriend before you're too fat to get out of the front door.

Jill   So basically all you want is for me to be a slut like you.

Mam   Listen, if it makes you a more pleasant human being, frankly I'd be delighted.

Jill   Mam. I hate you. And the stupid cake man.

Stuart *walks in in his pyjamas.*

Stuart   Morning.

They both look at **Stuart**.

Scene Eleven

Jill   Scene Eleven. Trivial Pursuits.

Jill *goes out leaving* **Mum** *and* **Stuart**.

Mam *and* **Stuart** *are playing Trivial Pursuits.*

Mam   A green piece of pie, please.

Stuart   Look, can we stop now?

Mam   What do you mean, we haven't even finished.

Stuart   But it's hypothetical. I haven't even got a bit of pie.

Mam   Play the game, Stuart.

Stuart   It's just I wanted to talk to you seriously.

Mam   What on earth do you want to talk seriously about?

Stuart   I mean, do you really think this is all right?

Mam   What do you mean all right?

Stuart   It just seems a bit weird.

Mam   Look. Your mam had to go into sheltered accommodation and there's more than enough room here. Come on.

Stuart   Geography. What are the cannibal tribes of Borneo known as?

Mam   Shit.

Stuart   But what about Jill?

Mam   What about her? She wants to mind her own business.

Stuart   But I don't think she likes it.

Mam   Of course she likes it. Christ, it's like a bloody mortuary with just the two of us. I think you've brought a bit of spice into our lives, Stuart.

Stuart   Are you sure it's not weird or anything? I mean you're a teacher.

Mam   Stuart. Teachers have lives, you know. Teachers have sex. Anyway, I didn't ask you to move in here because of your mind, Stuart.

Stuart   Didn't you?

Mam   The Dyaks.

Stuart   I beg your pardon.

Mam   The Dyaks of Borneo. Another piece of pie, please.

Stuart   But I was thinking. Look, I'm just ordinary sweet goods supervision manager. It's just all a bit sudden.

Mam   Look, Stuart. You could come out of your little cake factory tonight and get run over by a bus.

Stuart   I just don't know if it's right. I mean. It was all right coming round now and again. But living with him.

Mam   Fuck him, Stuart. Fuck you and your stupid ideas of what's proper behaviour. All I want is to come home and not have to sit with him stinking of formaldehyde. All I want is to have a drink. Watch the telly. Just be normal. Just forget. There's nothing weird about that, is there?

Stuart   No.

Mam   Can't you see how important this is. To have you here.

Stuart   So you don't want me to move out or anything.

Mam   You've got the run of the place. What more do you want?

Stuart   It's just I don't know where I stand. With him and everything.

Mam   Stuart. You don't stand anywhere. You don't have to think about anything. All you have to do is stop your whinging and be here for me. It's not a lot to ask. Is it?

Stuart   I don't suppose so.

Mam *comes over to him seductively.*

Mam   Don't worry, Stuart, you can do anything you want with me. I'll make sure you know which side your bread's buttered on.

Stuart   Really?

He grabs a card to deflect the amorous attentions.

History. Which historical figure gave their cook a city?

Jill *is in chef's hat standing with Stanley watching. She puts him down and comes upstage to make something extremely delicate – like icing-sugar roses or something like that. Dad is onstage through the next scene. He starts to get an erection.*

Scene Twelve

Jill   Scene Twelve. A speech about cooking. In the olden days they used to think that cooking was something special. Mark Antony once gave his cook a whole city cos Cleopatra liked his gravy. Those were the days when they really appreciated things. They went all over the world to get stuff to eat. Fantastic ingredients from all over the world. Camels' feet cooked in roses. Whole plates of nightingales' tongues, pigs that when you carved them doves would fly out, marinaded lentils wrapped in gold. You see, they appreciated food and it was good to be fat. It was sexy to be fat. When you see them old paintings of women in the nude – they weren't skinny, were they? They had something to be proud of. Big pink tummies, enormous soft thighs and they were always stuffing themselves with a bunch of grapes. Sometimes I have this dream, where I'm lying there in the middle of an enormous bowl of fruit, and I'm lying there in the kiwis and papayas, totally naked, eating chocolate puddings. I suppose, in that way, I'm quite old-fashioned, really. And when I grow up that's what I want to be, Dad. A cook and I'd have a husband who was a gourmet and we'd live in a little cottage with hams hanging from the rafters and every day we'd make the most exquisite recipes known to man. And you'd be there too. In the back. And we'd pass through your stuff through a little hatch in the wall. Delicious delicacies that'd we'd pass through to your bit. And then we'd be happy, Dad. Wouldn't we? Wouldn't we?

Jill is in her bedroom. A few cuddly toys and cookery books.

We hear a door close downstairs.

Stuart (*off*) Anybody home?

Jill ignores this.

Stuart   Anybody home?

Scene Thirteen

Jill   Scene Thirteen. The act-one twist. I'm upstairs.

Jill *continues reading. We hear* **Stuart** *come upstairs. he pops his head round the door.*

Stuart   Hija.

Jill   She's not in.

Stuart   When will she be back?

Jill   Dunno. She went to see Marg in Middlesbrough.

Stuart   What are you up to?

Jill   Nothing.

Stuart   Christ. You've got plenty books mind.

Jill   I collect them. What's that?

Stuart   What's what?

Jill   There?

Stuart   Oh. It's nothing. Here, you can have it.

Jill   Isn't it for Mam?

Stuart   I thought you'd prefer it.

Jill   Thanks.

Stuart   Well, open it.

Jill   It's a cake, isn't it.

Stuart   Not just any cake.

Jill   It's a Black Forest gateau.

Stuart   It's the fanciest one we do.

Jill   You nick these cakes, don't you?

Stuart   No one notices.

Jill   Did you really bring it here for me?

Stuart   Well, I thought you'd appreciate it.

Jill   Thanks.

Embarrassed silence.

Stuart   So how are you getting on at school?

Jill   All right.

Stuart   Get that project finished?

Jill   Nearly.

Stuart   Champion.

Jill   You can sit down if you like.

Stuart   No. It's all right. I mean, I just brought you the cake.

Jill   Stuart. How old are you?

Stuart   Twenty-six. Why like?

Jill   I just wondered why you were going out with a thirty-eight-year-old.

Stuart   Age doesn't matter. Anyway, when I met your mam I thought she was younger than me.

Jill   You were pissed.

Stuart   Still, it's the person that counts.

Jill   But isn't it more normal that a man goes out with someone younger than the other way round?

Stuart   So?

Jill   I'm just saying.

Stuart   Have you got a boyfriend?

Jill   I'm not really interested.

Stuart   It's not a crime, you know. Having a boyfriend.

Jill   I think I scare people off.

Stuart   Rubbish. You're dead easy to talk to.

Jill   Do you think?

Stuart   Yeah. Easier than your mam.

Jill   Lads my age aren't really into conversations.

Stuart   But you're quite attractive. You've got lovely bushy hair.

Jill   Have I?

Stuart   Yeah. It's the first thing I noticed about you, your hair. I wish I had hair like that.

Jill   Like mine?

Stuart   Well, a bit shorter, but you know.

Jill   I'm not exactly God's gift, am I?

Stuart   I wouldn't say that.

Jill   Mam's right, isn't she? I'm overweight.

Stuart   You're not overweight. Anyway, I prefer a bit of meat on somebody.

Jill   Serious?

Stuart   Course I'm serious.

Jill   Do you think I've got an attractive body?

Stuart   I think your body's very attractive.

Jill   Thanks.

Stuart   You're a very attractive person.

Jill   So are you.

Stuart   Really.

Jill   Would you like a bit of cake?

Stuart   You're all right for now. I thought you hated me.

Jill   I thought you hated me.

Stuart   No, I like you. I mean. You're a nice person. A caring person.

Jill   Not especially.

Stuart   Well, I mean, you're more of a caring person than say, your mam.

Jill   I thought you liked Mam.

Stuart   I do.

Jill   Well?

Stuart   All I'm saying is I feel comfortable with you. It's just nice to be able to have a chat now and again.

Jill   Do you think I'm as good-looking as Mam?

Stuart   Perhaps I'd better leave you to it.

Jill   No. You don't have to go.

Stuart   Really.

Jill   I don't mind. I like a bit of company.

Stuart *sits down.* **Jill** *eats a piece of cake.*

Stuart   You know your dad. What exactly did he do?

Jill   He used to be a surveyor, but he gave it up for entertainment.

Stuart   What sort of entertainment?

Jill   He used to be Elvis.

Stuart   Elvis Presley.

Jill   No, Elvis O'Connor. Who did you think?

Stuart   Christ.

Jill   I know.

Stuart   Do you not like Elvis, like?

Jill   I hate it. I still play it for him but it drives me mental.

Stuart   So he used to dress up and that.

Jill   Course. All his stuff's in there.

Stuart   You kept all his costumes and that?

Jill   Do you want a look?

Stuart   Sure. So what happened to him, like.

Jill   Who?

Stuart   Your dad.

Jill   His car hit a lorry and he went through the window. He'd only got round the corner. Everyone thought he was dead.

Stuart   Christ. He had plenty of gear then.

Jill   He used to do it every night.

Stuart   Look at this.

Jill   Try it on.

Stuart   You must be joking.

Jill   Go on. It'd look good on you.

Stuart   He must have been pretty serious about it.

Jill   I suppose.

Stuart   But he didn't think he actually was Elvis or anything.

Jill   You'd probably have to believe you're Elvis, wouldn't you. A bit.

Stuart   Would you?

Jill   To make it convincing.

Stuart   You reckon.

Jill   Everybody pretends they're someone else to make themselves more convincing. That's a fact of life.

Stuart   Is it?

Jill   Try it on.

Stuart   It's a bit weird, isn't it. With him being crippled and everything.

Jill   It's only a costume.

Stuart   All right then. As long as you don't tell your mam.

He starts to change and then gets self-conscious.

What are you looking at me like that for?

Jill   I'm just watching.

Stuart   You're a right bunch of perverts, you.

Jill   And the pants.

Stuart   Are you sure?

Jill   Go on. Look. They fit perfect.

Stuart   They're a bit tight round here.

Jill   They're supposed to be.

Stuart   What do you reckon?

Jill   You look great.

Stuart   Do you think I'm sexy?

Jill   What do you mean?

Stuart   You know, do I turn you on as Elvis?

Jill   I don't know.

Stuart   I've seen you look at iz.

Jill   Looking like what?

Stuart   Like you were interested.

Jill   In what?

Stuart   How old are you?

Jill   What difference does that make?

Stuart   Not a lot.

Jill   Why did you ask?

Stuart   I was just interested.

Jill   Fourteen.

Stuart   Do you usually invite strange men to get changed in your bedroom.

Jill   You're not a strange man.

Stuart   Am I not?

Jill   Not to me.

Stuart   What would your mother think?

Jill   I don't know.

Stuart   Do you not think she'd get the wrong impression with me in this suit and everything?

Jill   Maybes she'd think it was perfectly natural.

Stuart   Natural.

Jill   I don't see what's wrong with it.

Stuart   Really.

Jill   You look good in that suit.

Stuart   Maybe I should take it off now.

Jill   Maybe you should leave it on.

Stuart   Won't your mother be back.

Jill   She'll be at least another hour.

Stuart   Will she indeed.

Jill   Do you think I should put a record on?

Stuart   As long as it's Elvis Presley.

Jill *starts to go.* **Stuart** *grabs her arm. They kiss.*

Stuart   Do you really think we should be doing this.

Jill   I don't see why not.

They kiss again.

Elvis comes out of the wardrobe singing 'The Wonder of You'. Maybe he gets covered in dry ice and when it has cleared, he has disappeared and they are in the bed.

Scene Fourteen

Jill *appears on the bed standing up,* **Stuart** *on top of her, as if it's a bird's-eye view.*

Jill   Scene Fourteen. A Speech about Gravy.

Jill *is being fucked by* **Stuart***. She has a slice of cake that she nibbles on intermittently.*

Dad, I'm only telling you this because you won't tell anyone else. Look, even if you do get better you have to promise not to tell anyone. At all. You see, yesterday, I did it with someone. I mean, I didn't mean to. I mean, it's all right to have it off with someone even if you don't love them. Isn't it? I mean, you had it off with that woman from Tynemouth, didn't you, and you didn't love her. Did you? But the thing was, Dad, even though it was all right and that, even though I quite enjoyed it, well, it felt weird. Like I shouldn't be doing it. I could feel all this cold polyester against my leg and all I could think of was you. The sequins were sticking into me and all I could think of was you and Mam and Grandma. And I kept looking over to the wardrobe, and all the time he was on iz, all that I could think of was that Mam would jump out. That everyone would jump out of the wardrobe, Mam, Grandma, the cookery teacher, everybody. And they would catch iz, Dad. And he was kissing iz. And he was all hot. Smoky breath and his fly was like cutting into me leg. And I felt terrible, and all I could think of was you. And then I started to smell this smell, and the smell was this sweet smell of dough. And then I thought of a big plate of dumplings. Then I imagined Mam and she was eating the dumplings. And she was sitting there eating the dumplings and she was crying. And I was passing her the gravy and she was eating the dumplings. And he was saying she loved iz. And I didn't know what to do, Dad. And all I could think of was big sticky dumplings and gravy. Thick, salty gravy.

Stuart *is finished, zips himself up and leaves.* **Jill** *tidies herself up.*

Scene Fifteen

Kitchen. **Jill** *is cooking up a storm.*

Jill   Scene Fifteen. The Kitchen.

Mam   Jill.

Jill   Hang on a minute, Mam. I'm busy.

Mam   Jill, stop cooking.

Jill   I can't stop now or it'll be spoilt.

Mam   Jill, I said stop cooking. I want a word with you, young lady.

Jill   What's the matter now?

Mam   I need to talk to you. Look, sit down. It's something personal.

Jill   Have I done something wrong?

Mam   Look, Jill, I don't want you to think I've been snooping round or anything.

Jill   What have you been doing?

Mam   Jilly, there's something I just don't understand.

Jill   Mam, if you've been in my room.

Mam   Jill, I wasn't snooping around.

Jill   What were you doing in there?

Mam   I was cleaning up, Jilly.

Jill   You've got no right to go in there.

Mam   Jill, I have to talk to you about this.

She produces a bag which she holds at arm's length. **Jill** *blanches.*

I was so disgusted I have had to put it in a plastic bag.

Jill   Mam, I can explain.

Mam   But it was under your bed.

Jill   There's an explanation.

Mam   What the hell is going on, Jill?

Jill   It was fermenting.

Mam   Fermenting, Jilly, this is a salted fish.

Jill   They need a cool dark place.

Mam   It's disgusting.

Jill   It's Vietnamese.

Mam   Look, it's absolutely fetid.

Jill   That's how it's supposed to be.

Mam   I'm at the end of my tether here.

Jill   I won't do it again.

Mam   It's OK to keep these things in the kitchen, Jill. But no more food in your bedroom. It's absolutely unhygienic.

Jill   I'm sorry, Mam. I better carry on.

Mam   You don't have to do this, you know. I don't know why you're insisting on cooking for Stuart.

Jill   Mam, I want to.

Mam   I know it's very nice of you. But you don't have to do it all the time, darling.

Jill   Mam, I want to. It's a labour of love.

Scene Sixteen

Stuart, **Jill**, **Mam** and **Dad** *all sit down at the table.*

Jill   Scene Sixteen. Things Turn Nasty. What do you think?

Stuart   It's a nice bit of fish this.

Jill   It's sole veronique.

Stuart   I never thought grapes would go. Are you not eating any?

Mam   I've had plenty. It's quite rich, isn't it?

Jill   No, it's not rich at all. Is it, Stuart?

Stuart   No. I mean yes. I mean, it's just very nice, isn't it?

Jill   Don't you think it's weird how Mam hardly eats anything?

Stuart   Well, she's watching her weight, isn't she? She wants to look attractive.

Jill   You don't have to watch your weight to be attractive though, do you. I thought you said you liked a bit of meat on somebody.

Mam   When did you say that?

Stuart   I don't know. Maybe I mentioned it in passing.

Mam   Anyway, I think that's right. Don't you think she looks attractive in the new dress I bought her?

Stuart   Yes, she looks very nice.

Mam See. If you got yourself a new haircut, you could start attracting the fellas.

Jill Mam, I think you should change the subject.

Mam Why?

Jill Cos Stuart doesn't want to hear about me.

Mam Course he does. You're interested in Jilly, aren't you?

Stuart Yes. I mean . . .

Mam Don't you think if she just lost a couple of pounds she'd look great?

Stuart She does look great.

Mam But don't you think they'd be going wild for her if she was just a bit trimmer?

Stuart Mam. Will you shut up.

Mam I was just asking Stuart's opinion.

Stuart Anyway, I think it's the person that counts not what they look like.

Jill Do you think I'm not good-looking?

Stuart Of course I think you're good-looking. I was just saying.

Jill Look, if you don't think I'm attractive just say so.

Mam All we're saying, Jilly, if you lost a few pounds you'd be even more attractive.

Jill Is that what you're saying?

Stuart I'm not saying anything.

Mam I don't know why you're flying off the handle. I'm just trying to give you some friendly advice.

Jill I don't want your advice. You're the one he doesn't find attractive.

Mam   What on earth are you on about? Do you find me unattractive?

Stuart   Course not.

Mam   So what are you on about?

Jill   Mam. Basically, you are just ignorant.

Mam   Sit down.

Jill   Oh, piss off, Mam.

Mam   Gillian.

Jill   I'm taking him through, you can clear up, the pair of yous.

Jill *storms off, sticking a lump of food in her gob as she goes.*

Mam   I don't know what's got into her.

Stuart   Maybe I should go and talk to her.

Mam   Fuck her, if that's how she's going to be. Stuart, I want you inside of me.

Stuart   I beg your pardon.

Mam   Right here. On the table.

Stuart   In the middle of the fish and everything.

Mam   Fuck me, Stuart.

Stuart   But what about me trousers?

Mam   For Christ's sake. That'll do nicely, Stuart.

Mam *grabs* **Stuart** *on to the table. They make love.* **Mam** *grabs* **Stuart**'s *head and thrusts it down to her crotch. Crossfade to* **Jill** *and* **Dad** *upstage. We hear the burbled orgasmic noises coming from the kitchen table as if they were in another room.*

Scene Seventeen

Silence.

Jill   I didn't know you could hear so much through here.

*Suddenly **Dad** comes out of the wheelchair in Elvis gear and sings 'Suspicious Minds' with great aplomb.*

*The stage is cleared. Then it plunges into darkness. Pitch black. The bedroom door opens. **Mam** appears in her dressing gown. She is going to the loo. She suddenly sees **Jill**. She gets a shock.*

Scene Eighteen

Jill   Scene Eighteen. The Landing. Night.

Mam   What are you doing here?

Jill   I couldn't sleep.

Mam   You haven't been cooking, have you?

Jill   No.

Mam   What's that smell?

Jill   It's nothing. It's from before. I was looking for Stanley.

Mam   Jill, it's half past three in the morning. Go to bed.

Jill   Mam, do you think Stuart loves you?

Mam   Let's not get into that again. Go to bed, darling, I need the loo.

Jill   But do you?

Mam   This is neither the time nor the place.

Jill   But Mam . . .

Mam   Jilly, this is ridiculous.

Jill   Mam, I've got something to tell you.

Mam   What is it?

Jill   Mam. I've got a boyfriend.

Mam   That's wonderful, darling, is it anyone I know?

Jill   No.

Mam   I know exactly how you feel. It's perfectly normal not to be able to sleep. But really you should be in bed now. Take Stanley to your room if it makes you feel better.

Jill   Mam, do you love Stuart?

Mam   It's the middle of the night.

Jill   But how do you know if somebody really loves you?

Mam   You can just tell. Good night.

Jill   Good night, Mam.

Mam *goes to the loo.* **Jill** *then reappears and opens the bedroom door.*

Jill   Stuart. Stuart.

Stuart *appears at the door almost naked and pushes* **Jill** *into the corridor.*

Stuart   Jesus Christ. You can't come in here.

Jill   Stuart. I need to talk to you.

Stuart   Do you know what time it is?

Jill   It's the middle of the night.

Stuart   What do you want?

Jill   I want you, Stuart.

Stuart   Jesus Christ. Your mam's only gone to have a slash.

Jill   I don't care.

Stuart   Jesus.

Jill   You hardly looked at me all night.

Stuart   What do you expect?

Jill   I thought you loved me.

Stuart   I never said I loved you.

Jill   Yes, you did.

Stuart   Look, what's happened between us has been a big mistake.

Jill   What do you mean a mistake?

Stuart   I just got carried away.

Jill   But you said you loved me.

Stuart   Keep your voice down. I never meant to say that. It just came out.

Jill   Came out.

Stuart   Oh, I don't know. It's just what you say.

Jill   But I love you.

Stuart   No you don't. Look, you're a lovely kid but . . .

The toilet flushes.

Jill   Kid! I'm your lover.

Stuart   For God's sake, you're still at school.

Jill   Well, you had it off with me.

Stuart   She'll be out in a second.

Jill   Look, I've made you these.

Stuart   What the hell are they?

Jill   They're truffles. They've got your name on.

Stuart   Look, take them back, I don't want them.

Jill   They're a present.

Stuart   Look, this has to stop.

Mam *comes out.*

Stuart   Shit.

Jill   Well, stuff you then.

Jill *gives the truffles to* **Stuart** *and disappears.*

Mam   What are you doing?

Stuart   I was just going to the toilet.

Mam   What are you doing with those?

Stuart   I was just a bit peckish.

Mam *goes past and trips.*

Mam   That bloody tortoise. Put those down and come back to bed.

She closes the door. **Jill** *reappears.*

Jill   Stuart, I want you. Now.

Stuart   For Christ's sake.

Jill   Come on, we can go into the bathroom.

Stuart   Look, this is getting completely out of hand.

Jill   It's all right. Just bring the truffles.

Stuart   Jill, we are not going anywhere. This has to stop. I don't love you. Our relationship is going nowhere. Understand. Finito.

Mam *opens the door.*

Mam   What are you two up to?

Jill   I'm still looking for Stanley.

Mam   Get to bed at once, young lady. He's in my room because I nearly crippled myself with him running round the landing.

Jill *goes off.*

Mam   And for God's sake put those sweets down.

She goes back inside and stubs her toe on Stanley.

Ow! That fucking tortoise.

Stuart *is left alone.* **Jill** *reappears and grabs the truffles.*

Jill   I hate you.

Jill *storms off.*

Stuart   Fucking hell.

Dad *as Elvis appears on the balcony.*

Dad   It happened the first time when I was in Vegas and Priscilla was wearing her skin-tight, velour catsuit, it happened the second time in Phoenix when I was in the jacuzzi with the little fox from Reno. It happened at home in Graceland after breakfast. And I called for the doctor and I asked him, Doc, how can this be that the King who has all the riches of this world, all the girls he could dream of, I asked him, Doc, what could be wrong now, why do I have this erectile disfunction. And the doc said, son, you maybe the King, you may have Cadillacs and all kinds of foxy minxes, but son, all around you is despair, poverty, hurt and suffrin, and you must feel for them all. You must feel for the poor, the mean, the harelipped and the ugly, the sad, the dejected, the wounded and heartbroken and sodomites. Sodomites rutting in cornfields and in greyhound buses, in airplanes, on doorsteps, wiping their dirty little organs on the lily-white paper of our constitution. He said, son, it ain't no surprise you have that erectile disfunction, with all that weight on your poor shoulders. This ain't an easy time for any of us, and it ain't an easy time to be King.

Dad *disappears.*

Jill *alone. She takes the pie out of the oven in a demonic state. And prepares the meal for the next scene.*

Scene Nineteen

Jill   Scene Nineteen. Mr Kipling gets his Fucking Pie.

Jill *looks awful.* **Mam** *and* **Stuart** *sit down to eat.*

Stuart   Hiya.

Jill   Hiya.

Mam   Are you all right, Jill?

Jill   Fine.

Mam   You look a bit tired, that's all.

Jill   I'm absolutely fine, Mam.

Mam   Well, this looks lovely, doesn't it, Stuart?

Stuart   Oh yeh, I like a nice bit of pie.

Mam   It's got an unusual smell.

Jill   It's African.

Mam   That's very original.

Stuart   I've never had anything African before.

Jill   I thought I'd try something different.

Stuart   Well, it's quite tasty actually.

Jill   I'm not sure if it was a good idea. Mam, I'm starting to go off food.

Mam   Well, that's good.

Jill   I mean, it's terrible what people eat, isn't it?

Stuart   What do you mean?

Jill   Like tripe is sheep's stomach and black puddings are blood.

Stuart   Black puddings are lovely though.

Jill   Well, sheep's eyes and monkeys' brains.

Stuart   You're putting me right off.

Jill   And chicken's feet and woodlice and sperm.

Mam   Jilly. People do not eat sperm.

Jill   People do eat sperm. Cod roe.

Mam   Cod roe is fish eggs, darling.

Jill   But soft roe is sperm, Mam. Sperm from a fish.

Mam   Is there anything wrong, sweetheart?

Jill   No.

Mam   You seem a bit tense.

Jill   I'm fine.

Mam   How's this boyfriend of yours getting on?

Jill   OK.

Mam   Has something happened?

Jill   No.

Mam   Are you sure?

Jill   He's a complete bastard.

Mam   Well, it's all in the process of learning, dear.

Jill   I hate him, Mam, and I hate all the tortes and the omelettes and the custards and the stews and the puddings. All that chopping and pummelling and mincing, everything that's mashed and smashed and ripped apart. Mam, it's not natural, it's worse than animals. It's disgusting. We're all disgusting, Mam, human beings. I hate everything, every stupid last thing I ever wanted to cook for him.

Mam   What on earth's been going on, Jill.

Jill   It's like I saw all the things I've eaten. You know all the things that were alive and sudddenly I felt rotten. I mean, I thought what if there was something inside of me. No bigger than a pea. How would I like it if someone put that on a pizza? And then I thought about the Third World and all the starving children in Africa and there is Kate Moss without an ounce of fat to rub together. And I thought about all this and I just felt sick.

Mam   What do you mean there was something inside of you?

Jill   It was just something I thought.

Stuart   Maybe I should leave you alone.

Jill   Stay there.

Mam   What do you mean, Jill?

Jill   I don't know.

Mam   Have you been messing around with this boyfriend of yours, Jill?

Jill   No.

Mam   What's wrong, Jill?

Jill   I thought he loved me. He said that he loved me.

Mam   Who is this boy, Jill?

Jill   It's not a boy.

Mam   Jesus. It's not that Mary from across the road, is it?

Jill   It's a man.

Mam   A man. What sort of man?

Jill   I don't know.

Mam   Well, did you use protection?

Jill   I don't know.

Mam   What do you mean you don't know? How old is he, Jill?

Jill   I don't know. Stuart's age.

Mam   Stuart's age. Where on earth did you meet such a man?

Jill   I don't know.

Mam   Jill, this is serious.

Jill   What's serious about it? It's all right for you to sleep around.

Mam   I don't sleep around.

Jill   What about him?

Mam   Stuart and I have a relationship.

Jill   Well, so do I.

Mam   What?

Jill   Have a relationship. You think you're perfect sitting there all high and mighty looking down on me and everything. But you're the one to blame. Look what you did to Dad. But you won't admit it. You don't even care. You've got no conscience at all, have you? You're just a bastard.

Mam   All I do is have a conscience, Jill. I wake up every bloody morning and it's all I think about. What if we hadn't have argued. What if I'd never said I was leaving. What if. What if. But he did it, Jill. He was the one like a bat out of hell. I didn't ask him to. And what's worse is when I went round there and he was lying there, there was part of me that thought, it serves you right, you fucking bastard. It serves you right. Imagine how that makes me feel. All I do is have a fucking conscience. So get off my back.

Stuart   Perhaps I should leave yous to it.

Jill   Mam. I cooked Stanley in the pie.

Mam   You did what?

Stuart   For Christ's sake.

Mam   Gillian.

Stuart   You're fucking mental, you.

Jill   No, I'm not mental.

Stuart   You're off your dot.

Mam   Shut your mouth, son.

Stuart   I feel sick.

Mam   Just sit down there and shut your mouth before I shut it for you. What's going on, Jill?

Jill   I'm going to the toilet.

Mam   You're not going anywhere.

Stuart   Jill . . .

Jill   I don't give a shit about you any more.

Jill *glares at* **Stuart** *and then runs out.* **Mam** *follows.*

Stuart   Jesus Christ.

Jill *comes back on to announce, briefly.*

Jill   Scene Twenty. A Paranoid Speech by Elvis.

Scene Twenty

Dad *in spotlight as Elvis.*

Dad   You know it was never easy being King. There are bad and evil things in this world of mine. There is misery and there is pain but I was born to bring my people hope. So one day when I woke up and Priscilla was going on about me buying those ten Mercedes-Benz – and I just said, Priscilla, for gawd's sake shut up. What does my personal finance matter when there is a pestilence upon this nation. There is drugs and sodomising. This is no place for free men. And I said as America's number one American I'm going to see me the President. So I put on my Elvis cape and my Elvis belt and I caught the plane to Washington.

And then at the airport I saw this nigger sitting. And I said, boy, take me to see the President. And he said, ain't you the King. And I said, keep it under your hat, boy, cos this gun's undercover. And we went off to the White House by way of Dunkin Donuts where I had a couple o' dozen cos I'd dun missed my breakfast. And then the President came out and he said: Gee, Elvis, you sure wear some wayout clothing. And I said to the President, Mr President, sir, you've got your show to run and I got mine. And I said, Mr President, there is a pestilence upon this kingdom. My people are walking in a valley of woe. There is a darkness upon us. There's drugs and hippies and sodomites and every kind of evil. But where there is sadness I will bring hope, and where there is sorrow I will bring love, and where there is poverty I will bring the riches of the Orient, and where there is darkness I will bring light, and where there is hunger I will bring burgers. And all will be well and all manner of things will be well. And then I went home and was sick.

Dad *sits back down in his chair and adopts his comatose position.*

Jill *wheels him into position.*

Scene Twenty-One

Jill   Scene Twenty-One. Quite Near the Ending.

Stuart comes in and sits next to him.

Dad *is in his chair. He has an erection.* **Stuart** *comes over to him, takes out his dick and starts to toss him off.*

Stuart   Look, I know this must seem really weird, me wanting to talk to you and everything. But I just felt I had to, you know. I've got nobody else. And I know you must be thinking who's this bastard coming here seeing wor lass and the young un as well. But I never did it out of spite or nowt. I mean, I know I shouldn't have fucked the bairn. But she doesn't seem like a kid to me. I mean, in a way I thought I might be falling in love, you know.

Sorry, me hand's getting a bit sore. And I just want you to know like. I don't usually mess about with blokes, like. I'm only doing this because you're a cripple. And I just want you to know. I mean, even though I've been fucking your wife and everything. I want you to know you have my upmost respect. I mean, I wouldn't be doing this if I didn't respect you. And they love you. And they're both yours, you know that. I've fucked it now. I've got nobody, me.

Dad *comes all over* **Stuart**'s *hand.*

Stuart   There you go.

He wipes his hand on **Dad**'s *costume. A little bit is left.* **Stuart** *is curious. He sniffs the hand and then tastes a little bit of* **Dad**'s *cum. He thinks. He bends over, holds* **Dad**'s *head up and kisses him on the mouth.*

Jill *comes in.*

Jill   What are you doing?

Stuart   Nowt.

Jill   You were kissing me dad.

Stuart   No I wasn't. I was just giving him his medicine.

Jill   His medicine. Look at the state of him. What have you been doing?

Stuart   I haven't done anything.

Jill   I've had enough of you, you bastard. What have you been doing?

Stuart   I wanked him off.

Jill   You did what?

Stuart   He got an erection and I wanked him off.

Jill   Who do you think you are coming in here fucking me mother, shagging me, wanking me dad off. It's a good job I killed the fucking tortoise. I loved you. You fucking bastard.

Stuart   It wasn't what you think.

Jill   Wasn't what I think. A wank is a wank, Stuart. And you're the biggest fucking wanker I've ever laid eyes on.

Stuart   Hey. Don't call me a wanker.

Jill   You're sick. Get him out of here, take him next door.

Stuart   Look, stop ordering me around.

Jill   Do you want me to tell Mam? Eh.

Stuart   Listen . . .

Jill   What do you think she'll say when she finds out you've fucked her daughter and wanked her husband off.

Stuart   Look, there's nothing wrong with wanking your dad off.

Jill   You're out of your mind.

Stuart   They do it in the hospitals.

Jill   Well, two can play at that game, matey.

Stuart   Just calm down.

Jill   If everybody else is getting wanked off left, right and centre I don't see why should be left out.

Stuart   Look, Jilly, this has to stop right now.

Jill   Take off your clothes.

Stuart   What?

Jill   I mean it, take them off.

Stuart   You must be joking.

Jill   I'm serious.

Stuart   Your mam's upstairs.

Jill   She's gone out.

Stuart   But . . .

Jill   I want to fuck you on the table.

Stuart   Hang on a minute.

Jill   One last time and I'll never tell a living soul.

Stuart   But it's out of the question.

Jill   So you want me to tell her, do you?

Stuart   No. Jesus, no. But this is ridiculous.

Jill   Take your clothes off or I'll phone her now, she's at me nan's.

Stuart   This is ridiculous. Look, what about your dad?

Jill   Fuck me dad. I mean it. You could go to jail for what you did to me. Take your clothes off, Stuart.

Stuart   Look, one last time and that's that, OK?

Jill   Hurry up, she'll be back shortly.

Stuart *takes his clothes off. Down to his Y-fronts.*

Jill   Now get on the table.

Stuart   What's this?

Jill   I want you to rub it all over.

Stuart   But what is it?

Jill   It's a marinade. Rub it on you. Or else.

Stuart   You're a fucking pervert you.

Jill *pulls out a big kitchen knife.*

Jill   Rub it all over.

Stuart *looks at the knife, then at the jar and starts to rub on the marinade. Suddenly, we hear the door.* **Stuart** *starts.*

Jill   Stay there, you bastard.

Stuart   What are you going to do to me?

Jill   I'm going to fuck you good and proper.

Stuart   Please, put the knife down.

Jill   All over.

Stuart   Please, you're going too far.

Jill   You haven't a clue how far I'll go.

Mam (*off*)   Jilly!

She comes in.

What on earth is going on here?

Jill   Nothing.

Mam   What on earth are you doing?

Stuart   Look, I can explain.

Mam   What the hell is that stuff?

Jill   Marinade.

Mam   Jesus Christ. How long has this been going on?

Stuart   I think you've got the wrong idea.

Mam   How could you do this to me, Stuart?

Stuart   It wasn't on purpose.

Mam   What on earth were you thinking of?

Stuart   The whole thing was an accident.

Mam   An accident with that tub of lard?

Stuart   I'm sorry. Look, I'll go now. I'll never come back again.

Mam   Jesus Christ, Jilly.

Jill   Don't touch me. Leave me alone.

Jill *runs out.*

Stuart   Look, I'm sorry.

Mam   Where the hell do you think you're going?

Stuart   It's not what it seems.

Mam   She's only fourteen, Stuart.

Stuart   Honestly, I thought I loved her. I didn't know what I was doing.

Mam   You knew exactly what you were doing.

Stuart   Look at me. Look at me. I'm covered in fucking marmalade and you're having a go at me. Fuck this. Fuck you and your weirdo daughter and your spakker for a husband. I never even liked you. I never even liked her. I'm the victim here.

Mam   Victim!

Stuart   I've had a sheltered upbringing.

Mam   I'll give you a sheltered upbringing, you fucking monster.

She slaps him across the face. **Stuart** *picks up the knife. He holds it up. There is a stand-off.* **Mam** *grabs the blade and holds it tight, blood runs down.* **Stuart** *lets go of the knife.*

Stuart *stops dead.*

Mam   Get in that cupboard.

Stuart   Which one?

Mam   Get in the fucking cupboard. NOW!

Stuart *sheepishly goes into the cupboard.* **Mam** *rushes to* **Jill**.

Jill (*from inside the bathroom*)   Virtually the final scene. Jill is in the bathroom.

Scene Twenty-Two

Mam *outside the bathroom.* **Jill** *inside.*

Mam   Jill. What did he do to you? What did he do? Come on, sweetheart, open the door.

Jill   Please go away, Mam.

Mam   Jilly, open the door.

Jill   Mam, you don't want to see me now.

Mam   Jill, it's all right. Just open the door.

Jill *opens the door and comes out covered in blood. She is holding the knife and has cut her wrists.*

Mam   Jesus Christ.

Jill   I'm sorry, Mam. I couldn't even cut it properly.

Lighting change.

Jill   And then I fainted.

Mam *brings* **Jill** *a bowl of water. As she says the speech she starts to wash herself, cleaning up all the stage blood.*

Jill   And somehow Mam managed to pick me up. And she carried me across the landing. And everything was becoming too much. And Stuart was shouting from in the cupboard and her head was spinning and I was too heavy and she hadn't eaten for several days. And there we were at the top of the staircase. And she fell. And down we tumbled and I landed on top of her and she was shouting too because she couldn't get up and when we woke I was in the bed next to hers and we were both in hospital.

But somewhere in that fall. Somewhere in the middle of the staircase, something was irrecovably changed. And when I woke up I couldn't remember why it was that I'd tried to commit suicide. And I knew it was all right. Even if Dad was a cripple. Even if I was fat. Just as long as we didn't see that bastard Stuart any more. And Mam said she'd find a way so I never had to. And I asked Mam what had kept her going. Through everything that had happened. And she said she didn't know. But she said there was one time when she first brought him home. There was this one day when she just couldn't cope any more and she got all these pills and a bottle of whisky and lined them all up in a row. And just before she was going to take them, she heard Dad moan from next door and she went in to see him. And she looked down at his face and on it was a smile. Just a brief smile. For a second. And then it was gone.

And maybe life isn't about the tragedies. Maybe that's just what's normal, hurt and heartache, and loneliness and despair. Maybe life's about those tiny moments that keep us going through all that darkness. The little things. Like a delicious supper, or a tiny moment of kindness, or a smile – just for a brief second. Maybe it's about not giving up, and maybe we all have to try. But I'll tell you one thing life's bloody weird, isn't it?

By now a table has been prepared. **Mam** *dishes out some stew.* **Jill** *joins her. They both eat it.*

Scene Twenty-Three

Jill   Scene Twenty-Three. The Unbearably Glib Epilogue.

Mam   It's funny how things work out.

Jill   It's funny how all your problems can just 'disappear'.

Mam   I think we're actually quite happy now. Just the three of us. Me, you and your dad.

Jill   I think so.

Mam   I'm glad you've got that cooking thing under control.

Jill   I'm glad you're eating properly.

Mam   It's amazing what a good bit of catharsis can do.

Jill   It's funny that you can get rid of all your problems at one fell swoop.

Mam   I couldn't agree more, sweetheart.

Jill   Any more 'stew'?

Mam Don't mind if I do.

They look towards the audience breaking through the apple-pie image with vicious sneers. A fanfare plays.

Dad *as Elvis appears with a mike in a ridiculous costume.*

Dad Ladies and gentlemen, boys and girls, countrymen, comrades, brothers in arms, time is fleeting fast and as we move deeper into the night, we have finally come to the end of our humble show this evening. And good people all, I ask of you as you wend your weary way home this evening to stop and think about what you have seen tonight. Consider the marvels you have witnessed on our tiny stage, but I ask each and everyone of you to realise that what you have seen in these four walls tonight is only art. Don't weep or despair at the tragedy and horror we have depicted here. Instead remember that all the world's a stage and all of you good people in it are merely players and this vast and shimmering world of ours is all love and all light. And there are no cripple Elvises, no sad mams or Burger Kings, no fat girls or cake-makers, there are only people, human beings who love and hope and fear, who spend all their days in search of a little truth, a little happiness, a fragile little moment that will raise us up. And tonight, as you leave with your loved ones, raise up your voices and rejoice that we are all one, all snuggled together under the vast umbrella of God in the eternal kingdom of Heaven, transformed and exalted, ever glorified, ever uplifted, ever venerated in his everlasting love.

My name is Elvis Presley and you've been a very special audience.

He then sings 'Glory, Glory Hallejulah'.

He disappears.

Sound effect of 'Elvis has left the building'.

Bollocks

Bollocks was originally performed as the Radio 4 play *Gristle* on 19 January 1997. The cast was as follows:

Peter	Derek Walmsley
Mary	Tracey Whitwell
Ian	Trevor Fox
Lisa	Sharon Percy
Mr Happy	Shaun Prendergast
Man	Dave Whitaker

Director Kate Rowland

The stage play *Bollocks* was first performed as a rehearsed reading at Live Theatre, Newcastle-upon-Tyne, on 5 March 1998. The cast was as follows:

Peter	Derek Walmsley
Mary	Philippa Wilson
Ian	Trevor Fox
Lisa	Sharon Percy
Mr Happy	Shaun Prendergast
Man	Dave Whitaker

Director Max Roberts

Scene One

Monologue

Peter   I think it's only when you can't do something that you notice how weird it is. You know, like sex. How sex is everywhere. Everywhere you look it's on display. Every magazine, on the TV, everywhere. And you start asking yourself, what is it, this 'sex'? How to keep your man happy? Are you getting enough? Ten ways for the perfect orgasm. What does all this really mean? Why does it only happen to other people? Why is it always just out of your grasp? And the truth of the matter is I don't think all this sex even exists. In real life people aren't shagging each other senseless. Who do you know who's shagging all the time? In real life people are coming home from work knackered and reading about it in friggin' magazines. Nobody's got the time. And everybody knows that it's a load of bollocks, but it still doesn't stop you wanting it.

I'm reading all this stuff. Thinking all this mixed-up crap. And I can't even toss myself off. No secret little wank just to get it out of my system. It's just churning in my mind. A fucked-up churning. All I see is a sea of cocks and cunts and arseholes all getting fucked, all cumming all over. And at first it was sexy – feeling turned on all the time, but then it gets horrible, all these apertures disconnected from bodies. Like I'm being suffocated by hairy minges, like all these fat pricks are poking me in the face. And I want to scream. I want to say stop. I thought sex was something beautiful, I thought it was something sacred, I thought it was something you could touch and taste and feel. I thought it was the weight of another body. I thought it was the special privacy. I thought it was another person breathing in your face.

Intro to 'Banks and Braes' sung by Kathleen Ferrier.

Scene Two

Open ground, Northern Ireland.

The sound of feet tentatively creeping through broken rubble. We hear footsteps and nervous breathing as if someone was in danger. There is an air of unpleasant suspense. Suddenly there is gunfire.

A man lets out a blood-curdling scream. It is absolutely shocking and horrific. It goes on and on. As the scream goes on the singing gradually gets louder. The sound of the screaming is unbearable, but the singing crossfades and the beautiful elegy is all that remains.

Scene Three

Peter's *house.*

Mary   What have you been doing?

Peter   Just sitting.

Mary   You should have had a walk. It's a lovely day.

Peter   I didn't feel like it.

Mary   It'll do you good.

Peter   What good will it do me?

Mary   It might cheer you up.

Peter   Look, I don't need cheering.

Mary   I popped into me mam's on my way home. She's given us the three hundred quid.

Peter   What?

Mary   Here.

Peter   What did you say to her?

Mary   I told her we'd pay her back. But she says it's a present.

Peter   What a fucking bitch.

Mary   What are you on about?

Peter   You took it?

Mary   Of course I bloody well took it.

Peter   After what I said?

Mary   Yes, after what you said.

Peter   For Christ's sake.

Mary   What else was I supposed to do? Where else are we going to get three hundred quid?

Peter   Give her it back.

Mary   What are you on about, Peter?

Peter   We don't need charity. I've told you. I'll get a job.

Mary   Look, Peter. Normal blokes can't get work never mind . . .

Peter   A fucking cripple.

Mary   It's just to tide us over.

Peter   You realise why she gave you that money.

Mary   Because she . . .

Peter (*interrupting*)   To get at me. Don't you see?

Mary   Don't be so bloody stupid.

Peter   You don't even care.

Mary   Of course I care.

Peter   You've got a funny fuckin' way of showing it.

Mary   You're being ridiculous.

Peter   Look, just fuck off with your three hundred quid.

Mary   We can't go on like this much longer.

Peter   What do you mean? I'm fucking stuck with this for the rest of my life.

Mary   Come on, pet.

Peter   Don't patronise me.

Mary   I'm not patronising you.

Peter   I don't need fucking pity.

Mary   What about me, Peter?

Peter   What about you?

Mary   I'm the one that needs some pity. Have you ever thought I might need a bit of support?

Peter   Ah, fuck off.

Mary   Peter.

Peter   You and your frigging mother. A right pair of fucking martyrs.

Mary   Stop it.

Peter   At least admit it.

Mary   I can't take much more of this.

Peter   Just say it, will you. Just say you hate me. Just say the last thing you want to do is to spend the rest of your life with some cunt with half his fucking dick blown off.

Mary   Peter. Not again.

Peter   Just fucking admit it.

Mary   You'd prefer it if I did hate you, wouldn't you? Cos it would be easier. You could feel really bloody sorry for yourself. But it isn't that simple, Peter.

Peter   It is that simple. Of course it's fucking simple.

Mary   Look, I know it isn't going to be easy but we have to try and get back to normal.

Peter   Normal.

Mary   I'm trying my best, Peter, but you have to give me a break. (*Pause. Then in extreme frustration.*) Sometimes I want to just go upstairs and fucking top myself.

Peter   Sometimes I wish you would.

Long silence.

Peter   I'm sorry, pet.

Mary   It's all right, lover.

Intro to 'Drink to Me Only with Thine Eyes'.

Scene Four

A bustling pub.

Lisa   Peter, have you and Mary ever thought about having kids?

Peter   Why do you ask?

Lisa   I just wondered.

Peter   Not really. Why?

Lisa   I always thought you'd make a good father. And you could spend a lot of time with it.

Peter   What's that supposed to mean?

Lisa   Nothing. I'm just saying.

Peter   What about you?

Lisa   I don't know, Ian seems a bit weird about it.

Peter   Weird?

Lisa   You know what he's like. He's worried about his independence and that. He says it's the wrong time. But I mean, when is the right time. It's weird to think we've both got to this age without any kids. I think it helps keep people together, doesn't it?

Peter   But you've been together for about four year.

Lisa   But we're still not married.

Peter   But it's the same thing.

Lisa   Not really. I mean, I love Ian and that. But you know, things are never what you dreamed of.

Peter   What do you mean, like?

Lisa   I just thought he'd take care of things more. Things are a real struggle. He's earning some money doing guvvies, but you know, it's not what I expected.

Peter   Well, things aren't exactly blossoming for me either.

Lisa   You're doing all right.

Peter   Come on. I'm a bloody cripple, I can't get a job or they'll stop me sick, and I'm not even thirty.

Lisa   Well, you'd never tell.

Peter   Never tell what?

Lisa   That you got shot. You look pretty good to me. Plus you've got your pension.

Peter (*dismissively*)   Fucking happy days.

Lisa   At least you're alive. What more do you want?

Peter   I don't know what I want. That's the whole point.

Lisa   Just give it time, Peter. How's Mary?

Peter   To tell you the truth things are a bit difficult at the moment.

Lisa   How do you mean?

Peter   We're under each other's feet a lot.

Lisa   It's funny how things work out, isn't it?

Peter   What do you mean?

Lisa   I mean. How come I ended up with Ian instead of someone else? Instead of you even.

Peter   You wouldn't want to get stuck with me.

Lisa   It might not have been so bad.

Peter   Right.

Lisa   What's the matter, I'm still attractive, aren't I? For my age.

Peter   Of course you are.

Lisa   It's just I think I'd feel settled with someone like you. I mean, you're pretty straightforward.

Peter   You might be surprised.

Lisa   No. I think you're all right.

Peter   Everybody has their faults.

Lisa   What do you think my faults are?

Peter   I don't know.

Lisa   Come on. You can tell me.

Peter   What you see from the outside doesn't really tell you much. You never really know what's going on underneath, do you?

Lisa   That's a bit deep.

Peter   Look, Lisa, there's noting wrong with you. I'm the one who's screwed up.

Lisa   You're not screwed up.

Peter   Lisa. I'm a fucking cripple, man.

Lisa   You're not a cripple. I think you're just a bit depressed.

'Down by the Sally Gardens'. First verse.

Scene Five

Peter's *bedroom*.

Mary   Look, I'm sorry.

Peter   What about?

Mary   About before.

Peter   It was my fault.

Mary   Come here.

She kisses him.

Don't be so uptight. You can touch me, you know.

Peter   I'm sorry. I'm a bit distracted.

Mary   I love you, Peter.

Peter   Don't.

Mary   What do you mean, don't?

Peter   Don't touch me there.

Mary   It's all right.

Peter   I don't like it.

Mary   It's all right. There's nothing to feel embarrassed about.

Peter   There's nothing there.

Mary   Don't you feel anything?

Peter   I've told you.

Mary   I just want it to feel good for you.

Peter   Look, it doesn't feel of anything – it's just disgusting.

Mary   You're being ridiculous. Why would it disgust you?

Peter   Because I've got no dick. Why the fuck do you think?

Mary   Come on, Peter.

Peter   What's the fucking point?

Mary   I don't care. I just want us to be close.

Peter   Give it a rest, for Christ's sake.

Long silence.

Mary   Why don't you ever touch me any more? Just because you're injured doesn't mean we have to stop being intimate.

Peter   I'm just . . . you know. I just don't feel like it.

Mary   Where does that leave me?

Peter   I'm sorry. I'll get over it.

Mary   You keep saying that.

Peter   It just takes time. It doesn't exactly make you feel very sexy having your block and tackle blown off.

Mary   Peter. I don't care what you look like. I need to be physical.

Peter   Well, how am I going to fuck you?

Mary   I don't want to be fucked. I just want to be intimate.

Peter   Jesus.

Mary   We have to talk about it.

Peter   How do you think it makes me feel?

Mary   You need to talk about it. You need to get it all out.

Peter   Look. I've had half me fucking dick blown off. End of story.

Mary   You can still do things.

Peter   Shut up, will you?

Mary   It's not about fucking. You could put your fingers in me. You can lick me.

Peter   Jesus Christ, woman.

Mary   It's been so long, Peter. I just want something back. I'm the one who's been mutilated. I'm only twenty-five, Peter. I feel sore. All over my body sore. Just for a bit of contact. It might not be something you can see, but it's still fucking real. It's still mutilation.

Long pause

Peter   I'm sorry.

'Come Ye Not From Newcastle'. First verse.

Scene Six

Bustling pub.

Ian   Lisa said she took you out for a pint the other night.

Peter   Yeah.

Ian   She said you didn't seem too happy.

Peter   I was fine. I just had a bit of a row with Mary.

Ian   The trouble with you is you spend too much time dwelling on things.

Peter   I haven't been dwelling on things.

Ian   It's the same as last time we went out. You spend too long contemplating your navel. You want to stop all this moping around.

Peter   How many times do I have to tell you? I am not moping around. Look, what's wrong with the fact that I might think abut things?

Ian   You should spend less time philosophising and more time getting your end away.

Peter   For Christ's sake.

Ian   I'm just saying there's nothing better than a good shag to take your mind off things.

Peter   Give it a rest.

Ian   I mean, Mary's a game girl. You should try out a few new things. I bet she'd be up for it.

Peter   What would you know?

Ian   You can just tell.

Peter   Has she been saying anything?

Ian   She hasn't said owt, you stupid bastard. But it's obvious that you're not exactly Casanova.

Peter   What's obvious?

Ian   You're hardly going to charm anyone with that attitude. Looka. If Mary's not up for it, get some on the side.

Peter   Just shut it, Ian.

Ian   What's the matter with you?

Peter   How would you feel if you were in my position?

Ian   You have to think of it as an opportunity. I mean, right, you had your stint in the army. And then you came out, admittedly you took a drop. But you're all right. You're a hero, man. There's plenty of people with a lot worse than a limp going about. Anyway, just because you're a cripple doesn't say you're fucked. I mean, some people think it's an advantage. Look at that bloke in the wheelchair, he solved the mystery of the universe by writing through a straw. You've got to snap out of it.

Music. 'Blow the Wind Southerly'.

Scene Seven

Monologue.

Peter   When you think about it. If there isn't a God how can you judge anything? How do you know if something is good or bad, if there's no divine justice? If some guy shoots me, well, why shouldn't he? If there isn't a God what's to stop him?

I ask myself over and over. What was I doing in Belfast? And I still can't tell you. And what's happened to the Paddy that fired the bullet? Is he dead? Did he have his balls blown off? Or is he still down the Falls Road shaggin' like a fuckin' rabbit? And if it's true that there isn't a God, I should wish him well. Because everything we do is just an accident. If there isn't some divine justice then it's all just chance. There's wars and then they stop. You hate people and get over it. Things happen and they change. And no one gives a shit. It just happens.

Music. 'Blow the Wind Southerly'.

Scene Eight

Ian's *bedroom.*

Ian   Don't you fancy it?

Lisa   Now?

Ian   When else were you thinking of? What's the matter?

Lisa   There's nothing the matter. I just don't feel like it.

Ian   You never felt like it last night either. Or any night come to think of it.

Lisa   Well, what do you expect? You've been getting at iz all day.

Ian   Come off it.

Lisa   Come off it, what?

Ian   You've always got some pathetic excuse.

Lisa   Just let it lie, Ian. I'm just not in the mood.

Ian   I don't have to put up with this, you know.

Lisa   Well, maybe if you made me feel a little better about myself then it would be different.

Ian   What's that mean?

Lisa   You never touch me unless you want a screw. You never ask what I'm feeling. You never try and sort things out.

Ian   What's there to sort out?

Lisa   Jesus Christ. Our situation. Having a family. You know fine well.

Ian   Look, I'm doing me best.

Lisa   Why don't you just behave like a normal human being?

Ian   Would you rather be with someone else?

Lisa   I want to be with someone I can talk to.

Ian   I bet you'd rather be with Peter, wouldn't you? Mr Sensitive. Has he got a bigger knob or something?

Lisa   Shut up, Ian.

Ian   That's it, isn't it? You still fancy him, don't you? Your childhood sweetheart.

Lisa   I don't fancy anybody.

Ian   Is that right, though? Has he got a bigger dick than me?

Lisa   Please, Ian. I'm trying to talk to you. I've been thinking about our situation and everything.

Ian   What about the situation?

Lisa   Well, I was talking to Lynn Folger.

Ian   What about Lynn Folger?

Lisa   You know she's a dancer.

Ian   She's a stripper.

Lisa   Well, erotic dancing.

Ian   Stripping.

Lisa   She makes a hundred quid a night.

Ian   Bollocks. A hundred quid. That scrubber.

Lisa   I swear. She says I could get some work.

Ian   Who the hell's going to pay to see you?

Lisa   Just shut up. I'm serious. I'm asking you.

Ian   What?

Lisa   How you would feel.

Ian   Well, how do you think I'd feel? I can't even get me end up and you're parading your arse to every fucker in town.

Lisa   Well, how else am I going to make any money?

Ian   Jesus Christ, we're not that desperate.

Lisa   How else are we going to start a family.

Ian   Well, the first thing you've got to do is get pregnant.

Lisa   It would just be until we get ourselves on an even keel.

Ian   We're getting on an even keel.

Lisa   I'm only trying to help.

Ian   Help. By suggesting you bare your arse in public.

Lisa   You sound like me dad.

Ian   What do you expect? What if you're 'dancing' and your dad walks in?

Lisa   He never goes to the Ship.

Ian   You're fuckin' twisted. You won't have a shag because you're too busy worrying whether or not you should go strippin'.

Lisa   You're not even listening to me.

Ian   I'm not listening. Well, you're doing sweet FA for me, pet.

Lisa   Where you going?

Ian   To have a wank.

Piano intro to 'Come Ye Not From Newcastle'.

Scene Nine

Interview room.

Man   How old are you?

Peter   Twenty-nine.

Man   And you were in the forces.

Peter   Army.

Man   What happened?

Peter   I got hit by a sniper.

Man   Where?

Peter   In Belfast.

Man   No. Where?

Peter   In the groin.

Man   In the knackers.

Peter   In the groin area.

Man   Painful.

Peter   But I'm all right now.

Man   But they've pensioned you off.

Peter   I was in hospital a long time.

Man   That's hard lines.

Peter   I mean, I can get around and that.

Man   And you're after some work.

Peter   Yeah.

Man   Well, if you're fit enough to work, what's the matter with the army.

Peter   I'm not fit enough to fight.

Man   But you're fit enough to work.

Peter   Yes.

Man   What's the matter with you exactly?

Peter   I told you, I got hit in the groin.

Man   Do you have a limp?

Peter   It's hardly noticeable.

Man   But you do have one.

Peter   It's not my fault. Look, I'm telling you I'm fit enough to work.

Man   Look, don't expect any sympathy from me, mate. I just need someone who can do the job. What qualifications have you got?

Peter   Qualifications.

Man   O levels and that.

Peter   I never did O levels.

Man   Jesus Christ.

Peter   I've got some CSEs. Maths, English and Metalwork.

Man   That'll not do you much good.

Peter   Look, it was fifteen years ago. I learned a lot in the army.

Man   Look, mate. I'm not looking for marksmen, you know.

Peter   Well, what type of work is it?

Man   Normally we get students from the college.

Peter   Students.

Man   Are you reliable?

Peter   Of course I'm reliable, I was in the army.

Man   And you don't mind weekends.

Peter   What exactly is it you're looking for?

Man   The Metro Bunny.

Peter   You what?

Man   There's a special suit and that.

Peter   You're joking, aren't you?

Man   Didn't he tell you?

Peter   Christ.

Man   Look, you can get out now with that attitude.

Peter   No. Wait a minute. It's just. You know. I thought it was something different.

Man   You go round giving balloons to kids and stuff. There's Metro Bunny and Mr Happy. And I can tell for a start Mr Happy's out of the question.

Peter   It's just . . . I mean . . . I was a soldier.

Man   Take it or leave it. It's cash in hand.

Peter   I don't know.

Man   I'm supposed to be doing this as a favour.

Peter   But people'll see.

Man   Who'll see, you're in a friggin' suit, man. Those students are lining up for this job.

Peter   And you're sure nobody will know?

Man   Look, mate. Take it or leave it. I'm sticking my neck right out for you. And the last thing I want is someone taking the piss.

Peter   All right.

Man   Two fifty an hour.

Door opens. Someone comes in.

Man   Start tomorrow. Here's Mr Happy.

Peter   Hello there.

Mr Happy (*in a joyous mood*)   Hi!

Short piano intro to 'I Have A Bonnet Trimed With Blue'.

Scene Ten

'Hark the Echoing Air'. A verse about Cupid.

Scene Eleven

The park.

Lisa   The problem is, Mary. I don't know where it's going any more.

Mary   What do you mean, where it's going?

Lisa It's like I can't even touch him any more. I just feel disgusted by the whole thing. Not with him, more with me. I don't know, I just feel trapped.

Mary But you just moved in together.

Lisa I know. It's just made matters worse.

Mary What does he think?

Lisa I don't know. He never really talks. I mean, he's out most of the time. Whenever I see him all he wants to do is sleep, eat or have sex. He never talks about things. You know what he's like.

Mary You don't think he's got someone else, do you?

Lisa I think he's depressed. I know you've got your problems and everything but I look at you and feel jealous.

Mary Of me?

Lisa Well, it's obvious you love each other.

Mary Is it?

Lisa Have you ever thought of having children?

Mary We haven't really thought of it.

Lisa But you do want kids, don't you?

Mary I suppose so, but . . .

Lisa The thing is he knows it's what I want more than anything else. He just goes on and on that we can't afford it.

Mary Maybes he's right.

Lisa But there's never a right time. I've started saving.

Mary Where are you getting the money?

Lisa Promise not to say anything.

Mary OK.

Lisa   Well, you know Lynn Folger. She got me in doing some dancing.

Mary   Stripping.

Lisa   Mary.

Mary   Are you out of your mind?

Lisa   It's the only thing I can see is going to change things. If I get a bit money behind me, everything'll be a bit different.

Mary   What does he say?

Lisa   He doesn't know.

Mary   What do you mean, he doesn't know?

Lisa   He told me no way should I do it.

Mary   He told you not to and you still did it.

Lisa   How else am I going to earn that kind of money?

Mary   How much do you get?

Lisa   Fifty quid a night.

Mary   Only fifty quid.

Lisa   It's only ten minutes' work.

Mary   But isn't it weird? Taking your clothes off?

Lisa   It's a bit weird.

Mary   Don't you feel dirty?

Lisa   I don't see what's wrong with it. I've got a nice body.

Mary   But still.

Lisa   What is weird is that they're so close. Like at the Ship in the Hole. It was packed. You could feel the heat, the pricks in their trousers.

Mary   That's awful.

Lisa   In a way I enjoyed it.

Mary   Weren't you embarrassed?

Lisa   I didn't really think about it.

Mary   You must have done.

Lisa   I wasn't embarrassed. Look, Mary. It's awful. I have to tell somebody. You've got to promise not to say.

Mary   Are you all right, pet?

Lisa   It wasn't the stripping. I knew about that. It was after I'd been on.

Mary   What's the matter?

Lisa   Something happened.

Mary   What happened?

Lisa   Well, the manager locked the doors. And somehow he gave one of the other lasses some money.

Mary   Some money.

Lisa   You know, some extra. She was really pissed by then.

Mary   Calm down.

Lisa   It was for 'a bit extra'.

Mary   What do you mean a bit extra?

Lisa   She went on with hardly anything on to start with. I mean, she wasn't really stripping. I could see from the back. We got changed in the loos off the bar. She sort of ran on and took her clothes off. Then she was going up to people. These blokes and fondling them and that. She was taking their pricks out their trousers.

Mary   In the pub?

Lisa   It was late. And she was putting them in her mouth. These dirty blokes. They were shouting. I was watching from the back. And then she took one of the blokes on to the

little stage and she put him in her mouth. Then he turned
her round and he was fucking her. She was on this table and
he was fucking her. And they came out of their chairs and
they were queuing up. Queuing up to fuck the girl and she
was just laughing. And they were going wild. And the young
lass I was with started crying. I felt sick. The place was hot,
my face was burning. I could feel myself wanting to be sick,
and I couldn't breathe. I told the young lass not to watch. I
went in the toilet and after a while the girl came through
with cum all over her. She was pissed off her head. And I
couldn't speak. I couldn't even speak to her.

Mary   And you're still doing it.

Lisa   I told them I was finished. But they said I didn't
have to go those nights if I didn't want to. That I could
just do a few dinner times, you know, when it's pretty
harmless.

Mary   Have you been back?

Lisa   A few times. It's good money, Mary.

Mary   But how do you feel?

Lisa   I feel awful.

Mary   Jesus Christ, Lisa. You can't do this to yourself.

Lisa   I know.

Music. 'I Have A Bonnet Trimmed With Blue'. A verse.

Scene Twelve

Monologue.

Peter   It's not just that it's humiliating that's depressing.
It's that it cuts you off. Being inside this big suit and
everything. It makes you see things. It's like the whole
Metro Centre is a dream. Shops and shops of endless things.
And you can tell most of the people they can't afford it.

Even when they've just spent a bloody fortune you can see
in their eyes they can't *really* afford it. It's something I hadn't
noticed before.

There's no proper light, there's no proper air. They've got a
fake antique village with a fake river and a fake stone bridge
made out of fibreglass. Where you can buy fake antiques,
fake miners' lamps made in Hong Kong. And you're in this
village where you can't see the sky. You can't see anything
except all these stupid bastards who think it's a treat to be
there. Nothing better to do. And I'm in a rabbit suit looking
at them on the fibreglass bridge and I can hear the taped
ducks quacking. And I try and imagine myself in a real
village just to enjoy it. And I realise to these people the
village *is* real. It's better than real because there's no duck
shit, no rain, no problems. And I realise that these people
think they're enjoying themselves. There's nothing better,
except if they were drunk. And you might say what's wrong
with it. It's only natural. But I realise there isn't anything
natural in the whole bloody place.

And you know how you can tell. The kids. The kids are
always miserable. That's why they need someone in a bunny
suit. Because they're screaming and crying and you look in
their mothers' eyes and there is real despair. Not just when
you're having a hard day. This is real desperation. There
they are on their own, with screaming kids, exhausted,
surrounded by things they can't afford, and this is their life
and there's no way out, and even if they didn't have the
kids, and even if they did have the money, or a nanny – you
know they know that this is all there is. The limit of their
imagination. Somewhere they can't find their way out of, in
the artificial light being approached by a six-foot rabbit.

Reprise of 'I Have A Bonnet Trimmed With Blue'.

Scene Thirteen

Peter's *house. The party.*

Ian   All right. Which star would play you if they made a picture of your life?

Lisa   That's stupid.

Ian   It isn't. It's a question.

Mary   Do you want another beer?

Ian   Peter.

Peter   I don't know. Who would play you?

Ian   Bruce Willis.

Peter   Bruce Willis. More like Danny DeVito.

Ian   Divvint talk daft. That shortarse?

Peter   Who do you think you are, like, 'Garth'?

Lisa   What about you, Mary?

Mary   I never watch films.

Peter   Of course you do.

Mary   On the telly. But I don't know who's in them.

Peter   Julia Roberts.

Mary   That skinny cow. She looks like she's ready for the morgue.

Lisa   Well, who else?

Mary   I don't know. Meryl Streep.

Ian   For fuck's sake.

Mary   What's the matter with Meryl Streep?

Ian   You've got to be joking, haven't you? She's about as horny as a kick in the nuts.

Lisa   Does she have to be sexy, like?

Ian (*to* **Mary**)   Well, you're sexy.

Mary   Give over.

Ian   Don't you think so?

Peter   Of course she's sexy.

Ian   You're at your prime.

Lisa   What about me?

Ian   What about you? Just because Mary's sexy doesn't say you aren't. Peter always thought you were sexy. Didn't you?

Peter   No. I mean.

Lisa   You don't think I'm sexy?

Peter   I'm not saying that.

Ian   He's always had a hot spot for you if you ask me. Since you were at school.

Peter   Howway, man, Ian.

Ian   Come on, admit it.

Mary   Peter.

Peter   This is stupid.

Ian   What's stupid about it? Anyway. You never said yours.

Peter   What?

Ian   Film star.

Peter   There aren't any Geordie film stars.

Ian   Don't be a complete twat.

Peter   Harrison Ford.

Mary *laughs.*

Lisa   Harrison Ford.

Ian   Well, you know what they say about Harrison Ford. Don't you?

Lisa   What?

Ian   He's got a dick like a baby's arm.

Peter   What are you trying to say.

Ian   You see, these games are very revealing.

Lisa   Is it true, Mary?

Ian   She's blushing.

Lisa   It must be true.

Ian   Look, she's went beetroot.

Peter   Who would you be?

Lisa   Sharon Stone.

Ian   Look, she's still thinking about his dick.

Peter   Leave her alone.

Ian   Look.

Mary   I wasn't. Anyway.

Ian   Well, it's not how long it is it's what you do with it. Isn't that right, love?

Lisa   Why don't you see if you can shove yours up your arse?

Ian   I'll have to unwrap it from round me leg first.

Peter   Just leave it be.

Ian   What's the matter with you?

's just getting a bit crude.

hell. You're a bit prudish these days.

, there's women.

Ian   That's sexism, that is. Mary, you're not embarrassed, are you?

Mary   Well . . .

Ian   See. Lisa?

Lisa   What's good for the goose is good for the gander.

Mary   You mean the other way round.

Lisa   What?

Mary   The goose is a woman.

Ian   What?

Mary   What's good for the gander is good for the goose.

Ian   You've lost me. Anyway, Peter, about your dick . . .

Peter   Shurrup, will you?

Mary   Peter.

Ian   There's no need to be like that.

Lisa   He was only joking.

Peter   I think it's worn a bit thin.

Ian   'Funaah-funaah.'

Peter   I just don't know why you have to turn everything into an innuendo.

Ian   I was only having a bit fun.

Peter   But you always take things too far.

Ian   You're embarrassed, aren't you? Anybody would think you're scared of sex or something.

Peter   I'm not scared of anything.

Ian   Maybe you feel inadequate.

Peter   What do you mean inadequate?

Ian   Cos you're a cripple or something.

Peter   I'm not the one who's inadequate. At least my lass hasn't got to go stripping.

Ian   What.

Silence.

What do you mean? Go stripping?

Lisa   Mary.

Mary   Peter.

Lisa   You promised.

Ian   I told you.

Lisa   It was only two or three times then I stopped.

Ian   You stupid bitch.

Mary   What did you have to say that for?

Ian   Am I the only one who doesn't know?

Lisa   It was for the money.

Ian   But I said.

Mary   Just let it lie.

Ian   Shut up, you.

Peter   Don't tell her to shut up like that.

Lisa   I can't believe you told him.

Ian   I expect you've paid three quid to see her snatch 'n'all.

Peter   Don't start getting funny, Ian.

Lisa   I did it for the money. You lot. All of you. All you do is sit round and moan. At least I went and did something.

Ian   What you going to spend it on, like? A new sequinned G-string?

Lisa   I've put it away. You stupid bastard.

Ian   For a rainy day.

Lisa   For a kid.

Ian   Well, thanks for telling me, like.

Lisa   I don't have to ask you.

Ian   Don't you think it might be helpful to include me in this if you want to get pregnant.

Lisa   I don't have to include you any more.

Ian   Who the hell do you think you are, the Virgin bloody Mary?

Mary   Shut up – both of yous.

Ian   You'll not be able to bare your arse down the Dog and Parrot when you're eight months pregnant.

Lisa   All I want is to have a kid. Is that too much to ask? All I want is to have someone to love without having to get their permission. Someone who's not so depressed they don't even talk to iz. I want a reason to get out of bed in the morning. It's only natural. I mean. All these excuses, Ian. What's the matter with you?

Silence.

Mary   Another beer, anybody?

Lisa   Fuck off, Mary.

Music. 'Go Not Happy Day'. First few lines.

Scene Fourteen

Monologue.

Peter   I have these dreams. Nightmares really. That people are fucking Mary. I'll be in the living room and then I'll go to bed. And there she is being fucked by somebody. Usually people I know. Like the binman or my old sergeant major. And they're giving it rice in the bed and I just stand there frozen. And they carry on as if I'm not there. Then suddenly they'll look up and laugh. Some bloke shaggin' my wife laughing at me. In my own bed. And I want to die. Not out of embarrassment. I want to die because of what Mary's gone through. The last thing she'd do is be unfaithful. I know it's me. There's something sick in my mind. Something in me that wants to be humiliated. That wants to humiliate other people. And it makes me sick. I think I must be sick. I think there's something sick in human nature.

Verse beginning 'He wears a blue bonnet' from 'The Keel Row'.

Scene Fifteen

Office, Metro Centre.

Man   You're late back again.

Peter   Sorry. I got held up.

Man   I'll give you held up. You're supposed to be the Metro Bunny. There's people queuing up to have this job.

Peter   Look, I was only five minutes late. I'll make it up.

Man   I don't have to take your lip, just cos yer a war hero.

Peter   I'm sorry. It'll not happen again.

Man   You bet it won't.

Peter   I'll get changed then.

Man   You better hop to it. Get it. Hop to it.

Piano out of 'The Keel Row'.

Scene Sixteen

The pub.

Mary   Look. I don't know what I'm doing here in the middle of the afternoon.

Ian   I thought you might want to talk about things.

Mary   What do you mean?

Ian   What do I mean. Peter.

Mary   What about Peter?

Ian   Well, he seems to be going off the deep end.

Mary   He's just depressed.

Ian   He seemed more than depressed to me.

Mary   It's fine, honestly.

Ian   Are you OK, Mary?

Mary   I'm fine. It's you and Lisa I'm worried about. Where is she?

Ian   She's gone to her brother's in Middlesbrough.

Mary   Oh.

Ian   Do you want another?

Mary   No, I'm fine.

Ian   Well, don't sound so depressed about it.

Mary   Thanks for the drink. I think I should be going.

Ian   Is there something you're not telling me?

Mary   No.

Ian   Mary.

Mary   Ian. I'm desperate. He's never satisfied. It's morning, noon and night. Picking at me. I know I should have more patience.

Ian   All you need is a good fuck, the pair of yous.

Mary   Jesus Christ.

Ian   What are you Jesus Christing about? It's true.

Mary   Ian. The accident.

Ian   What?

Mary   He can't do anything. He's not all there.

Ian   No bloody wonder he's going round like one o'clock half struck.

Mary   I should never have told you.

Ian   The selfish bastard.

Mary   What do you mean?

Ian   So there's nothing there. Not even a little bit.

Mary   Keep your voice down.

Ian   Christ.

Mary   Please don't say anything.

Ian   As if I'm going to say anything. So you can't make love?

Mary   It's not as if that's all you have to do.

Ian   What do you mean?

Mary   I can't stand it any more. He's switched off. It's deformed him.

Ian   Come on, lover.

Mary   I'm at the end of me rope.

Ian   You just need someone to hold you, Mary.

Mary   Ian. You must never tell anyone. It would kill him.

Ian   Shh. The poor bastard. He doesn't deserve you.

Ian *kisses* **Mary**.

Mary   What are you doing? You can't kiss me here.

Ian   Nobody's looking.

Mary   Look. I don't think we should do this.

Ian   Mary. You need someone. You need me. You want to be fucked. I can see it, Mary.

Mary   I just want everything to stop hurting. Screwing you won't help me. It'd only make matters worse.

An apposite (second or third verse) of 'The Stuttering Lovers'.

Scene Seventeen

Ian's *bedroom.*

Ian   Don't worry, she won't be back until tomorrow.

Mary   Jesus Christ, Ian.

Ian   I want you.

They kiss.

Mary   What about Lisa?

Ian   I don't want Lisa. I want you. I need you. I want to put my tongue inside you. I want to fuck you, Mary.

Mary   He mustn't find out.

Ian   Nobody will ever know, Mary. Nobody will ever know.

Next verse of 'The Stuttering Lovers'.

Scene Eighteen

Changing room, Metro Centre.

Mr Happy   You know your trouble, don't you? You're morbid. That's your trouble. I'm not saying I'm not sorry for you and I'm not saying you don't do a good job. But

you're the most miserable Metro Bunny we've had.
Anybody would think you'd be happy. You know, pleased
with the fact you were bringing pleasure into people's lives.

Peter For Christ's sake, leave me alone.

Mr Happy Cheer up, man.

Peter Listen, you're getting right on my tit end.

Mr Happy Just listen to Mr Happy. Whatever way you
look at it life's not that bad. It's just ways of seeing. The
trouble is, my friend, you just see the problems. One man
sees a glass half empty, the other sees the glass half full.
You're playing right into their hands by this self-pity. That's
exactly what they want you to do. Collective action, that's
the only way forward.

Peter Look, you've lost me there, pal.

Mr Happy You were wounded, right. So you've got
something to complain about. But what's the point of
keeping it to yourself? Have you ever discussed with me
how you feel?

Peter I don't want to discuss my problems.

Mr Happy What's the matter with you?

Peter I got hit in Northern Ireland.

Mr Happy Show me your wounds.

Peter I can't.

Mr Happy Show me your wounds. Look, until people
are prepared to come out and admit to each other they're
imperfect, as long as they are determined to keep themselves
to themselves and perpetuate the myth that somehow
there's such a thing as normality, things will never change.
Look. Do you see that? That's a colostomy bag. Now you
wouldn't have expected that, would you? But I'm not
ashamed to show you.

Peter I don't see why that makes you any happier.

Mr Happy   At least I'm not hiding anything. I'm working for a better society where people can lose their inhibitions and just enjoy themselves.

Peter   But even if you turned the whole bloody world upside down – you can't make people happy.

Mr Happy   You can but try.

Peter   Listen, every morning you'd wake up and worry about something, however fine the weather is.

Mr Happy   There is nothing we can't provide for each other.

Peter   What if you're a cripple? What if you lose your legs in an accident?

Mr Happy   Then we'll get you a wheelchair.

Peter   Well, what if you have cancer or some incurable disease.

Mr Happy   Then we will give you somewhere to convalesce. And we will do research. Christ, it's all just a matter of resources. I'm not saying we'll not die. I'm just saying we can stop the misery of being alive.

Peter   But what if someone is insane?

Mr Happy   Well, give him somewhere to be. Care and consideration. Medication if it helps. But you can still treat them like a human being.

Peter   But what about people who are sick even if they seem fit and well?

Mr Happy   What do you mean?

Peter   What if somebody's lost their genitals?

Mr Happy   Jesus Christ. You don't give up.

Peter   But it must happen.

Mr Happy   Well, they'd be buggered. But the important thing is you have to care. You have to share our pain.

Peter   What do you know about it? How the hell can you know what I feel? No matter how bloody clever you are. No matter how dedicated. You can never know shag all. What do you know about the bleeding? About the shame? Or the embarrassment? Or operations? Or the arguments? Or the frustration? You can't understand a bloody thing. And if you don't understand I don't want your sympathy, or your highfalutin ideas. I'd much rather you shut your hole. I'd much rather you all just fucked right off.

Mr Happy   Look into people's eyes, Peter. Today when you walk through here. Look and see the damage. We're all cripples somewhere deep down.

Peter   You make me sick.

Mr Happy   What do you mean?

Peter   You sanctimonious little bastard. Just because you piss into a plastic bag you feel as if you can tell me what's right and wrong. If I didn't need this job I'd kick your fucking arse for you.

Mr Happy   That's it. Let your anger out, my man. It's the only way to heal. Why should you suffer alone?

Intro to 'Have You Seen Owt a Ma Bonnie Lad'.

Scene Nineteen

Peter*'s house.*

Peter   Where have you been?

Mary   I just had a drink, with Lisa.

Peter   It's just you seem to be seeing a lot of Lisa lately.

Mary   Shouldn't I?

Peter   What's happened?

Mary   What do you mean what's happened?

Peter   You've been dressing up more lately.

Mary   I thought you liked me dressing up.

Peter   But you stopped.

Mary   Well, I've started again.

Peter   Who is it?

Mary   Who is what?

Peter   I'm not stupid. Who are you seeing?

Mary   I'm not seeing anybody.

Peter   Don't deny it.

Mary   I'm not denying anything.

Peter   You think I'm a fuckin' idiot. That I'm going to sit round here while you go round like some ten-bob whore.

Mary   You're being ridiculous.

Peter   Tell me who it is?

Mary   Honest, it isn't anybody.

Peter *grabs her.*

Peter   Tell me who it is or I'll knock it out of you.

Mary   Please, Peter. You've got it all wrong.

Peter *whacks her.*

Peter   Bitch.

Mary   Stop it.

Peter *whacks her again.*

Mary   Stop it, Peter. Please.

Peter *hits her again and again.* **Mary** *screams. She sobs quietly.* **Peter** *goes to sit down.*

Mary   Stop it. Stop it. There isn't anybody else.

Peter   What are you doing to me? What are you doing?

Mary   It's hard enough as it is.

Peter   Jesus. I'm sorry.

Mary   You have to control yourself.

Peter   I'm sorry.

Mary   I'm going to the bathroom.

Mary *goes to the bathroom and locks the door.*

Peter   Oh God, Mary. I'm sorry. I know there isn't anyone else. I'm sorry.

Reprise of 'Have You Seen Owt a Ma Bonnie Lad'.

Scene Twenty

In bed – fucking

Ian *straining.*

Mary   Harder.

Ian   Look at me. Look at me.

Ian *comes. Long pause.*

Mary   If you could wish for one thing in the whole world right now. What would it be?

Ian   I don't really know. What about you?

Mary   I don't want to say.

Ian   Go on, you can tell me.

Mary   I wish he was dead.

Ian   For fuck's sake, Mary.

Mary   Well, you asked.

First verse of 'Down by the Sally Gardens'.

Scene Twenty-One

Metro Centre.

Lisa   Peter.

Peter   What are you doing here?

Lisa   I came to see you.

Peter   How did you know where I worked?

Lisa   I asked a few people. I thought you said it was security.

Peter   It's undercover.

Lisa   Undercover.

Peter   Yeah. You know.

Lisa   What exactly do you do?

Peter   Look. Will you promise not to tell anyone?

Lisa   I suppose so.

Peter   I'm the Metro Bunny.

Lisa   What?

Peter   You mustn't tell Mary. Or Ian.

Lisa *laughs.*

Lisa   I'm sorry.

Peter   What's so funny about that?

Lisa   Well, you know, the Metro Bunny.

Peter   Jesus Christ. Don't tell Mary.

Lisa   I didn't mean to upset you.

Peter   I don't know why you came. Why you've been snooping around.

Lisa   Look, Peter. I know you're not happy.

Peter   How can you say that?

Lisa   What?

Peter   How can you know?

Lisa   I want to help you.

Peter   You can't help me.

Lisa   You could help me.

Peter   What do you mean?

Lisa   You mean an awful lot to me. All I want is some comfort. I've always had a soft spot for you.

Peter   Don't be ridiculous.

Lisa   I'm just tired. Of it. He's a monster, man. I need to be treated different from that. I know I'm worth more than that. I'm sensitive to things. You know. I think about things. You've always thought about things. It's what I like about you.

Peter   Lisa, pet. I think you've got the wrong idea.

Lisa   Please, Peter.

Peter   You're just being ridiculous.

Lisa   Will you just hold me? I just want someone to hold me.

Peter   Why me?

Lisa   I just want a man to hold me. That's all.

Peter   I can't.

Lisa   I thought.

Peter   Well, you thought wrong.

Lisa   But the way you look sometimes.

Peter   But that doesn't mean anything.

Lisa   I'm sorry.

Peter   You don't understand.

Lisa   I know that.

Peter   You can't possibly understand.

Lisa   You need help, Peter.

Peter   Listen, pet. I'm not myself.

Lisa   Peter.

Peter   You better leave me alone.

Lisa   I'm terrified. What are we becoming?

Peter   We'll look back on this in a few years and have a good laugh.

Lisa   Will we?

Peter   Have a good fuckin' laugh . . . It's funny where you end up, isn't it? Who you end up stuck with. I mean, none of us are bad people. But we certainly make a fucking mess of things, don't we? The thing is I can't even put into words properly what the problem is.

Lisa   I just want somebody close to me.

Peter   Please, don't touch me.

Lisa   I just want somebody close.

Long pause.

Peter   Lisa. I'm sorry. You have to leave me alone.

Lisa   But you said yourself things weren't good with Mary.

Peter   It's not Mary that's the problem.

Lisa   I don't understand. What is the problem?

Peter   I'm the problem.

Lisa   I don't understand.

Peter   I think an affair with me would be more trouble than it's worth.

Lisa   How do you mean?

Peter   The accident. Lisa.

Lisa   The accident.

Peter   I'm sorry, Lisa. I can't be close to anyone. Please don't tell anyone.

Lisa   What do you mean?

Peter   I'm sorry, Lisa. I have to go.

Reprise of 'Down by the Sally Gardens'.

Scene Twenty-Two

Monologue.

Peter   Sometimes I am just walking. Along a street. And I see a child. And maybe the child has only one leg. Or a broken arm. Or is blind in one eye. Or has had part of his head removed in some operation. And the child looks at me. And comes running in his callipers.

And then I see a woman. With one of her breasts removed. Or someone from a car crash. Or she's had a hysterectomy. Or a bone-marrow transplant. And she's running too. And there's a man with elephantiasis. And a guy with a wonky spine. And there's people with leukaemia and diabetes. People with open wounds and septic sores and bleeding gashes. And they are all running and they are all standing next to me singing. In their croaked voices, with their tracheotomies and their ruined lungs and we are all singing.

Standing upright – or as best we can. And I am surrounded by cripples and invalids, the corrupt, the flatulent, the weak and the dying. And we all rise and sing as one voice: 'It's a long way to Tipperary'. It's that song. And they are doing the best they can. And their hearts are right there. But I can never understand why it's me. I can never understand why it's that song.

Music: 'Kitty Will You Marry Me?'.

Scene Twenty-Three

The park.

Lisa   Mary. I think we should talk.

Mary   Talk.

Lisa   Mary. I know everything.

Mary   What do you mean you know everything? Who told you?

Lisa   Nobody's told me anything. Not directly. Who would, it's too painful. I worked it out.

Mary   I'm sorry.

Lisa   For Christ's sake, Mary. Don't apologise. You deserve much more than this. If there's anything I could do. I'd do anything to make it better.

Mary   What do you mean? I fuck your boyfriend and now you tell me that's OK.

Lisa   Fuck my boyfriend?

Mary   You said you'd worked it out.

Lisa   Jesus Christ.

Mary   What had you worked out?

Lisa   Peter. I know what happened to Peter.

Mary   He told you?

Lisa   You bitch.

Mary   I'm so sorry.

Lisa   How could you do that to Peter? How could you do that to me? You're a little whore, Mary.

Mary   I'm sorry. Honestly. I don't know what I've been thinking.

Lisa   I know exactly what you were thinking. You dirty slut.

Mary   It's been well over a year, Lisa. And he told me things weren't good between you.

Lisa   A year.

Mary   I'm sorry.

Lisa   I'd wait ten years. Twenty years. A lifetime for Peter. And to do it with Ian. You know what he's like with me.

Mary   I haven't been thinking.

Lisa   He's a bastard, Mary. Do you think he cares about you? Do you really think he cares for you any more than he cares for me. The bloke is a headcase. He's a sick bastard, Mary. And if that's what you want. You can have him.

Mary   Lisa.

Lisa   You can both go and fuck yourselves until you're blue in the face. It's your funeral.

Mary   But Lisa.

Lisa   You asked for it.

Mary   I didn't ask for any of this. I didn't ask for anything.

Speech by John Major.

Scene Twenty-Four

Metro Centre.

Peter   I've been thinking about what you said. About suffering alone. Sorry about what I said. About the colostomy bag and everything.

Mr Happy   It's all right. I've got nothing to be embarrassed about.

Peter   It's just that maybe I've been a bit depressed and that.

Mr Happy   I'm privileged that you're sharing this with me.

Peter   It's just I think I've been unfair to Mary. You know, everything she's done. Everything she's put up with. She's like a bloody saint and all I've done is pick at her and ignore her.

Mr Happy   Well, you have to tell her.

Peter   But what can I say? How can I make up for all the shit I've given her?

Mr Happy   You'll find the words. Just go. Go now and the words will come.

Peter   I can't go now. I've got to work.

Mr Happy   Give me that suit.

Peter   What are you doing?

Mr Happy   I'll cover for you.

Peter   But . . .

Mr Happy   Lend me your ears, Peter. Lend me your ears.

Scene Twenty-Five

Peter's *bedroom*.

Ian   Come on then. Get your kit off.

Mary   Ian, I brought you up here to talk.

Ian   We can talk any time.

Mary   Please, Ian. Listen. Lisa knows.

Ian   I don't care, Mary.

Mary   How can you say that? I didn't want this to happen.

Ian   Just forget it. She doesn't mean anything to me.

Mary   How can you say that?

Ian   Because it's true.

Mary   Oh God, Ian. Can't you just try to be more understanding?

Ian   Understanding. Is that what you want from me?

Mary   What do you think I want?

Ian   To be fucked.

Mary   Christ. What are you doing here, Ian? He's your best mate.

Ian   He's your husband. Come on. I need you, Mary.

Mary   Stop it, Ian. It's disgusting.

Ian   I'll tell you what's disgusting. A young woman crippling herself over something that didn't even happen to her.

Mary   Of course it happened to me. It happened to all of us.

Ian   Look, it wasn't your fault. What good is fucking yourself over when you could be fucking me?

Mary This is serious, Ian. I'm pregnant.

Ian You're what?

Mary It's true.

Ian Are you sure?

Mary Of course I'm sure.

Ian Have you seen a doctor.

Mary I've took enough tests.

Ian You'll have to get rid of it.

Mary Hang on a minute.

Ian You can't keep it.

Mary It's not that simple.

Ian Of course it is.

Mary It's not that likely I'm going to get pregnant again very easily.

Ian But he'll kill you.

Mary But he always wanted a child.

Ian But not like this.

Mary But what about me? Why should I be barren?

Ian Mary.

Mary Maybe I should leave him.

Ian What, when you're pregnant?

Mary It's your child too.

Ian Now hang on a minute.

Mary But you said.

Ian I never said I was going to get you up the stick.

Mary You bastard.

Ian   Look. I thought this was different. I thought we needed each other. That we were stuck in relationships that were suffocating us. I thought it was all clear. That for once in our lives we were being honest with each other. And now you spring this on me.

Mary   Listen, you were the one who sprung this on me. I thought we were being careful.

Ian   What more do you want me to do?

Mary   You don't understand anything, do you?

Ian   What do you want me to do? What did you expect me to say? Eh?

Mary   I don't know, Ian. I don't know.

Ian   Do you really want to go and live in some shit heap with me and raise a bairn? Is that really what you had in mind?

Mary   Ian. I never had anything in mind. That's the trouble. I was always getting through and I was always waiting for life to happen. I always thought it was just around the corner; one day it'd be different. And I'd imagine it in the distance and I'd put out my hands to touch it. It was such soft wonderful silk. And then I'd see my hands and they were rough and dirty and I pulled back in horror. Not at life. But at my own hands. I don't know if I can go on like this. Maybe I have to grasp things warts and all.

Ian   Jesus Christ.

Mary   I think we should tell him.

Ian   You can't. It'd kill him.

Mary   But he has the right to know.

Ian   Just think about this a minute.

Mary   All I do is think about it.

Ian   He'll crucify you.

Mary   Maybe I deserve it.

Ian   You can't do this. What about me? What will he do to me?

Mary   Is that all you care about, Ian? I always thought you were just some insensitive pig. You know, always the ladies' man. Always the one with the joke. But I've seen more than that. I know there's more to you. I see there is something special in you and I need you to help me. I need some support.

Ian   What are you trying to do to me? You don't know anything about me. This was all meant to be a bit of fun and all you do is whine. What do you expect me to do? You're not going to trap me. You can go back to cockless bastard.

Mary   Oh my God.

Silence.

Mary   I thought you loved me.

Ian   I never even liked you.

Sound of **Peter** *coming in downstairs.*

Peter (*off*)   Mary.

Ian   Shit.

Peter   Mary.

Ian   What are we going to do?

Mary   Shh.

Sound of **Peter** *coming up the stairs.*

Peter (*off*)   Mary.

Mary   Peter.

Peter   What the . . . What's he doing here?

Mary   I'm sorry, Peter.

Peter   What are you doing in my bedroom?

Ian   It's not what you think.

Peter   I can't believe this is happening. After what you said.

Mary   I was going to tell you.

Peter   How long?

Ian   About three months.

Peter   But you promised.

Mary   I didn't know how to tell you.

Peter   Get out.

Mary   Please listen.

Peter   Out.

Mary   Peter. I think we should go downstairs and talk about this rationally.

Peter   There's nothing rational to talk about.

Mary   Please.

Peter   You cow.

Slap. **Mary** *starts to cry.*

Ian   Get off her.

Peter   Don't dare touch me. If I start I'll kill you.

Ian   Peter, she's pregnant.

Peter   What did you say?

Ian   Look, you've got no right to take it out on her. You're ever so pleased with yourself, aren't you? Because you're a fuckin' cripple. But look what you've done.

Peter   You're monsters.

Ian   You're the monster. Look what you've done to her, man.

Peter   I don't understand. Do you love him?

Mary   Don't be stupid.

Ian   She doesn't give a shit about me.

Peter   What the fuck is she doing in bed with you, then?

Ian   She needs some warmth, Peter.

Peter   What do you know?

Ian   Are you blind?

Peter   But how could you do this? How could you humiliate her?

Ian   You don't humiliate a woman by screwing her, but you do by ignoring her. You don't even deserve her.

Mary   Get out. Get out, you bastard.

Scene Twenty-Six

Peter*'s living room.*

Mary   I'm sorry.

Peter   I bet you had a good laugh, didn't you?

Mary   Peter.

Peter   I bet he laughed his balls off. I bet he laughed his knob off when he heard.

Mary   Nobody laughed.

Peter   You did. You just can't admit it. You used to laugh. I remember when we were married. Do you remember at the reception and we laughed till we both cried.

Mary   Peter. Stop it.

Peter   And you cried when I went to Ireland. You kissed me and cried. But when I left this house you were laughing. You were laughing because we had such great hopes. But you know something, Mary. When they brought me back, when I was in the hospital. You didn't cry once. You didn't laugh. You didn't cry. Not when I was there.

Mary   You have no idea how much I cried.

Peter   Mary. There used to be a time when you were jealous. When you used to worry about other women. Now that's something to laugh about now, eh. Remember how you used to be jealous. Eh?

Mary   Yes.

Peter   Well, no need for that now. No need to worry that I'm going to go screwing around. To me that's something to laugh about.

Mary   Shut up.

Peter   Laugh when you see some poor down-and-out bastard. Laugh when you see somebody worse off than yourself. Shall I show you? Shall I show you something to laugh at.

Takes off his pants.

There, there's something to laugh at. Look at the state of that. No, look, Mary. Face facts. Look at me. What can you see? They're not genitals. It's a joke. It's just burned-up, mutilated flesh. It's a joke. A sick ruddy joke. Go on. Have a good honest laugh.

Mary   Cover yourself up.

Peter   What's the matter?

Mary   Peter.

Peter   You don't seem to be finding it funny.

Mary   You're scaring me.

Peter   How could you be scared of me when I haven't even got any balls?

Mary   Stop it.

Peter   What do you see, Mary? Be honest, tell me what you see.

Mary   Nothing.

Peter   Mary, for Christ's sakes, look at me. Just tell me what's left?

Mary   A body that's scarred.

Peter   Tell me what it's like, Mary.

Mary   It's just scar tissue. Where your cock should be is just rubbery skin, it's contorted and smooth, it's pink and red . . . Peter, it's not an ugly body, it's beautiful. But when I look at you now, I don't even see it, all I see when I look is your eyes. The same eyes when we first met. You always had sad eyes. But when you used to look it felt like I had strong arms around me. Like you would never let go. All I ever wanted was someone to protect me and never let go. And you were so strong, Peter, you were so tough . . . Now I look and all I feel is alone.

Peter   Are you scared?

Mary   I don't know. I still love you.

Peter   It's just you've got a funny way of showing it.

Mary   Peter. I'm sorry. I'll never forgive myself.

Peter   Look. I don't blame you for going with Ian. I think you're quite entitled.

Mary   I'm not asking for you to understand. All I want is for you to say you love me.

Peter   Look. You can go ahead. I'm going to move out. You can keep the lot. The house. The furniture.

Mary   No. Peter. It's you I want. You just have to forgive me. I didn't know what I was doing.

Peter   Of course you knew what you were doing. Why are you lying to me now? Maybe my fucked-up body makes you sick. But believe me, you make me sick. Your slimy hands, your sagging tits, your fat arse, your stinking gob. Everything about you. You repulse me. You're rotten to the core.

Mary Why don't you just hit me again? That's what you want, isn't it? Go on.

Peter You're not worth the effort.

Silence. Over a long time. **Mary** *starts to cry.*

I used to think you were so strong compared to me. But you're just as broken as I am.

Mary I don't want to leave you.

Peter You're just a poor pathetic cunt like me, Mary. Look, I'll leave you alone.

Mary I'm not leaving you now.

Peter I think we should just go our separate ways.

Mary Peter. Be reasonable.

Peter There's something in us deeper than reason. I just need to be alone.

Mary Are you serious?

Peter Of course I am.

Mary But what am I going to do?

Peter At least you're strong and healthy. But if you're tied to me, pet, you haven't got a snowball's chance in hell.

Mary Where are you going? Don't leave me alone.

Peter I haven't the strength to look after you. I haven't the imagination. I'd been blind to all this before. It's got nothing to do with you and Ian. It's got nothing to do with us. It's just me. I can see too clearly.

Mary For Christ's sake, don't do anything stupid. Not after what we've been through. Look everything's going to be all right again. Just the two of us.

Peter   Look, Mary. I don't want to see you again.

Mary   But we can make it work, Peter. No matter what you put me through, I'll still love you. I'll do anything to make things better. Just tell me you love me. Just say you still love me and it will all be all right.

Silence from **Peter**.

Mary   Just tell me, Peter.

Silence.

All you have to say is you love me.

Long silence.

Scene Twenty-Seven

Monologue.

Peter   I remember when I was small. The canary my granny had. I'd been out running around. Soldiers – some daft shite. And as I came in running I saw her standing with this pin. And the little thing was flapping at the bottom of its cage. And its eyes were just bloody lumps. And she was shaking like she didn't know what she'd done. And I grabbed her. I was shouting. And she kept saying it's what her mother did. It makes them sing better. And I was standing and I couldn't believe it. How she could be so cruel? And I was shaking too and I didn't know what to do. So I hit her, in the face. And I ran upstairs. I could hear her crying. And I was crying too, not for punching her. But because I understood. Something about why she had done it and to this day I've tried to put it into words. But it seems so hard. But it was something about how the world seemed clearer in the dark.

Final verse of 'Down by the Sally Gardens'.

Spoonface Steinberg

Spoonface Steinberg was broadcast on Radio 4 in January 1997. It was directed by Kate Rowland and performed by Becky Simpson. This stage version premiered at the Crucible Theatre, Sheffield, in December 1999 and transferred to the New Ambassadors Theatre, London, in January 2000. The cast was as follows:

Spoonface Steinberg   Kathryn Hunter

Co-Directors Marcello Magni and Anne Castledine
Designer Liz Cooke
Lighting designer Tina McHugh

The music in the play is taken from *Callas: La Divina 1* and *2* (EMI Classics).

MUSIC: *Maria Callas singing 'Casta Diva' from* Norma *by Bellini*

Spoonface *talks over the music.*

Spoonface   In the olden days – when they wrote the songs and the operas and that, it mattered how you died – when the singers singed and went about – and they sang like beautiful birds and they fell over and everything – and she was all quavery and beautiful and everyone holded their breath – and there she was in the special light with her boobs and everything – and everyone would be looking and they would cry and in their hearts they would weep for the poor lady – the poor poor lady who dies so well.

And if I could ever grow up I would be one of them sad singers and do the dying and everybody would clap and cheer – and in all of the singing when people heard it they would have a little piece of beauty – which is very important – to have the little piece of beauty what's in the music – and this is what I realised – even though the beautiful singing is sad – it is still happy in a way – the saddest things fill you up – like in a big way and you feel so full as in no happiness can bring such – and all such sadness is beautiful – as beautiful as the singing – as beautiful as the dying – and it would make a meaning – and I would sing the dying and people would love me – and I would sing the dying and out come the angels to take me away – and I would sing the dying and there would be a lovely piece of beauty in the world – and I would sing the dying and be as free as a little bird floating up to heaven.

MUSIC: *Maria Callas singing 'Casta Diva' from* Norma.

I never heard such singing before except for when Doctor Bernstein brought the tapes – even though the other children like such music as Take That and that – even one little girl has this tape of Take That and Take That sent her this picture and they were all blowing her a kiss and all she ever does is play the music and she can't even hear because she is in a coma and then Take That made her a tape which said 'Hello this is Robbie' and she still wasn't better – and I said this was no surprise on account of the tape – but I play the proper music – it is so sad – and it is about the dying and it makes me so clear.

I was never right ever since I was born – this means that I do very bad writing and that I can't speak proper and that I am backwards and that I am a special child – but why is a mystery for what they have not got an answer – but Mam said when I was born it was at a dark night and it was raining and thundery and all the cats and dogs and things were under the tables – and the wind was screeching round everywhere – and everything was quite horrible – but I didn't mind because I was just little and I was in the hospital and Mam kissed me and when she looked at my face she noticed that it was round – and everyone came and looked at my face – and they laughed and said I was Spoonface because when they looked at my face it was round as a spoon and when you look into a spoon you see this face just like mine – and that is how I came to be Spoonface Steinberg – because my other name is Steinberg – but I never even knew because I was just a little baby and all the stars and planets were moving inside of me and I was looking up and the world was as bright as colours and as shimmery as light and I was just a baby – and when you're a baby you have a soft head and that – and that's what makes you backwards. Sometimes when it's very late at night – when they think I'm asleep, Mam says to Dad that maybe it is his fault that I am not right – on the fact that on the day Dad came back when he was out with the floozie, I did fall off the chair – Dad came back and it was quite late for our tea and I was sitting on the chair and Mam said that Dad was out with someone – and Dad says he was in the office doing the meeting – and Mam said she phoned the meeting and he was off with the office doing a floozie – and that this was one of his students – and she was going somewhere – off with the final straw – then there was all this crying and screaming and Dad went like a beetroot and Mam said that the student was just a baby and had big boobs and I fell over – it was like when you bump your head only worse – and then everything went white like lightning – and this was bad on account of my softness – and they were crying there with me and I was silent as a worm

– and Dad told Mam he would not ever have another floozie if Mam would be nicer and Mam said she would be nicer – and then it was that everything was alright – except I started going backwards – but I am not sure if this is to do with it or not – maybe it is – maybe it is not – I think I was backwards before the fall – before Dad came back and everything – I think I was always backwards ever since I was born and there was all the thunder and that, and I think ever since I was born that my brain was quite special – I think I have a special brain what is quite different in how it was and stuff – but nobody knows for sure – all the experts with all their computers and all the doctors who poke in your ear and look into your brain and all the people who do the quizzes and all questioners and such like – none of them know for certain – they all said no one can know can ever know for certain – and that's what Dad says – he says there is only one thing for certain – nobody knows anything for certain – what is true I think – on account that he is a lecturer of philosophy – the thing is even now I am old I cannot read proper or to write and am very bad at games and that I cannot go to a proper school as I am not allowed on account of my brain – but I am quite a special little girl, though – that's what Mrs Spud says – Mrs Spud does the cleaning – and she says that I am quite one of the special girls she has ever known and every time she comes she brings me a sweetie which is very nice for she has so many problems of her own – she says that everybody is different and that it is quite good indeed and that we should all be happy and that – for every person is a very special person and that it is good to be different as if there's no difference we would all be the same – and Mrs Spud told me not to worry about my brain because to be different is to be who you are – so I do not believe that I fell on my head – I do not believe that I was affected – or it was Dad's fault for the floozie or Mam's fault 'cos I was unattended – I believe that I was supposed to be backward – I believe it was all part of what is supposed to be – and when I was born God came and touched me on my head – down he came and touched my soft spot and made me me.

MUSIC: *Maria Callas singing 'Mon cœur s'ouvre à ta voix' from* Samson et Dalila *by Saint-Saëns*.

One day I started to do the numbers. This was when Dad came back from the university and he was with a calculator for doing the marks. He was sat doing the marks when he said two numbers and I went 42 – because it was the answer of the two numbers – and then he goes – goodness me – and then he said two more numbers and I said 147 – which was another answer – and then he did more and more – and some of the answers he had to do on the calculator – and then he started shouting of Mam – and Mam came running as if there was something bad – but it was only me doing the numbers and I did more and more – and Mam kissed me and was crying and that – and Dad kept doing more and more and he was laughing – and Mam said he had to stop – and I said what was it that had made her cry? – and she said that it was because of the numbers and never in the world did they know I could do the numbers – but I could do them now – and I was a genius – and it was of my brain.

And then I had to do them in front of a doctor – and then the doctor said – if Spoonface can do numbers then she can do dates – and then I did some – this is how I do it – what is the day of July the 4th 2010? – Saturday – amazing, absolutely amazing – and that is how I do the dates and they have to look it up in a book as soon as I've said the answer and there it is – and they say how do I know so many numbers? and I say I don't know – and how do I know so many dates? – and I also say I don't know – but it's just obvious like colours – and that is why – and Mrs Spud says that is why we are all different – to me the numbers are obvious and to her some other stuff is obvious – like how to clean the loo and that – but at least that means we're all different.

So this is all because I am autistic – and that is quite a big strain on Mam and Dad which was account of why they did split up – for a start Mam was quite sad – she was in the house when Dad went to work and she did look at her books and such like as she was getting a Ph.D also like Dad – only he finished quicker on account of women have to have babies that men can't have – this meant that hers was much slower – and she would sit in the room and when ever she was just to do some work I came in and then she had to stop – and it wasn't fair of me to do the Ph.D – and Dad was on the committees – so Mam had to drink the vodka – and she used to sit with the book and the vodka – and Dad came back and she said – that he was not of attention – and maybe he wasn't.

Then one day Dad said he had met one person who was doing a different Ph.D to Mam and that she was very nice and that he would go away to live with her for a bit – and Mam said she was glad of him to go – and even though I was backwards and that – it would be better than his stupid face – and off Dad went for a bit until sometimes he came back for a few minutes on a Saturday.

Then Mam used to have more and more – and she would come to me and say 'My poor sweet angel, my poor sweet angel' – and then drink the vodka – and then she had to take tablets off the Doctor and would stop the vodka at the same time – except one time she had the pills and the vodka and went to sleep on the stair and I put on her a nice blanket in case anyone tripped – but nobody did trip as there was only me – then the next day Mrs Spud came and tidied up where she had been sick.

MUSIC: *Maria Callas singing 'Teneste la promessa' from* La Traviata *by Verdi*.

When I first started feeling funny that is when I still had hair – it was hardly noticeable at first – that was there was hardly nothing wrong except I was tired a bit – but then Mam was very worried that I was thinner and thinner and one day I might fade away to a speck – and that I was looking peaky – but because I'm backwards then I wasn't very good at saying what is wrong – so she took me straight to the doctor in case I disappeared – and the doctor looked at me like this . . . and he said – 'Oh deary me, Spoonface will have to go straight to the hospital' – which is where I went – it was alright as I had been before to do the numbers – they were all very nice to me and the doctors held on to my hand and stuff and they all smiled which means something is wrong – and then Mam looked greyish and they said they were going to have to put me in a tube, which was quite horrible as I am only little – I did not wish to go into the tube but they said I would have to on account of being so thin – and inside the tube they would find out what it was – so I went in the tube and Mam was watching when I went in and waved bye bye – and then all these computers went off and stuff – and they did all this dialling and whirring and then there was some rays or something – and I was in there like it was a space machine but it never went anywhere except in the hospital even though it took ages – and I waited and all the computers were doing different numbers and all the information was going everywhere and that – and then it came time for me to come out and when I came out there was Mam and the doctor waiting and they said hello and I was allowed out – the doctor said he would have to check the switches and that we should all go into a room where Mam could cry and I could play with Lego – when I was in the room I got a drink of pop and Mam said it was unexpected that we would go straight to the hospital and go into a tube – then the doctor came back and said that he had got an answer off the machines and the answer was – that I was going to die.

MUSIC: *Maria Callas singing 'Addio, del passato' from* La Traviata *by Verdi.*

Mam looked very sad and said the doctors must have wonky computers and that they needed to put me in the tube again – but then they said how the computers were only new and that they were very expensive and that it was definite what they said – and it was that I was still going to die – only they said there was hope – that there was always hope – and anyway, it would take a long time for me to die so we went home for some tea – when we went home in the car there was rain and wind and everything and we passed this accident where a man on a motorbike had got his head smashed off –

and Mam said that even if I was supposed to die there would still be hope 'cos there was millions of people that were saved by God everyday – even if the poor man was smashed on the road – and so it was better not be too worried about it – so I said I wasn't worried and we had fish fingers.

Then Mam had to phone Dad – he was with the granduate – in a little flat and everything – and Mam rang and the granduate answered and said that she would still like to meet Mam as there was no hard feelings but Mam said she had to speak to Dad quick – normally she used to shout at him saying, 'What did I do? What did I do?' – but this time she said to the granduate to get right off as she needed to talk to Dad immediately – then on came Dad and Mam said there was something terrible wrong with Spoonface and that she'd been in a tube and had been playing with the Lego and they said she was going to die and he must come at once – and then she put the phone down – and Dad came and said this was the last thing he expected – especially as we had so many troubles and he kissed me and he also kissed Mam and said – what such troubles we had – first I wasn't born right, and that even though I did numbers, I wasn't very good at games and stuff – and then he went off with a graduand too young for him and stuff and Mam was living here with only me – and now I was going to die.

Mam said she was sorry and that deep down she really loved Dad, and Dad was sorry that he really loved Mam and they all loved me over and over – I was supposed to be asleep by now but I could hear them and of everything they said – it was so terrible for everyone and this was the change of everything – and then they came in at the door and looked at me in the dark where I was supposed to be asleep – and I was lying in my beautiful bed with all the covers up and they would stare like this at me . . . and have their arms holding each other and they whispered that I was a poor little soul – but they never knew I was wide awake and I could see them through the crack in my eye as not to scare them – and when I looked at them and I saw that they were crying – and then

Dad said: there I was fast asleep not a care in the world – but this was ridiculous because I was there awake all the time.

MUSIC: *Maria Callas singing 'Ebben? ne andrò lontana' from* La Wally *by Catalani.*

After a while Dad came back to see us quite a bit – some nights he used to stay in Mam's bed and everything and he would see me in the morning – and the Ph.D said that she had a new boyfriend who was quite young and played in a musical group and that Dad was quite old to be living at her house and Dad was to live all alone except when he came to see us – and when he came he was nicer than ever – and Mam was quite happy sometimes but she would cry at night when I couldn't hear who she was – I kept going to the hospital and they would do all these checks on me and go, 'Oh well, it is very bad indeed' – Mam would be worried and tell me to be brave – then one day they said, 'Spoonface is going to die, except we might put her in this machine and she would get some rays and stuff and then she would be better' – but I couldn't go in straight away on account of the list so I waited a few days and stuff – and Dad came round every night and that – and he said that Mam was to go out to see her friend and he would stay and watch me – but he never 'cos he was downstairs and he found Mam's vodka – I was feeling quite sickly and I was all wobbly because I was thin as a stick so I went straight to bed – then I was asleep – then there was this noise and in came Dad and he smelt really weird – and he came right up to my nose – like he has flying over my nose which was horrible – and his eyes were sort of fat and soft – and he had one of the glasses from downstairs and the vodka what Mam kept in the freezer – and he took this huge gulp and went pink – I just looked at him like this – wishing Mam was back – then he grabbed my arm and it was quite hard – he did grab me tight like this . . . and I looked up and was frightened of what he would do – and then I thought I was going to faint of the pressure – and he started rocking backwards like this – and then he said I had suffered the worse out of anyone in the world and it was all his fault – that he didn't know what he was doing – that he was such a young man and he was just a poor philosophy man because he couldn't think of what else to do – and that he loved Mam even though when they had such a young baby as myself it was before things were settled – but then he said that he loved me and he didn't know what he was doing except for that he was sorry for it all – and especially sorry for his whole life – but then I was Spoonface from his own sperm and that I was the most loved child in the whole world – and even if I never understood a word I was still the most loved child in all the world – and he went like this for ages – and all of a sudden he stopped doing his grip and fell backwards and plopped on to the floor – I wanted to go to the loo, but I didn't ask in case he tried to grab me again – and I saw he was sitting back like this ... on the floor and his face was bright red and he sort of shook – he was shaking and he did these gasps like he couldn't breathe – and no tears would come from his crying just these shakes – then I heard the door and Mam came up the stairs in her coat and she saw Dad on the floor doing the shaking and she just left him and picked me out of bed and put me in between her bosoms and she pressed me there for a long time and kissed the tip of my head – after that she took me to her room – she said that Dad was over-whelmed and that he was reading of Kierkegaard which was too bad for him – and the next day I was in Mam's bed and Dad was in mine.

And she said that not to worry about Dad that he was very sorry from gripping me so hard and it was all 'cos of the vodka – and he promised he would never shake again.

MUSIC: *Maria Callas singing 'O mio babbino caro' from* Gianni Schicchi *by Puccini.*

I love the beautiful women who do the operas and how they sing and they flutter their voices like this – because it is the saddest things are the best things of all – and that is because God made all the sad things for to make us human and this is what Doctor Bernstein said at the hospital when I went in – he was quite old and stuff and he said that I was very brave and I should be very brave because when his Mam was little she was very brave as well even though she was in a concentration camp.

Concentration camps were these places where they took Jewish people to burn – this is what the doctor said – he said that there were loads of people and they all had to sleep on one bunk and that – and the Nazis shot them and then they starved them and it was horrible for his poor Mam because she was just little – in the whole history of the world there has never been anything as awful as the concentration camps, but what happened to the poor people there was to show that they never gave up hope – and that never mind the worse thing that could happen to people they could not stop them from being human beings – some of the little children were skinnier than I am now with the cancer, and all that was wrong with them was they didn't eat – just this soup what didn't have any vegetables in it – and they'd just be standing there and their Mammies and Daddies would be bashed – like there was one little girl who was with her Mam and the soldier came and hit her Mam on the head and shot her and then she died and the poor little girl just had to stand there – that little girl was the Mam of the doctor – and there were millions and millions of people like this – so in comparison to me it is much worse – and I felt sorry for the doctor when he told me these things as he had a little cry in the corner of his eye – and he never said any of this to scare me – he said all of this to help me because the whole lesson of the stories was that little children were braver than everybody else (*underneath her voice we hear Maria Callas singing 'Casta Diva' and then 'Mon cœur s'ouvre à ta voix'*) and all the little children all played games in the middle of mud – in the middle of the concentration camp they played – and this was the human spirit – in the middle where their Mams and Dads was getting gassed – and they could kill their Mams and stuff but they couldn't kill what was in the minds of the children – this was the lesson – that no matter how bad it is for us while we are dying it is still a wonderful thing that we are alive – this is what the doctor said – and he said when the soldiers came and took the poor little children to the ovens and the poor children and everything thought they were going for a wash but every body knew really that they were going to get gassed – because they had seen the smoke of burning bodies – then the children were waiting outside and all the little children wrote things on the walls – on the walls of the gas chamber where they were about to be cooked. And some little children wrote poems – and some little children drew pictures – and even today you can see the pictures of butterflies on the outside – little butterflies that were flying up to God – beautiful butterflies with tender wings that would brush their faces and kiss them better before they flew – careful little butterflies in all the death and the mud and every thing – and that day when he told me this I cried for the butterflies and the little children – and all their sad faces drifting up to heaven.

And the doctor said that his Grandma used to be a singer of the opera before she went to this place – and in them days everyone loved the opera – not like now when everyone likes Take That – and when they would put the lights out – all the poor women on the bunks would think of their husbands who were never to be seen – and they would ask Grandma Bernstein to sing – and in the sad dark she would sing – sing to all the poor skinny women – and she sang all the songs what she knew in the opera – and she sang for the poor people in the bunks – and all the poor people who had died – and she sang for the children of the people to come – and that was very important to everyone to have such songs to be sung – and then I would play the music and in the heart of it I could hear the singing of the poor Grandma on her bunk – and the poor children who wrote their pictures on the wall – and even in the darkest place there was someone with such a beautiful song to sing.

MUSIC: *Maria Callas singing 'O mio babbino caro' from* Gianni Schicchi.

By the time I had to go into the machine I was quite upset that I was going to die but then Mam told me not to be because it would zap me and then I would be alright – but I knew that maybe there was a chance that I would not be zapped proper

– but I never said anything – so I went in and got zapped – I went in every day for three weeks they said that was quite enough as they didn't want to zap too much as they might do a mischief – they gave me centigrays – these are special rays which get the cancer and make it better – they put me in the machine and then zapped the centigrays straight into me – and I felt so small as if I was travelling all through the history of time to another place where all the things were different – and in this place then everybody was laughing and happy and there was no more hospitals or concentration camps and everybody had ice cream and watched the telly and there was opera people and everything – and all of a sudden I believed that maybe I had died in the zapper and when I looked around that I was in heaven – but then I came out and I had not died at all and I was still in the hospital and there was Mam and Doctor Bernstein and I remembered this was the hospital and there were concentration camps and I was still going to die – and then everybody said how I was – and I said quite well – and they said what a brave little girl I was in the zapper and that I should have a special little present – and that it was a special CD player what the nurses had bought me 'cos they knew I liked the opera – but I couldn't wear it inside the machine on account of the interference – after a few days they told me the zapper was not really such a zapper at all – and in fact it was called an accelerator – which means to go very fast – but it is for to slow the cancer down – and I sat for hours – but the cancer never slowed – in fact that the centigrays hardly stopped it at all – and they said I had to go home for a while.

I started getting even worse than I was – really woozy and everything and virtually as soon as I had got out of the hospital they said I had to go back in – this time they said there'd be no more machines and stuff – but they would give me this special thing in my arm and that would make me sick and have diarrhoea and all my hair would fall out – this was the chemicals and such and they said that if that didn't save me, that was that – so I went and had the diarrhoea – and they put the thing in my arm – like a tap which they had all bags and special machines which had these chemicals that they put in my arm and made me ill – I was feeling quite sickly and then I had to have this medicine to stop me puking up – it is quite hard to have the diarrhoea and want to puke up at the same time because you don't know which one to do first – and this was called a side-effect – but it effected all over – and I would sit in the bed with the arm thing and my new CD and then I would poo myself and my hair all fell out and I was quite weird – then one day Dad came and he had this hat for me to wear it had a picture of these opera singers on the front and I wore the hat even though I was inside – and everyday I was sicker and sicker and I goes to God – Please God, why are you making me so sickly? – and I never found out – because he never said – then I was quite depressed – and my eyebrows fell out.

Doctor Bernstein came to see how I was and he said it must be horrible having diarrhoea – but I said I didn't mind that much, and anyway that's what Beethoven had when he wrote his music – he had diarrhoea and deafness – and he was quite ill a lot of the time – but he wrote the beautiful music – and the doctor said how did I know such things and I said someone told me what looked at my tapes.

Then Doctor Bernstein said there was this man, Job, and he had a horrible time except he put up with it and he was alright. Doctor Bernstein said that Job was a Jew too and so was Jesus and so was all these famous people – and that there was a lot to suffer in the history of the world – which is true – and one day he came to me and took off the drip and said that the good news was that my hair would grow – but the bad news was I was still full of cancer and there was nothing to be done – all the chemicals and the centigrays and everything was useless.

When I went home I was in bed a lot and I used to watch everything through the window – and had lots of time to be by myself and think about things and that.

First – when Mam brought me home, then Mam said that I was a brave little girl indeed because of my baldness and everything and that my hair would be growing in soon – but then when there was Dad there and that he was allowed to stay on the sofa downstairs for every day that I was alive – then I was in bed and then I would have the pills and stuff which is called morphine – and I would be propped so I would look out of the window – then she said that she did hate God and how could he do such a thing to poor Spoonface who was in bed – which was me – only I could hear and everything and Dad said to her for to be philosophical and Mam said that philosophicals could just go away and that she did hate God – as basically God is a bastard – this is what I heard and then I looked up and saw the wind.

MUSIC: *Maria Callas singing 'Voi lo sapete, O mamma' from* Cavalleria Rusticana *by Mascagni.*

And when we went home the doctor gave me this book to me – but I can't read so I had to get Mam to read it to me – and then I found all this stuff out – like you had to pray to God – and that this would help get on his good side and even if you did die then he'd look out for you afterwards – and in the book it said there was different ways you can pray – there is like when you get up and sit and say things – that is one way of praying – and then there is like you go to the synagogue and then everybody does it all together and that – and then there is this different way what was invented by these people in Poland quite a while ago – this is when everything you do is a prayer – and you have to do everything you do the best you can because it is not just normal, in fact it is a prayer straight to God – when you smile that is a prayer – when you talk that's a prayer – and when you walk that's a prayer – and when you brush your teeth and when you give someone a kiss – and Mams and Dads when they go to bed that is a prayer – and when you pray that is a prayer – and when you spit, when you suck, when you laugh, when you dance, when you snore – everything you do is a prayer – specially what you do when you meet other people because all the people in the world are in God's kingdom – and it doesn't even matter if they're Jewish – and all the animals, all the birds and bees and fishes and swans and llamas and piglets and worms and trees and buses and cars and people and that – because when the world was made, God made it out of magic sparks – everything that there is, was all made of magic sparks – and all the magic sparks went into things – deep down and everything has a spark – but it was quite a while ago since it was made and now the sparks are deep down inside and the whole point of being alive – the whole point of living is to find the spark – and when you meet someone and say hello – or if you tell them a joke or when you say that you love them or try and help someone or you see someone who is sad or injured or maybe they have lost all their money or have been battered up or maybe they're just a bit glum or hungry or you ask the time or maybe they've missed the train – all these people, all they need is help to find the spark – and the people what invented this – the Hassids a long time ago, when they saw people that were having a chat they saw the sparks jump in the space in between them – the sparks were jumping like electricity – sparks God put there – and the sparks were put there for each other 'cos God wanted people to find them in each other – and doing this making sparks – this was to pray – and the old people a long time ago they saw the sparks and when people met and the sparks jumped right up into the air from the place they were hiding and they leapt up through the firmament and through the clouds and past the sun and they shone over the whole universe – and when people kissed there were sparks and when people held each other there were sparks and when they waved as they were going away in a car there would be sparks and they would all be prayers – they would all be prayers for the babies and the sad people with cancer – and for the kings to be good – and the experts to be clever – and all the Mams and Dads and the cleaning ladies and the milkmen – and if only you could see the spark then there was a meaning – because what was the meaning of anything? – if you were going to die, what was the meaning? – all the trees and the bushes and the famines and wars and disasters and even pencils or pens – what was the meaning of all these things? – and the meaning was if you found the spark – then it would be

like electricity – and you would glow like a light and you would
shine like the sparks and that was the meaning – it wasn't like
an answer or a number or any such – it was glowing – it was
finding the sparks inside you and setting them free.

This is what it said in this book what the doctor gave me – the
doctor what's Mam was the little girl whose Mam got shot –
and it meant that the meaning that everybody thought was
somewhere else was right here – and all you had to do was do
the sparks and become like a lightbulb – and the meaning
wasn't that I was going to die but that I was still alive – and I
could make everybody shine – the bus boys and the milkmen
and Mrs Spud – and I thought, if I wasn't scared of when I
wasn't born why would I be scared of when I wasn't existed
at the other end – you can't feel the end or touch the end –
'cos it was just nothing – the end of things is not the problem
'cos there was really no ends to find – that was the meaning
there are no real ends – only middles, and even if I was at the
end I was still in the middle – 'cos it wouldn't know it was the
end then – because it would be ended – so everything is in the
middle – even if it was at the middle of an end – it didn't
matter because I'm in it.

And when I looked to my middle and I saw underneath there
was a belly and bones and muscles and veins and cancer and
intestines but in the middle of the middle was sparks – the
sparks what would save me – the sparks what I could make
shine – the sparks that knew there was no more endings – the
sparks what would be as a huge light in the world and the
sparks would fly up and take me to heaven.

MUSIC: *Maria Callas singing 'Vissi d'arte, vissi d'amore' from* Tosca
by Puccini.

During the day Mrs Spud comes in and sees me – she makes
me stuff and that and helps out Mam with the laundry and
the cleaning and she makes the house spick and span and that
– if I was to grow up, I would be like Mrs Spud and everyday
I would clean the fridge and the oven and the shelves and the
steps out to the garden and some of the skirting boards, but I

would leave the shelves where nobody looks and everything would be clean.

I asked Mrs Spud where I got my cancer from and she did not know – I said, I think I might have caught it off God and she said God does not have cancer as far as we know – I said, maybe he's just not telling anybody – Mrs Spud says that if God has got cancer we're all in trouble – I think maybe he has or he has not.

She said she has a son who is a little angel and a husband who is dead – he had the cancer too – only his was of a difference – she did weep when she told me about him and how when they were just children they met and he kissed her on the neck and that – and on those days that the sun shone forever – she said that the trouble is when people are around – you forget that they are quite special and when they are gone it is too late to tell them and you must always tell them – she said there was nobody like her husband and that he was a very kind man to her – and when she spoke of him you could tell as her eyes were sparkly and her breath was warm – and although he was gone away he was also here – and that every day they had a little chat – and how was the weather and in heaven it never rained – she said we would all be there in the same place one day and maybe I'll get to meet him – I said I didn't know if I could go to there on account of being Jewish – but she was sure I would – his name was Mr Spud.

Then I said that I quite liked the rain when it was wet and it blew so grey on the ground and I would watch from the bed when the trees would weep and bend in the day – and I saw how the shed wobbled in the wind – and I would see the cloud for all the silver there was in it – and every day of the rain, the sun even in its little bits made the world spark like diamonds and glisten in the weather – and if I was in heaven there would be no dull to shine out in the sad days – but Mrs Spud said she liked the sun and when she could afford she would go on a nice holiday in Ibiza – although Jimmy – which is her son – would not go on account of the price – which is a shame.

I asked her if she was lonely without poor Mr Spud – she said a bit and that she would lie and remember him whenever – but then again we are not gone – then I said, did she see that there was blackness and she did not – she said there was sadness and stuff but that's what there is – but if you look there is also happiness – like little children having a smile – or someone with a birthday – and even in a graveyard there might be a little butterfly flying round the gravestones – and these are the things what is important – and poor Mr Spud would be sad in heaven if he thought that Mrs Spud didn't look at the day and see that in the trees and in the sky there was a little piece of heaven.

I felt sad for Mrs Spud as she had three hungry mouths to feed – her and Jimmy and someone else – and one day she came into my room to do the hoovering and I had poo'd in my pants and it was a disgusting smell and she cleaned my bum and the bed for me – and I made her a card the next day – and it said 'I love You Mrs Spud' – and she cried – and she cried when she got it – she said, what a lovely card – and I said I did my best considering the crayons I had which was not very many and there was no blue so there was no proper sky – but she said it was quite a beautiful card for a cleaner.

MUSIC: *Maria Callas singing 'Vissi d'arte, vissi d'amore' from* Tosca.

When you think about dying it is very hard to do – it is to think about what is not – to think about everything there is nothing – to not be and never to be again – it is even more than emptiness – if you think of emptiness it is full of nothing and death is more than this – death is even less than nothing – when you think about that you will not be here for your breakfast – and that you will never see Mam or Dad or Mrs Spud – or the telly or hear the sweet singing opera ladies or feel anything any more – but you won't feel sad as there will be nothing to feel of – and that is the weird point – not that there is even anything but there is not even nothing – and that is death.

Sometimes it is scary – but to think that I'll not be is impossible because I'm here – and when I'm not here there'll still be cows and grass and vegetables and radios and telephone machines and cardiologists and soup tins and cookers and hats and shoes and Walkmans and Tiny Tears and synagogues and beaches and sunshine and walks in the rain and films and music and my coat and my shoes and cars and underpants and necklaces and my Mam and Dad and flowers – everywhere there'll be something in the whole world everything will be full except me – and there isn't even a hole somewhere where I used to be – and apart from people what remember me and what I was like there is nothing missing from when I was here – there is no space in the universe where people have dropped out – it is all filled in as full as ever – there is nothing to know, as is everything that there is, is all around us – there is nothing to know because there it is – in the world everything is divided – everything divided one from the other one, from the many – from the mother and from the father – there is day and night and black and white and all these things but in the very beginning and in the end – everything will not be divided and there will be no me or you – there will be no this or that, no little puppy dogs or anything, there will only be that everything is the same – and every moment is forever – and it will shine and it will be everything and nothing – and that is all there is to know – that all of us will end up being one – and that is nothing – and it is endless.

MUSIC: *Maria Callas singing 'Ebben? ne andrò lontana' from* La Wally *by Catalani.*

Blessed and lauded, glorified and lifted and exalted and enhanced and elevated and praised be the Name of the Holy One,
Blessed be he although he is high above all blessings, hymns and uplifts that can be voices in this world.
May his name be blessed for ever and ever.

(*The Kaddish*)

THE END

I Love You, Jimmy Spud

I Love You Jimmy Spud was first performed on 27 February 1998 at the Live Theatre, Newcastle-Upon-Tyne. It was part of a season of his work entitled Radio Live. Other plays performed included *Bollocks*, *Spoonface Steinberg* and *Dancer* the original working title for the film *Billy Elliot*. The cast was as follows:

Jimmy Spud	Gus Brown
Scout	Adam Pearson
Dad	Trevor Fox
Mam	Charlie Hardwick
Gabriel	Paul James
Granddad	Donald McBride
Various other characters	Joe Caffery and Phillippa Wilson

FADE IN:

EXT. OVER THE SEA. WHITLEY BAY. EARLY MORNING.
It is a bright but cold morning. We are flying high in the sky above the sea which is gently lapping underneath us. We pass a seagull in flight that seems to look at us as we swoop down towards the Spanish City. In the background, we hear the clicking of a clock as in a TV game show.

GABRIEL (*V/O*): Let's start with general knowledge. Who was the first president of the United States of America?
JIMMY (*V/O*): George Washington the First.
GABRIEL (*V/O*): Biblical studies.

EXT. AMUSEMENTS. WHITLEY BAY.
As the cosmic game show continues in voice-over, we have passed the fairground and are flying past Fat Sam's chippy with a huge plaster fish rocking in the breeeze.

GABRIEL (*V/O*): Where did Judas Iscariot kiss Jesus Christ?
JIMMY (*V/O*): On the nose?
GABRIEL (*V/O*): Gethsemane. Arithmetic.
  Having exhausted the sights of Whitley Bay we fly out towards the Tyne and up to Newcastle.

INT. SPUDS' HOUSE. MUM AND DAD'S BEDROOM.
The room is in darkness. Two figures sleep. MUM *and* DAD *are sleeping the sleep of babies.*

EXT. OVER THE DISUSED SHIPYARDS.
We are now flying up the Tyne towards the abandoned shipyards of Howdon and Wallsend. A cavernous basin where the ships would be built appears below us.

GABRIEL (*V/O*): If it takes four men four hours to dig a hole four by four. How long does it take two men to dig the

same hole two by two?
JIMMY (*V/O*): One hour fifty minutes.
*The ticking behind the theological quiz is getting louder. We pass an
old crane.*
GABRIEL (*V/O*): Theology. Does God exist?
JIMMY (*V/O*): Erm?

INT. MUM AND DAD'S BEDROOM.
Close-up of the bedside clock. DAD *coughs and turns over.* MUM *pulls
the pillow over her head.*

GABRIEL (*V/O*): I'm going to have to hurry you on this one.
JIMMY (*V/O*): Yes. No. Pass.

EXT. OLD RAILWAY TRACK.
*Flying shot down an old railway line past rows of pigeon crees towards
rows and rows of sooty terraces.*

GABRIEL (*V/O*): Relativity. Which is lighter a pound of
    feathers or a pound of lead?
JIMMY (*V/O*): A pound of lead.
The ticking becomes more insistent.
GABRIEL (*V/O*): Which is better: to have loved and lost or
    never to have loved at all?
JIMMY (*V/O*): To love at all.

EXT. SCHOOL PLAYING FIELD.
Flying shot over the playing field. A solitary figure, GABRIEL, *is
marking out the pitches.*

GABRIEL (*V/O*): Which came first the chicken or the egg?
JIMMY (*V/O*): The chicken.
GABRIEL (*V/O*): The egg.

EXT. ROWS OF TERRACED HOUSING.
Flying shot over the rooftops of row after row of terraces.

GABRIEL *(V/O)*: Is the redemption of the proletariat in Marx,
    through the transformative value of human labour,
    merely teleological mystification or does it have real
    claims to a materialist theology?

INT. MUM AND DAD'S BEDROOM.
*Close-up on the second hand of the clock clicking even closer to the
twelve.*

JIMMY *(V/O)*: Yes.
GABRIEL *(V/O)*: If I spat in your face would you turn the
    other cheek?
JIMMY *(V/O)*: What?
GABRIEL *(V/O)*: If you had all the money in the world what
    would you do?

EXT. STREETS.
We are heading for the Spuds' house.

JIMMY *(V/O)*: Buy things and give the rest away.
GABRIEL *(V/O)*: You are shipwrecked on a desert island.
    Which ten records would you have with you in
    descending order of preference?
JIMMY *(V/O)*: 'Bohemian Rhapsody' by Freddie Mercury.
    *We swoop towards the window with the curtain flapping in the wind
    and fly straight in.*

INT. MUM AND DAD'S BEDROOM.
Close-up the bedside clock. The alarm goes off.

JIMMY *(V/O)*: That one by Michael Bolton.

INT. JIMMY'S BEDROOM.
JIMMY, eleven, sits bolt upright in bed. Next to him is his goldfish, Stanley, in a little bowl. The curtains are blowing in the wind. MUM opens his door and pops her head round. JIMMY smiles nervously.

MUM: Jimmy.
   MUM looks at him suspiciously.

INT. KITCHEN. LATER THAT MORNING.
GRANDAD and JIMMY are sitting around the kitchen table. DAD is at the end. He is fiddling with a piece of wood for his etchings. He coughs badly. MUM is trying desperately to cook breakfast and smarten herself up ready to go out at the same time. She puts a fried egg on JIMMY's plate, while opening her lipstick.

JIMMY: What does eschatology mean?
GRANDAD: What did he say?
   GRANDAD fiddles with his earpiece. It whistles. MUM is putting on some lippy but gets disturbed by the noise.
MUM: For Christ's sake.
JIMMY: Radgie Patel says it.
MUM: I'll stop you going in that shop.
   MUM hands GRANDAD a sausage.
JIMMY: I was only asking.
   Beat.
   Mam, can I have a note for games.
MUM: You already had a note.
JIMMY: Don't be stupid. That was last week. Dad.
   DAD coughs.
MUM: Leave your dad alone. He's going to the doctor's.
GRANDAD: What?
DAD: Listen, when I was your age I was running for the
   county.
JIMMY: But I've got a bad foot.
DAD: You'll get a bad foot right up your backside.
MUM: You're going to be late, Jimmy.
   JIMMY picks himself up in a sulk and heads for the door.

MUM: Your kit.

> JIMMY *stops.* MUM *is holding his gym bag.* JIMMY *grabs it and goes out the door.*

MUM: What time's your appointment?

DAD: I don't know.

MUM: Jesus Christ.

> MUM *shakes her head and grabs her coat.* GRANDAD *leans over and steals a sausage from* DAD's *plate.* MUM *prepares to leave. She looks over her shoulder at* DAD *who is concentrating uncommunicatively on his piece of wood. He splutters yet another cough. She kisses his forehead.*

EXT. STREET. ON THE WAY TO SCHOOL.

JIMMY walks along the street in the drizzle struggling with his big black bag. He passes the corner shop at the end of the street. MUM *comes down the street walking rather briskly.*

MUM: Are you all right, Jimmy?

JIMMY: I suppose so.

> MUM *takes out her hanky, wets it on her tongue and wipes a mark from* JIMMY's *cheek.*

MUM: Well, why are you looking so miserable?

EXT. WASTELAND.

JIMMY struggles onwards towards school. Suddenly, a tiny stone hits him on the head. A group of BOYS *are behind him in the distance. They laugh as* JIMMY *turns.*

BOY: Wanker.

> JIMMY *hurries towards a fence. He looks back and spots the gang of* BOYS *in the distance. He turns the corner and pushes his big bag through a hole and then disappears through it himself.*
>
> JIMMY *is in the industrial graveyard of a magnificent old dock. The yard is overgrown and he stalks through the old relics of industry. We hear the gang of boys pass unseen.* JIMMY *heads towards a warehouse and goes inside.*

JIMMY *walks inside the old building. It has the feeling of an old church. The light streams through. It is covered in debris. And is the home for whole flock of pigeons which fly around high in the rafters. The shafts of light catch* JIMMY *as he passes through. He sits on a bench and unpacks his rugby kit. He stores it an old wooden chest. He takes out his pen and paper and begins to write himself a note. Suddenly a bird flies past and startles him.*

Close-up of JIMMY *writing:*

Dear Mr Charlton, Jimmy cannot do games today as his kit is still in the wash.
Yours Mrs Spud.

The wind whistles through and catches the door. JIMMY *gets scared and hurries out.*

INT. METRO. PULLING INTO WHITLEY BAY.
MUM *yawns as she looks out of the rain-splattered window at an old guy carefully inspecting the contents of the bins.*

INT. CLASSROOM.
MISS *is marking the register. The class are half listening.*

MISS: Sproat?
SPROAT: Here, Miss.
MISS: Spud. Where's Jimmy?
   The door opens. JIMMY *rushes in. He is dirty and wet.*
JIMMY: Sorry, Miss.
   JIMMY *walks to his seat passing the boy who threw the stone.*
MISS: I warned you, Jimmy. Detention.
   JIMMY *sits glumly. The gang look at* JIMMY *as* MISS *carries on.*
MISS: Trevelyan?
TREVELYAN: Here, Miss.
MISS: Underwood?

INT. WAITING ROOM. DOCTOR'S SURGERY.
DAD *is sitting glumly waiting for his appointment. Next to him is a* WOMAN *with a screaming* TODDLER. *On the other side a* FAT MAN *with half of his face bandaged. The whole clinic is full with a completely motley collection of the walking wounded.* DAD *takes out his tobacco and begins to roll up. The* RECEPTIONIST *notices this and interrupts* DAD.

RECEPTIONIST: Excuse me, sir.
   She indicates a NO SMOKING sign which is directly above a poster of a skeleton enjoying a cigarette.

INT. CHANGING ROOM.
Pan along a row of skinny boys' legs in shorts and rugby boots. At the end of the row JIMMY'S *legs are fully clothed.* MR CHARLTON, *the games master, suddenly swipes the head of* SPROAT, *the boy next to* JIMMY. CHARLTON *holds* JIMMY'S *note.*

CHARLTON: Pathetic.
   CHARLTON *throws the letter away.* CHARLTON *blows his whistle and the boys leap to their feet and canter past* JIMMY. *The* BOY *who threw the stone clatters past on his studs.*
BOY (*under his breath*): Puff.
   The boys file out and JIMMY *is left on his own. He stands up and hangs from the coat hangers. He wanders around. Eventually, he sits down in a toilet cubicle to read the graffiti. 'Mr Charlton is a wanker.'*
   Suddenly, we hear a stern voice from outside of the cubicle.
GABRIEL: Hello there.
JIMMY: Who is it?
GABRIEL: I just need a few more details.
   From JIMMY'S *POV we see the feet of* GABRIEL *pace back and forth under the door of the cubicle.*
GABRIEL: Date of birth.
JIMMY: Twentieth of September 1985.
GABRIEL: Occupation?
JIMMY: Schoolboy.

GABRIEL: Marital Status?

JIMMY: What?

The feet stop directly facing the booth.

GABRIEL: Single. Any hereditary illnesses? Formal debilities.

Close-up of JIMMY's *face. Nervous.*

JIMMY: I had the mumps as a toddler.

The feet start moving again.

GABRIEL: Annual yearly income of household.

JIMMY: I don't know.

JIMMY *tries to peer through the crack in the door. It is impossible for* JIMMY *to get a complete view of* GABRIEL.

GABRIEL: Just a ballpark figure.

JIMMY *stands on the toilet seat to look over.*

JIMMY: Well, my dad's on the dole and me mam's a chippy.

He is too short to see.

GABRIEL: Are your parents happy, Jimmy?

JIMMY: I don't know.

GABRIEL's *eye peers in.*

GABRIEL: I'm just trying to get an overview. Nothing to get shirty about.

JIMMY: I wasn't getting shirty.

GABRIEL: Did anyone touch you as a child, Jimmy? Make you do anything you didn't want to do?

JIMMY: Look. Can I go now?

GABRIEL: We have to ask. It's standard procedure.

JIMMY: I'm completely normal.

GABRIEL: OK. That's all.

JIMMY *sits in silence. The sound of flushing from the cubicle next door.*

INT. ROW OF CUBICLES.

Bird's-eye view: An empty cubicle. The water spiralling down the bowl. JIMMY's *head appears looking under the partition.*

INT. CHANGING ROOM.

Outside the cubicles, JIMMY *looks both ways but* GABRIEL *is not to be found.*

INT. DR BROWN'S EXAMINATION ROOM.
DAD *is sitting on the couch with his shirt off.* DR BROWN *is examining his chest with his stethoscope.* DAD *breathes heavily.* DR BROWN *puts his tube away and goes slowly to the desk. He looks at* DAD *grimly.*

INT. FAT SAM'S CHIP SHOP. WHITLEY BAY.
MUM *is staring out of the window into the bleak wind and rain.* FAT SAM *is having a fag by the fryer. They both listen to an incessant creaking.*

EXT. FAT SAM'S.
A giant haddock is creaking in the wind.

EXT. SCHOOL PLAYING FIELD.
JIMMY *walks out into the rain. In the distance he sees an* OLD MAN *(possibly* GABRIEL*) riding his bike across the field. The* OLD MAN *looks back momentarily. The* BOYS *are splattering about in the mud playing rugby. The scene is an obvious homage to the football sequence in* KES. *The* BOYS *are miserably playing rugby. They are being continually hectored by the indomitable* MR CHARLTON. CHARLTON's *frustration with the boys' laxity gets too much for him and he picks up the ball and runs into a crowd of* BOYS *as if he was taking on the All Blacks.*

CHARLTON: Come on, then, tackle. Tackle.
   Despite several BOYS *clinging to each limb,* CHARLTON *smashes through their defences. He lumbers towards the try line and scores a try and rejoices triumphantly. The* BOYS *look on in wearied disdain.*

EXT. DR BROWN'S SURGERY.
DAD *leaves the surgery. He looks a little shaken. He takes out of his pocket the cigarette he rolled earlier and lights up nervously.*

INT. CHEMISTRY LAB. SCHOOL.
JIMMY *very carefully fills a test tube up with a chemical. He very carefully holds it over the Bunsen flame. He peers at it through his goggles. He very carefully drops in some liquid from a syringe. The whole thing explodes.*

MISS: All right. Time to write up.

INT. CORRIDOR. SCHOOL.
JIMMY *emerges from the classroom.* MISS *is behind him. She switches off the lights.*

MISS: We'll forget the detention. Just try to be on time, Jimmy.

EXT. STREET. OUTSIDE THE DOCKYARD. NEWCASTLE. LATE AFTERNOON.
JIMMY *runs along the street constantly looking behind him to check that the coast is clear.* JIMMY *slips into the hole in the fence and emerges in the yard.* JIMMY *heads towards the warehouse.*
He collects his kit and kicks it around in the dirt to make it look like he did do games.

EXT. DOCKYARD.
JIMMY *tries to climb through the hole. We hear his trousers rip.*

EXT. A TERRACED STREET. A LITTLE LATER.
JIMMY *is rushing home. As he turns the corner he spots the gang of* LADS. *He stands stock still as if he knows exactly what is coming.*

INT. SPUDS' LIVING ROOM.
GRANDAD is fixed to the telly although the sound is turned down.
MUM is talking to DAD from the adjacent kitchen where she is
peeling potatoes. DAD is smoking a cigarette.

MUM: You'll have to give that up for a start.
DAD: They haven't said what's wrong with me yet.
MUM: It can't be doing much good.
DAD: Look, it's the one bit of comfort I get in this house.
MUM: They don't send you to the hospital for nothing.
DAD: It's just tests.
  JIMMY *comes through the door.*
DAD: Look at the state of you.
JIMMY: I fell over.
DAD: Well, you'll have to start taking balancing lessons.
  MUM *notices his trousers.*
MUM: These are ripped. Has someone been hitting you,
    Jimmy?
JIMMY: No.
DAD: What do you mean, no? How did you get in that state?
MUM: Who was it, Jimmy?
JIMMY: It was nobody.
DAD: What do you mean, nobody?
JIMMY: I just slipped.
DAD: And you just stood there and took it. You're a sitting
    duck now, Jimmy.
JIMMY: Dad, nobody hit me.
DAD: Where the hell do you think I'd be if I just let people
    stand around and rip my pants?
JIMMY: I don't know.
MUM: Are you all right, Jimmy?
DAD: If you made more of an effort in games you wouldn't
    have these problems.
JIMMY: I do make an effort.
DAD: You need to defend yourself.
  DAD *gets up and stands in front of* JIMMY.
DAD: Say someone's coming at you.
  DAD *demonstrates. He 'clips'* JIMMY.
DAD: You have to block, Jimmy.

JIMMY *puts up his arms.*
DAD: That's it.
   DAD *manages to get past* JIMMY's *guard and taps him on the head.*
DAD: You've got to be faster.
   JIMMY *reluctantly tries again.* DAD *manages to tap him again.*
DAD: Come on, Jimmy.
   Again and again DAD *taps him.* JIMMY *is becoming frustrated and
upset.*
JIMMY: Stop it, Dad.
DAD: You'll never get anywhere with that attitude.
JIMMY: I was trying my best.
MUM: Look, if you two are going to carry on like that, will
   you kindly do so outside.
DAD: Come on, Jimmy. We'll have a bit of a knockabout.
   JIMMY *gives a despairing look.*

EXT. BACK LANE.
DAD *is kicking a football. He is running round doing fancy tricks
keeping the ball up in the air. Heading the ball in succession.* JIMMY *is
looking around aimlessly.*
   DAD *kicks the ball to* JIMMY. JIMMY *kicks it reluctantly.* DAD
coughs.
   The ball has spun off at an angle and DAD *has to run to get it.*

DAD: Try to use the side of your foot, Jimmy.
   DAD *passes the ball back to* JIMMY. JIMMY *returns it hopelessly.
They pass the ball backwards and forwards.* JIMMY *is obviously
frustrating* DAD *with his lack of effort.*
JIMMY: Dad. What's polymorphous mean?
DAD: Jesus Christ, Jimmy. Try and concentrate.
JIMMY: I don't like football.
DAD: Well, what do you like?
JIMMY: Netball.
DAD: Netball. I hope you're not turning into a fruit, our
   Jimmy.
JIMMY: What do you mean, a fruit?
   DAD *runs for the ball. He is out of breath and breaks into a coughing
fit.*

JIMMY: Maybe we should go inside.

INT. LIVING ROOM. LATER.
GRANDAD *and* JIMMY *sit in the darkness. They listen to a scratched record of Al Bowly. The TV flickers in the darkness but its sound is turned off.* GRANDAD *is lost in his own world,* JIMMY *is watching. The record finishes. They sit listening to the needle rasp around the groove again and again.*

INT. WORKING MEN'S CLUB.
DAD *is talking to* RIDLEY *who serves behind the bar. He has a pile of his wood burnings with him.*

DAD: What do you reckon?
RIDLEY: I don't know.
DAD: But they're good, aren't they? Look at the perspective on that.
DAD *shows him a picture of an old mill with an interesting – almost cubist – perspective.*
RIDLEY: It's interesting.
DAD: I could do them to order if there's a particular scene you fancy.
RIDLEY: Look. It's not up to me. We'd have to ask the committee.
DAD: Well, will you ask them?
RIDLEY: I'll have a word with Harold when he comes in. Here.
RIDLEY *hands* DAD *another pint.* DAD *goes in his pocket, pulling out some change.*
RIDLEY: It's on the house.

INT. LIVING ROOM.
JIMMY *is watching the TV in the darkness. The film is* It's a Wonderful Life. GRANDAD *is fast asleep in his chair.* MUM *looks in at* JIMMY *from the light of the kitchen.*

MUM (*whispers*): It's time for bed.

INT. MUM AND DAD'S BEDROOM.
MUM *and* DAD *lie in bed. With the lights off next to each other.* DAD *splutters a cough.*

EXT. A ROAD IN TOWN. MORNING.
JIMMY *and* GRANDAD *stand watching a marching juvenile jazz band – twirling batons, huge bass drums and a million kazoos – blasting 'When the Saints Go Marching In'.* JIMMY *looks on in amazement.*
   JIMMY'*s POV. The brilliance of the shiny kazoos in the rare sunshine. The band streams past – and* TWO PUNKS *who had previously been obscured are seen snogging, oblivious to anything when the band passes. Finally a lone* FAT GIRL *some distance behind the others passes trying to keep up with the rest but weighed down by an enormous drum.*

INT. FAT SAM'S.
MUM *is preparing the fryer for the day. She yawns.*

EXT. ROAD LEADING TO THE YARDS.
JIMMY *and* GRANDAD *walk through the yards.* GRANDAD *is walking proudly,* JIMMY *dawdling behind.* GRANDAD *looks round to encourage* JIMMY *to keep pace with him.*

EXT. OLD SHIPYARDS.
   GRANDAD *and* JIMMY *sit on the edge of a huge basin. This is where the huge ocean-going ships would have been built. It completely dwarfs the two frail figures. The dock itself is surrounded by old cranes, dilapidated buildings and rusty machinery.* GRANDAD *takes out his sarnies. He passes one to* JIMMY.

GRANDAD: I used to work that crane, you know.
JIMMY: What?
GRANDAD: I used to work that crane. You could see right out

to sea.
JIMMY *looks up.*
JIMMY: It's massive.

EXT. OLD SHIPYARDS. A LITTLE LATER.
GRANDAD *and* JIMMY *are in the bottom of the basin.*

GRANDAD: There used to be thirty thousand blokes worked
these yards. Just a few years ago.
JIMMY *is wandering around in awe.*
GRANDAD: They built the *Mauritania* here, you know.
JIMMY: Does it make you sad?
GRANDAD: No. It was total exploitation.
GRANDAD*'s lace is undone.* GRANDAD *bends down to fasten it but
he is too old and stiff.* JIMMY *fastens it for him.*

EXT. A DISUSED RAILWAY LINE. LATER.
GRANDAD *and* JIMMY *walk down the steep bank. It is overgrown
with grass and bushes. The perilously steep path is littered with brightly
coloured cabins. They are makeshift and ramshackle. They meander
down the bank.* GRANDAD *opens one of the many cabin doors on the
side and goes in.*

INT. PIGEON CREE.
*The light is pouring in and they are surrounded by the pounding and
flapping of pigeons. It is a warm chaos of feathers and down.*
GRANDAD *feeds his pigeons as* JIMMY *looks on at the purring
creatures in wonder.*

JIMMY: You know Dad?
GRANDAD: Yeah.
JIMMY: Why does he keep doing them burnings?
GRANDAD: He's just trying to keep himself busy.
JIMMY: But why does he only do old-fashioned pictures?
GRANDAD: He's trying to make something out of his past,

isn't he?

JIMMY: Like recycling?

GRANDAD: I suppose so.

The birds perch on JIMMY's *head.* GRANDAD *sits to tend his pigeons.*

JIMMY: I'll see you later.

INT. METRO.

JIMMY's *face is pressed up against the glass.*

EXT. SPANISH CITY.

JIMMY *walks through the funfair. As it is out of season most things are shut. The odd hoopla booth is open, but it is rather sad and empty.*

EXT. FAT SAM'S.

FAT SAM *is up a ladder oiling the haddock.* JIMMY *walks past.*

FAT SAM: Afternoon.

INT. FAT SAM'S. LATER.

JIMMY *is aimlessly standing around looking bored.* MUM *is behind the counter.*

MUM: Why don't you go home and see your dad.

DAD: He'll just get at me.

MUM: Your dad just wants what's best for you.

JIMMY: What's that?

MUM: I don't know. He's just taking an interest.

JIMMY: Do you think he's depressed?

MUM: I think it's more complicated than that.

   FAT SAM *comes in from outside.*

JIMMY: Mum. Why did you marry Dad?

FAT SAM: I think you should go home now, Jimmy. Your mum's got work to do.

JIMMY: But there's nobody here.
MUM: Do you want a bag of chips?
FAT SAM: What do you think this is, a bloody charity?
JIMMY: It's all right. I'll see you later.

EXT. FAT SAM'S.
JIMMY *walks away. After a couple of steps, we hear a 'creak'.* JIMMY
looks up to see the haddock swaying gently in the wind.

EXT. FUNFAIR. WHITLEY BAY.
JIMMY *walks through the funfair with all the rides covered up. The old
waltzer has its cars covered in tarpaulins. Only a ride for tiny children is
working. A solitary* CHILD *turns round and round in a toadstool
watched by a bored* PARENT *at the side. As he passes a stall, an old
neon light, obviously broken for years, flashes momentarily.*

EXT. HALL OF MIRRORS.
JIMMY *sees that a side door to the hall of mirrors is open. He looks
around him. No one is watching. He furtively walks in.*

INT. HALL OF MIRRORS.
JIMMY *walks into the hall of mirrors. He looks at himself. He appears
to be a midget, then appears to be as thin as a pencil. Then suddenly, his
face is as wide as a melon. A voice disturbs him.*

GABRIEL (*OOV*): Excuse me.
   JIMMY *swings round but all he can see is an infinity of* JIMMYS.
GABRIEL: Just another few questions.
   JIMMY *swings round again.* GABRIEL *appears, clipboard in hand,
   with an enormous head and elongated feet, distorted by the mirrors.*
GABRIEL: OK. What do you think are the most pernicious
   obstacles to leading a moral life?
   JIMMY *turns.* GABRIEL *has disappeared, then suddenly appears at
   the other side of the room – now as tall as a rake.*
JIMMY: What?

GABRIEL: What do you think's really bad?

JIMMY: Tidying my room. Cilla Black. I hate Cilla Black.

GABRIEL has disappeared again and JIMMY follows him through the hall – their reflections change shape every few steps.

GABRIEL: Things that are really evil, Jimmy.

JIMMY: Like Hitler?

GABRIEL: Why have you applied, Jimmy?

JIMMY: I thought it would be cush.

GABRIEL: 'It would be cush'!?

JIMMY: Yeah. Helping people, flying around everywhere and that.

GABRIEL: You really think you're ready?

JIMMY: In the olden days by the time people were my age they were miners and sailors and stuff. Some of them had babies.

GABRIEL: That's not strictly true, Jimmy.

JIMMY: My dad would be dead proud.

GABRIEL: You know being an angel is quite a responsibility.

Finally the mirrors catch JIMMY and GABRIEL face to face. As they look one another in the eye, the image is repeated all over the room.

INT. ARCADE.

GABRIEL is shooting ducks with one hundred per cent success. Between each batch he reloads his cork gun.

JIMMY: But I want responsibility and to make things better and stuff.

GABRIEL: It's a little more complicated than that.

JIMMY: Was that the wrong answer?

GABRIEL shoots the last duck and wins a bottle of whisky.

GABRIEL smiles at JIMMY.

INT. BUS HEADING UP THE COAST ROAD.

JIMMY and GABRIEL are sitting on the bus. GABRIEL is clutching his whisky. JIMMY is sitting near the back. GABRIEL is behind him. They are talking surreptitiously, as if they didn't want anyone to know they were connected in anyway. A WOMAN keeps looking at them suspiciously.

GABRIEL: It isn't a simple case of right or wrong, Jimmy.

JIMMY: But it must be. You're an angel, aren't you?

GABRIEL: Listen, son. Things aren't that simple any more.

GABRIEL *rings the bell.*

JIMMY: Wait. Is that it then?

GABRIEL: Look, I'll see what I can do.

GABRIEL *stumbles down the bus and alights.* JIMMY *moves to the window to see him go. But as the bus moves off it seems as if* GABRIEL *has simply disappeared.*

INT. SPUDS' LIVING ROOM. EARLY EVENING.

MUM *is doing the ironing again.* GRANDAD *is watching the TV with* DAD *who is smoking roll-ups.* JIMMY *is doing weird exercises.*

DAD: Out of the road, will you.

JIMMY: I'm just doing my exercises.

DAD: I'll exercise the back of my hand in a minute.

GRANDAD *turns the telly down.* MUM *gives* GRANDAD *a look.*

GRANDAD: The opiate of the masses. That's what this is.

DAD: Christ, here we go. Ho Chi Minh.

GRANDAD: If you took more notice of me in the first place, you'd still have a job.

MUM: Peter. Have you farted?

DAD: What are you on about? I never fart. It's that little bastard.

JIMMY: Mum, it wasn't me.

DAD: Less of your backchat.

GRANDAD: Do you ever listen? What about high-rise housing. I predicted that back in the sixties. But oh no, take no notice.

DAD: Give it a rest, Dad. Jimmy doesn't want to hear you wittering on.

JIMMY: I do want to hear.

DAD: I'll clip you in a minute.

JIMMY: But . . .

DAD *reaches over and gives* JIMMY *a clip round the ear.*

JIMMY: What was that for?

DAD: For being clever.

JIMMY: I wasn't being clever.

DAD: But you thought you were.

   DAD *bursts into a coughing fit.* MUM *has no sympathy.*

MUM: I've told you about them fags.

GRANDAD: Paying to bloody well kill yourself.

DAD: For christsake, all I want to do is watch the telly.

MUM: Where are you going?

DAD: Down the club. I'm not staying here with Chairman
    Mao ranting down my lughole.

GRANDAD: Here. Take my tickets for the meat draw.

   GRANDAD *proffers the raffle tickets and* DAD *takes them*
   begrudgingly and leaves. JIMMY *gets up.*

MUM: Where are you going?

JIMMY: Upstairs.

   GRANDAD *turns the telly over. He stares at the screen, the sound*
   still off. MUM *sniffs suspiciously.*

MUM: Grandad.

EXT. GARDEN OF THE SPUDS' HOUSE.

JIMMY *is lying on the roof of the old coal shed with his huge Bible. He*
closes the Bible and rolls over to look at the stars.

GABRIEL: Jimmy.

   JIMMY *looks down into the lane and there is a dark figure standing*
   by an ancient bicycle. It is GABRIEL.

GABRIEL: You weren't so hot on the general knowledge,
    Jimmy, but overall your spiritual co-efficient wasn't too
    bad.

JIMMY: What does that mean?

GABRIEL: You can forget being a seraph. But I've put in a
    special plea with the boys upstairs.

JIMMY: And?

GABRIEL: They'll accept you on a traineeship.

JIMMY: Cush.

GABRIEL: You realise it's for a trial period only. Prove
    yourself, you get the halo no questions asked. Screw up
    now and it's game over.

Suddenly GABRIEL *is sitting on the wall next to* JIMMY. *He reaches in his pocket and pulls out a pen and paper.*

JIMMY: Don't worry, I'll do my best.

GABRIEL: Just sign here. I'll sort you out with the regular clobber – wings, all that nonsense – in the fullness of time.

JIMMY: Can I have a harp?

GABRIEL: Sorry, reserved for cherubs. I might be able to rustle up a trumpet or something.

GABRIEL *puts on his bicycle clips.*

GABRIEL: Any questions?

JIMMY: Well . . . does God exist?

GABRIEL: I couldn't possibly say.

JIMMY: But you're the angel Gabriel.

GABRIEL: Exactly. It's classified.

JIMMY: But isn't it important to know for sure?

GABRIEL: Just be thankful for small mercies, young man.

JIMMY: But, you'll help me, won't you? To do stuff right?

GABRIEL: Sorry, Jimmy. I'm afraid it's all down to you. I'll be around to see how you're going on, but I'm afraid I'm just not allowed to intervene.

JIMMY: How will I know if I've passed or not?

GABRIEL: You'll know.

GABRIEL *smiles up at* JIMMY *who is very perplexed by now. He gives him a wink and then starts to cycle away.* JIMMY *looks away for a second as a black cat crawls across the roof next to him. When he looks back, the lane is empty; just an old newspaper blowing in the night breeze.* MUM *comes out of the back door.*

MUM: What are you doing up there?

JIMMY *positions himself to hide the Bible from his mother's view. He smiles down innocently.*

JIMMY: Nothing.

INT. WORKING MEN'S CLUB. LATER.
DAD *is sat at the bar talking again to* RIDLEY. HAROLD, *an elderly man with a ginger toupee, takes the microphone.*

HAROLD: Attention please. And first prize in tonight's draw

is this lovely leg of lamb. And it goes to . . .

HAROLD *dips his hand in a bucket held by* ERNIE.

HAROLD: Number two hundred and forty.

Suddenly NORMAN BANKS, *a fat balding fellow, stands up.*

NORMAN: Yes!

HAROLD: Norman Banks.

As NORMAN *goes to collect his prize to limp applause,* RIDLEY *beckons to* DAD.

RIDLEY: That's the third ruddy week in a row.

As NORMAN *is handed the leg of lamb.* HAROLD *gives a surreptitious wink.* RIDLEY *spots it with disgust.*

RIDLEY: Listen, Peter. I've got a little something that might interest you.

INT. ATTIC. SPUDS' HOUSE.

JIMMY *shines a torch on dusty boxes.*

EXT. WORKING MEN'S CLUB.

People come out of the club in dribs and drabs. NORMAN *walking proudly with his leg of lamb.* DAD *and* RIDLEY *are standing by* RIDLEY*'s Ford Cortina.* RIDLEY *furtively opens the boot. Hands* DAD *a box from a pile.* DAD *slips* RIDLEY *some money.* RIDLEY *quickly closes the boot, winks at* DAD *and gets in the car.* DAD *walks off drunkenly down the street.*

INT. JIMMY'S BEDROOM.

JIMMY *is surrounded by material. Sheets, an old dress, what looks like an old tent, tinsel and a large pot of glue. He is wielding a large pair of scissors.*

INT. DOWNSTAIRS.

MUM *is putting her feet up with a nice cup of tea.* DAD *sings to himself as he staggers in.*

MUM: You're paralytic.

DAD: What you on about, I've had two pints.

  DAD *nearly falls over.*

GRANDAD: What happened in the meat draw?

DAD: Where's Jimmy?

MUM: He's in his room. What's that?

DAD: Jimmy! (*To* GRANDAD.) Norman Banks won a leg of
   lamb.

GRANDAD: I reckon he knows somebody. That's the third
   time running.

JIMMY (*off*): What?

DAD: Come here, son.

GRANDAD: It wants reporting.

MUM: Leave him alone.

DAD: Jimmy!

MUM: It's eleven thirty.

GRANDAD: You can't stand for that sort of thing week after
   week.

  JIMMY *comes in.*

DAD: Jimmy. What have you always wanted? Eh?

JIMMY: I don't know.

GRANDAD: I've been putting into that raffle for five years.

DAD: Come on, think.

MUM: Don't encourage him, Jimmy.

JIMMY: A violin?

DAD: No. Not a bloody violin.

MUM: Language.

JIMMY: A dictionary.

DAD: Come on, not a dictionary. What would any normal
   kid give their right arm for?

MUM: Go back to bed, love.

JIMMY: An organ?

DAD: An organ!

JIMMY: I don't know? A tape deck? A chemistry set? . . . An
   encyclopaedia?

DAD: A GameBoy.

JIMMY: Oh.

DAD: Look.

  DAD *gives* JIMMY *a cardboard box.*

MUM: Where did you get that?

DAD: Never mind. (*To* JIMMY.) Well, open it.

MUM: It's knocked off, isn't it?

DAD: No, it isn't. I bought it off Ridley.

MUM: Then it's definitely knocked off, isn't it?

JIMMY: Thanks.

MUM *grabs the box.*

MUM: Give me that here.

JIMMY: Mum.

DAD: Is that all you can say? 'Thanks.'

MUM: You can take it back where it came from.

DAD: Give the kid back his GameBoy.

MUM: Over my dead body.

DAD: I've just bought it, for Christsake.

MUM: I've told you, I'm not having stolen goods in this house.

DAD: What about the telly?

MUM: That's different.

DAD: Give him back his GameBoy.

DAD *and* MUM *struggle over the GameBoy.*

DAD: Let go, will you?

GRANDAD: You know what Marx said don't you. You have to change all prevailing conditions.

DAD *wrests the GameBoy free and gives it to* JIMMY.

DAD: Here.

JIMMY: I don't want it.

GRANDAD: I'm going vegetarian.

DAD: You're bloody well having it.

JIMMY: Honest, I don't want a GameBoy.

DAD: I'll thump you in a minute.

MUM: Ignorant sod.

DAD *bursts into a coughing fit. They all sit for a second in silence.*

DAD: Look. Stuff the bloody GameBoy. I'm going to bed.

DAD *storms out of the room.*

JIMMY *is jumping on and off a small pouffe.*

GRANDAD: Tabula rasa. It's no good rearranging the furniture, you have to knock down the house.

JIMMY *seems to float for a split second in mid air.*

MUM: Jimmy, what did you just do?

JIMMY: Nothing. Night night.

MUM *watches* JIMMY *go out as if she didn't quite trust her own senses.*

EXT. METRO STATION. LATER.
Drizzle.

JIMMY: Mam, do you have to work in Whitley Bay?
MUM: It wasn't easy you know when your dad got laid off. It was supposed to be temporary. Sam only took me on as a favour. I knew him from school.
JIMMY: He's quite fat, isn't he?
MUM: Jimmy. He's been very good.
JIMMY: Mam, are you happy?
MUM: Of course I'm happy.
JIMMY: Do you not get a bit sick of Dad?
MUM: We all get a bit sick of each other.
JIMMY: But do you not think he's scary.
MUM: Jimmy, he's softer than the lot of us.
   A metro approaches.
MUM: My mam used to hate him. 'You can do better than a common welder.' To me he seemed like Marlon Brando. Just shows you, eh?
   MUM *gives* JIMMY *a peck on the cheek.*
MUM: What have you got in that bag?
JIMMY: Nothing.

EXT. ROAD TO THE SHIPYARDS.
JIMMY *wanders along carrying his bag.*

EXT. DISUSED WAREHOUSES. BY THE DOCKS.
JIMMY *peeps round the corner of one of the warehouses dwarfing him.*

JIMMY (*V/O*): It has been really boring recently.

JIMMY *rushes across the disused wasteland. He is wearing an angel costume. As the camera pulls back to follow* JIMMY*'s journey, we see the stunning skyline against the Tyne.*

INT. OLD WAREHOUSE.
JIMMY *is in a huge warehouse. He appears on the top of a huge wooden spool that once held rope. He dives off on to a pile of cardboard boxes.*

JIMMY (*V/O*): All Dad does is cough his guts out.

EXT. OLD SHIPYARDS.
JIMMY *appears on a section of crane ten feet off the ground. He leaps off flapping his arms. He lands on an old mattress.*

JIMMY (*V/O*): And all Mum does is get in a nark.

EXT. RIVER BANK.
JIMMY *is standing on a large wall in his angel garb.*

JIMMY (*V/O*): If I was Dad I would get a divorce.
    JIMMY *leaps off the wall and lands flat on his face on the grass below.*
JIMMY (*V/O*): Come to think of it, if I was Mum I'd get a divorce as well.

INT. LIVING ROOM. SPUDS' HOUSE.
DAD *doing his wood burnings.* GRANDAD *watches him.*

JIMMY (*V/O*): If it goes on like this I'm going to get one of those where you divorce your mum and your dad.

INT. FAT SAM'S.
MUM *sweats at the fryer.*

EXT. RIVER BANK.
JIMMY *brushes himself off. He seems determined to carry on with his practice.*

JIMMY (*V/O*): Then they'd be sorry.

EXT. TOP OF A CRANE, OVERLOOKING THE RIVER.
Close-up of JIMMY*'s eyes.*

JIMMY (*V/O*): I had been practising like mad and nothing
     had gone right. Then something cush happened.
     Pull back to show JIMMY *standing very still, his hair blowing in the wind.*
JIMMY (*V/O*): The other day I was looking down over the
     river. Over all the smashed-up stuff and that.
     Pull back to reveal JIMMY *on the very top of the crane overlooking the river. The whole of the yards are directly below him. Further away we have a stunning view of the city beyond.*
JIMMY (*V/O*): And in the distance I saw this terrible accident.
     We realise JIMMY *is very high. Our breath is almost taken away by the wind and a tumbling sense of vertigo.*

EXT. QUAYSIDE. BY THE RIVER.
We see JIMMY *looking down towards the Tyne.* JIMMY*'s POV: He sees* SCOUT, *a plump Asian boy, riding his bike along the river.* SCOUT *is paying more attention to stuffing a sandwich into his mouth than he is to balancing properly.*
     SCOUT, *concentrating on his ingestion rather than his perambulation, drives off the edge of the quayside and falls into the water.*
     JIMMY *watches anxiously.* SCOUT *fails to resurface. There is just the dirty lapping of the water.*

JIMMY (*V/O*): No one seemed to notice. So I waited, and
     waited for him to come back up. And he never. Then I
     thought he must have been drowning. So I swooped . . .

Flying shot swooping from the crane, as if from JIMMY*'s POV,
down towards the river. We see the buildings flashing before us and
very rapidly the river rushing up to meet us. We are flying down to
where* SCOUT *has fallen.*

JIMMY *falls clumsily head first into the water, as if he'd just leapt
in from the pathway.*

JIMMY (*V/O*): . . . like a dipper bird. I could hardly believe it.
Underwater. JIMMY *swims down to* SCOUT *and tries to hold on to
him.* JIMMY *is still in his angelic outfit. The whole thing is in slow
motion and is elegiac and beautiful.*

JIMMY (*V/O*): It was horrible.

*There is a desperateness about the rescue which seems like some
cosmic battle to save the poor* SCOUT *from being snatched by the
darkness underneath.* SCOUT *is sinking.* JIMMY *holds on but*
SCOUT*'s weight drags him down.*

JIMMY (*V/O*): I could hardly see. It was like dancing but
without any floor.

JIMMY *and* SCOUT *disappear out of the frame.*

JIMMY (*V/O*): Then I realised I was drowning too. I was all
dizzy and my lungs was bursting.

Bubbles float from the bottom of the frame to the top.

JIMMY (*V/O*): All I could feel was this body and the pitch
black. Then all of a sudden we rushed up like we was a
gun going off. Then I noticed it was a Boy Scout with a
hat and all sorts . . .

JIMMY*'s POV: Bursting into the daylight.* SCOUT *emerges
unconscious covered in weeds and debris.* JIMMY *bends towards him
and they both sink again.*

JIMMY (*V/O*): . . . so I quickly gave him the kiss of life.

They reappear. This time SCOUT *is coughing.*

JIMMY (*V/O*): And he was saved.

EXT. PIGEON CREE.
GRANDAD *is covered in pigeons as if they were bright and risen angels.*

EXT. QUAYSIDE.
JIMMY *pulls* SCOUT *on to the bank further up the river.*

JIMMY (*V/O*): When I dragged him out – he said –
SCOUT: Jesus Christ. Are you an angel?
JIMMY: I'm just a trainee.
SCOUT : But you're wearing a dress.
JIMMY (*V/O*): So I said –
JIMMY: Don't tell my dad.

EXT. KITCHEN. SPUDS' HOUSE.
DAD sits staring into space.

EXT. PATHWAY. BESIDE THE TYNE.
SCOUT on his bike. He is drenched and still covered in weeds. He puts his cap on, water squelches out.

SCOUT : Maybe I could show you a few knots sometime?
JIMMY: Cush.
SCOUT : OK, then.
JIMMY: See you.
   SCOUT smiles and cycles away, squelching water as he goes. JIMMY watches him disappear along the impressive riverside setting.

EXT. OTHER SIDE OF THE RIVER.
GABRIEL stands by his pushbike writing carefully in a notebook. He watches JIMMY from afar.

INT. JIMMY'S BEDROOM. NIGHT.
Two soggy shoes by the bed.

JIMMY (*V/O*): Any road, lifesaving, that's like being a
   guardian angel, plus rescuing a Boy Scout is pretty good
   in itself.
   JIMMY kisses Stanley's bowl.
JIMMY: Night night. Stanley.

INT. CORRIDOR.
MUM *is in her nightie. She turns and suddenly gets a shock as*
GRANDAD *is standing in his pyjamas in a state of tired confusion.*

MUM: Are you all right, Ted?
GRANDAD: Champion.

INT. MUM AND DAD'S BEDROOM.
MUM *and* DAD *in bed.* MUM *tries to kiss* DAD. DAD *coughs.*

MUM: This is driving me crazy.
DAD: I'm going to the bloody hospital tomorrow.
MUM: Are you OK?
DAD: Don't you think he's acting weird lately?
MUM: Who's acting weird?
DAD: Jimmy. He's all disconnected.
MUM: I wonder where he gets that from?
DAD: What's that meant to mean?
MUM: Are you sure you're all right, lover?
DAD: I think we should go to sleep now.
  MUM *turns out the bedside light.* DAD *turns over.* MUM *stares at the*
  ceiling.

INT. HOSPITAL. AFTERNOON.
DAD *walks into the entrance.*

INT. SCHOOL CORRIDOR. AFTERNOON.
JIMMY *is running down the corridor. Suddenly he is stopped by* MR
CHARLTON.

CHARLTON: I see you're well enough to be running round
  here like Steve Cram.
JIMMY: I'm sorry.
CHARLTON: Look, if you're coming to the game, Spud.
  There's going to be trouble.

EXT. BACKYARD.
JIMMY *is helping* MUM *bring in the washing.*

JIMMY: What if God exists but He doesn't want us to know
    He does, so He pretends that He doesn't?
MUM: What?
JIMMY: What if God's just pretending not to exist?
MUM: Where have you been getting these ideas from,
    Jimmy?
   They carry the clothes inside.
JIMMY: I just thought of them.
MUM: It's no good asking me, Jimmy, I'm not even religious.
    DAD *comes in.*
JIMMY: Dad. Do you think God exists?
MUM: Leave him alone, Jimmy, he's been to the doctor's.
JIMMY: You're an atheist, aren't you, Grandad?
GRANDAD: Well, if there was a God why would there be war
    and disease and kids starving?
JIMMY: So all the wars and stuff mean there's no God?
GRANDAD: Well, if He existed He'd stop them, wouldn't He?
JIMMY: He might be busy.
MUM (*to* DAD): Are you OK?
JIMMY: Can there still be miracles if there isn't a God?
MUM: The only miracle around here will be when you shut
    up for thirty seconds.
GRANDAD: Listen, son. Christianity's a complete bloody
    mess. For a start Jesus was Jewish.
JIMMY: Do Jews believe in God?
MUM: You'll have to ask a Jew.
JIMMY: I don't know any Jews.
DAD: Go and help your mum set the table.
JIMMY: How come God never had a wife?
GRANDAD: What does He want a wife for, He's God isn't
    He?
JIMMY: So how was Jesus born?
MUM: The Virgin Mary.
JIMMY: Do Jews believe in the Virgin Mary?
DAD: I've warned you. Everybody has different ways of
    looking at things – so shut it.

GRANDAD: He was only asking a reasonable question.
DAD: Just let it lie.
JIMMY: It was a reasonable question.
DAD: Jimmy, go upstairs I want to talk to Mum.
GRANDAD: You have to let him think for himself.
MUM: What's the matter, sweetheart?
DAD: I got the X-rays back today and there's tumours all
    over my left lung.
MUM: Peter.
GRANDAD: Son.

   EVERYBODY *is stunned.* DAD *lights a cigarette.*
JIMMY: Dad. If there is a God, He'll probably save you.
DAD: Well, if you ask me, God's a bastard.

   DAD *leaves, slamming the door.*

EXT. DISUSED CRANE. SUNSET.
JIMMY *sits with* GABRIEL *watching a magnificent sunset over a
panorama of Newcastle. They are miraculously sitting at the end of the
crane's long arm.*

JIMMY: So you're saying that the Devil used to be an angel.
GABRIEL: One of the top dogs. I told you it wasn't going to
    be straightforward.
JIMMY: So I might be evil and not even know.
GABRIEL: 'Fraid so.
JIMMY: That's terrible.
GABRIEL: Sometimes life's a bitch, Jimmy.
JIMMY: It seems a bit weird to me.
GABRIEL: That's why you're just a trainee.
JIMMY: This angel business is a bit more complicated than I
    thought. I imagined it'd just be flying around doing a
    few good deeds and stuff.

   *The letter 'O', of the neon sign for 'Hope Metals', flashing on and off
   in the distance, gives* GABRIEL *the appearance of having a flashing
   halo for a few seconds.*

JIMMY: Will Dad get better?
GABRIEL: We'll just have to see.

Below them the city fades into the distance and the girders of the crane creak eerily in the wind.

EXT. DISUSED SHIPYARDS. AFTERNOON.
JIMMY *cycles round the perimeter of the huge basin. He is in his angel costume and rides through the disused warehouses and the panorama of Newcastle towards the crane which overlooks the river. For a second the crane seems to move infinitesimally.*

We see GABRIEL *looking down at him protectively as if he was an industrial gargoyle sculpted into the side of a warehouse.*

INT. EXAMINATION ROOM. HOSPITAL.
A DOCTOR *examines* DAD *in a room filled with equipment.* DAD'*s X-rays are behind him on a screen.*

EXT. DISUSED SHIPYARDS.
A seagull is perched on the huge iron gate. SCOUT *is sitting on a magnificent stone pillar waiting for* JIMMY. JIMMY *comes rushing along on his bike, his costume flashing in the wind.*

SCOUT: Hello.
JIMMY: How did you know it was me?
SCOUT: I recognised your dress.
JIMMY: This isn't the full whack, you know. It's just what
    angels wear on their time off.
SCOUT: It's really quiet.
JIMMY: Cush, isn't it?
SCOUT: Fancy a chip?
JIMMY: Thanks very much.
SCOUT: You must get hungry with all that flying around.
JIMMY: Can I have another one?
SCOUT: Why don't you finish them?
JIMMY: I hope you don't think I'm a starver.
SCOUT: It's all right, I've got another packet.
    JIMMY *takes the packet,* SCOUT *reaches in his pocket and pulls out
    another bag of chips.*

INT. HOSPITAL.
The DOCTOR *examines* DAD *further.* DAD *has to blow into a tube. It causes him to cough.*

EXT. DOCKYARD.
JIMMY *and* SCOUT *walk through the yard. They are dwarfed by the scale of the buildings.*

SCOUT: Anyway, thanks for saving my life.
JIMMY: How's your arm?
SCOUT: All right. I can't get it right up here like I used to.
JIMMY: You just did.
SCOUT: What?
JIMMY: Get it right up there.
SCOUT: It was a joke. That's a smashing bike you've got.
JIMMY: Thanks.
SCOUT: Don't angels fly everywhere?
JIMMY: Yes. But I'm just a learner.
SCOUT: I bet it's quite tiring flying about.
JIMMY: Of course. You have to do physical fitness and all
       that.
SCOUT: Are angels strong?
JIMMY: Feel me arms then.
SCOUT: They're rock.
JIMMY: I know.
SCOUT: Are you really an angel?
JIMMY: Well, I'm doing training.
SCOUT: I'm a scout, you know.
JIMMY: I know.
SCOUT: I bet scouts and angels have loads in common.
       Haven't they?
JIMMY: I suppose. I like your toggle.
SCOUT: That's my woggle . . . Have you saved lots of people?
JIMMY: Well. Not really. You're the only one so far.
SCOUT: Really?
JIMMY: Well. The first proper one.
SCOUT: Does your dad know?
JIMMY: He's got cancer.

SCOUT: Oh.
JIMMY: Does your dad know?
SCOUT: He's dead.

EXT. HOSPITAL.
The DOCTOR *shakes* DAD*'s hand.* DAD *stifles a cough as he leaves the room. He looks devastated.*

JIMMY (*V/O*): Are you lonely?
SCOUT (*V/O*): A bit.

EXT. A HUGE WINCH. YARDS.
JIMMY *and* SCOUT *sit looking down the river.*

JIMMY: Maybe, I could be your guardian angel?
SCOUT: I don't know. Haven't you got any friends?
JIMMY: Not that many.
SCOUT: Does your mum know?
JIMMY: No one really knows.
SCOUT: All right. You can be my guardian angel.
JIMMY: Promise not to tell anyone? Not even Akela?
SCOUT: OK.
   JIMMY *kisses* SCOUT *on the forehead.*
JIMMY: Was it all right to kiss you?
SCOUT: I suppose so. Is it all right to see your wings?
JIMMY: I'm not sure if I should.
SCOUT: Go on. I'll not tell anybody.
JIMMY: OK, but I'll have to take my top off.
JIMMY: There.
SCOUT: Wow.
JIMMY: What do you think?
SCOUT: They're lovely. Can I feel them?
JIMMY: I don't know if you should.
SCOUT: Go on.
JIMMY: OK then.
SCOUT: They're sort of soft.

JIMMY: Aren't they fluffy?
SCOUT: If I took my top off would you flap them on me?
JIMMY: If you want.

Flapping sound. The camera cranes round.

JIMMY: What's it like?
SCOUT: It tickles.

A bird flaps into frame, obscuring the boys as we get up to their level.

SCOUT: Can you not flap them faster?
JIMMY: No. I'd take off.

Beat.

I have to stop, I'm puffed.

SCOUT: Can't you stay out any longer?
JIMMY: My mum will kill me.

JIMMY *jumps down.*

SCOUT: But I haven't shown you the knots or anything.
JIMMY: Don't tell anyone about my wings or I'll get into
   trouble.
SCOUT: I won't.

JIMMY *gets on his bike and turns to* SCOUT.

JIMMY: Maybe, you'll help me do some angel stuff through
   the week.
SCOUT: See you around then.
JIMMY: Bye.

JIMMY *cycles away.* SCOUT *puts on his cap and tightens his woggle
and watches* JIMMY *ride off into the distance.*

INT. LIVING ROOM. SPUDS' HOUSE. EARLY EVENING.
GRANDAD *and* DAD *are both sitting watching the silent TV.* JIMMY
is playing Handel's Messiah *loudly on the record player.* MUM *pops
her head round the door.*

MUM: What do you want for supper?
DAD: I don't care. What the hell is this, Jimmy?
JIMMY: It's Handel.
GRANDAD: That old crank.
DAD: It's bloody murder.
JIMMY: It's good.
GRANDAD: Geddit? Handle. Old crank.

DAD: Turn it off.

GRANDAD: You have no appreciation for the finer things in life.

DAD: I'd appreciate a bit of peace and quiet of a teatime.

GRANDAD: There's no need to be like that.

DAD: For Christsakes, just leave me alone for once.

> GRANDAD *leaves the room.* MUM *comes through with a frozen pizza.*

MUM: Don't you want your dinner?

GRANDAD: I'm not hungry.

> GRANDAD *shuts the door behind him.*

MUM: What's the matter with him? Look, I've got this frozen pizza?

DAD: Whatever.

MUM: Or there's those chicken pieces?

DAD: Screw the bloody chicken pieces.

MUM: Sweetheart.

DAD: And turn that music off.

JIMMY: Mum.

MUM: Now.

> JIMMY *turns the music off and leaves hurriedly.*

INT. STAIRCASE.
JIMMY *walks upstairs and finds* GRANDAD *sitting at the top.*

JIMMY: What's the matter, Grandad? Are you crying?

GRANDAD: No. I'm OK.

JIMMY: Why are you sitting here?

GRANDAD: I was just thinking.

JIMMY: I hate him.

GRANDAD: He used to hate me when I was your age. I think this place is just too small for all of us. We're like fish in a bowl.

JIMMY: What's going to happen?

GRANDAD: I don't know, son.

JIMMY: Will he go to heaven?

GRANDAD: He's not dead yet, Jimmy.

JIMMY: Grandad. Is it true that if you really believe in

something enough you can make it happen?
GRANDAD: Maybe.
JIMMY: Can I tell you something?
GRANDAD: Go on.
JIMMY: I'm training to be an angel.
GRANDAD: That's good, Jimmy.
JIMMY: And I've got a friend who I saved.
GRANDAD: Who's your friend?
JIMMY: He's a Boy Scout.
GRANDAD: Your dad was a Boy Scout.
JIMMY: Cush, eh?
GRANDAD: His tent's still up in the attic. Well, good luck
     with the training.
JIMMY: You won't tell anybody, will you?
GRANDAD: You won't tell anyone you saw me crying.
JIMMY: Not a soul.

INT. LIVING ROOM.
MUM *and* DAD *are in silence.*

DAD: Sorry.
MUM: It's all right, sugar.
   She stares at him.

INT. JIMMY'S BEDROOM.
JIMMY *is polishing a trumpet.* MUM *taps on the door. He hides it under his bed.*

MUM: You should be asleep by now.
JIMMY: Mum. Do you think Stanley's happy?
MUM: I don't know, he's just a fish.
JIMMY: You know I love him and everything.
MUM: It's time you were asleep
   MUM *turns off the light.*

INT. MUM AND DAD'S BEDROOM.
MUM *is in bed.* DAD *is getting undressed.*

MUM: Lots of people get better.
DAD: But you slowly suffocate.
MUM: You're not going to suffocate.
DAD: What'll you do?
MUM: What do you mean, what'll I do?
DAD: I'm worried about Jimmy.
MUM: Come on.
DAD: He's not normal.
MUM: Of course he's normal.
   JIMMY *appears at the window in his angel costume.*
DAD: He doesn't play football.
MUM: Is that all you can worry about? Whether Jimmy likes
   sport.
DAD: He needs a man's influence.
   JIMMY *moves out of view.*
MUM: Let's get some sleep now. It's all going to be fine.
   MUM *puts out the light and cuddles up to* DAD.

EXT. SPANISH CITY.
It is deserted as usual. JIMMY *is waiting for someone.*
   SCOUT *arrives in a hurry, rushing past a coconut shy. He has a huge
bag of crisps with him.*

INT. FAT SAM'S.
MUM *is cleaning the top of the counter. She knocks over the huge bottle
of ketchup. It flies everywhere.*

MUM: Shit.

EXT. BOATING LAKE. TYNEMOUTH.
JIMMY *and* SCOUT *are in a boat, in the middle of the lake. Around the
edge are boats in the shape of swans. The whole atmosphere is*

heightened and almost surreal.

JIMMY: I found out there are angels everywhere, you know.
SCOUT: Are there?
JIMMY: Even in Africa. When somebody dies the people get
　　　something the person wore and leave it out for the
　　　angels. And in the night the angels come and plant it
　　　and it grows and the person comes back to life.
SCOUT: Really?
JIMMY: Honest.
SCOUT: Maybe it's the heat.
JIMMY: I thought we could try it on your dad.
SCOUT: How?
JIMMY: Just get one of his old shoes.
SCOUT: Do you think it'll work?
JIMMY: It's worth a try. Do you want to see my celestial
　　　trumpet?
SCOUT: OK. Where is it?
　　*JIMMY produces the plastic bag and unties the top. As SCOUT starts
　　to row back to shore, Stanley plops into the pond.*
JIMMY: It's at home.
　　*As we pull back, GABRIEL's head appears out of the water. He is
　　wearing a snorkel and is still taking notes.*

INT. FAT SAM'S.
MUM *starts to cry into the fryer.* SAM *puts his arm around her.*

FAT SAM: It's all right.

INT. JIMMY'S BEDROOM.
SCOUT *and* JIMMY *are looking at the trumpet in* JIMMY's *tidy
bedroom.*

SCOUT: Can you play it?
JIMMY: I'm just learning.
SCOUT: And it cures people?

JIMMY: Yeah.

SCOUT: Go on then.

GRANDAD *and* DAD *are sitting on the settee.* Grandstand *is on TV.* GRANDAD *is asleep. The sound of a trumpet squeals.*

DAD: What the . . . ?

INT. JIMMY'S BEDROOM.

JIMMY: I'm puffed.

SCOUT: Maybe you should take a breather.

JIMMY: Do you think it'll make him better?

SCOUT: Dunno.

JIMMY: If I practise maybe?

SCOUT: Would you play for me if I was ill?

JIMMY: Course. I'm your guardian angel. I'm gonna try again.

JIMMY *starts to play. There is banging on the door.*

DAD: Jimmy.

DAD *bursts in.*

DAD: What the hell's this?

JIMMY: I'm practising.

DAD: Practising what?

JIMMY: My celestial trumpet.

DAD: Your what?

JIMMY: Cush, eh?

DAD: It's bloody murder, Jimmy.

JIMMY: It's music of the spheres, Dad.

DAD *notices* SCOUT *eating another sandwich.*

DAD: What's he doing here?

JIMMY: Practising as well.

DAD: He hasn't even got a trumpet. I'm not having this nonsense in here.

DAD *turns to leave, then he double-takes.*

DAD: What have you got on?

JIMMY: It's my tunic.

DAD: A tunic?

JIMMY: Do you like it?

DAD: It's a frock, for Christsakes.

JIMMY: It's like spiritual overalls.

DAD: It's coming off this minute. You're not dressing like a
fruit in this house.

JIMMY: Dad.

DAD: It's going the journey. You can play your trumpet in
jeans and a t-shirt like every bugger else.

DAD *takes the angel costume.* JIMMY *is left in his undershirt.*

DAD: What's that?

JIMMY: What's what?

DAD: Those. What have you two been up to?

JIMMY: It's nothing. Just feathers.

DAD: Feathers? What have you been doing to our Jimmy?

JIMMY: He didn't do anything. It's just natural.

DAD: Son, this isn't natural.

JIMMY: What's not?

DAD: You should know better. You're a scout.

JIMMY: But . . .

DAD: This is sick.

JIMMY: Dad.

DAD: Sticking things on Jimmy. You're banned in future.

SCOUT: But Mr Spud.

JIMMY: What did he do wrong?

DAD: I'll speak to your Akela. (*To* JIMMY.) And don't pretend
you don't know what this is about.

JIMMY: What what's about?

DAD: You know fine well.

JIMMY: I don't know fine well.

DAD: You know exactly, you lying sod. Dresses.

JIMMY: Please, Dad, you're just upset because of your cancer.

DAD: I'm not upset because of my cancer. Has he been
messing around with you?

JIMMY: What?

DAD: How old are you?

JIMMY: Dad. I've become a beautiful angel.

DAD: Jimmy, you've become a little pervert. It's disgusting.
I'm downstairs barely able to catch my breath and
you're up here with a Boy Scout.

JIMMY: But it's natural.

DAD: I'll give you bloody natural.

DAD *takes the trumpet and smashes it violently, until he collapses on to the bed in a coughing fit.*

JIMMY: It's to save you.

DAD: Next time it won't be the trumpet that goes for a burton. Understand?

JIMMY: You're just surprised at the wonderment.

DAD: You little bastard.

MUM *runs upstairs and into the room.*

MUM: What are you doing?

JIMMY: He smashed my celestial trumpet.

MUM: I'll smash your bloody heads together – upsetting your dad like that. (*To* DAD.) Come on, lover. (*To* JIMMY.) And put some clothes on when you've got guests.

EXT. TYNE BRIDGE.

SCOUT: Some guardian angel you are. Your dad throws a wobbler and you didn't even do anything.

JIMMY: I tried.

SCOUT: Was your dad really a Boy Scout?

JIMMY: I think he's gone mental.

SCOUT: Maybe we should run away. I mean, I'm practically an orphan.

JIMMY: They'd never let me be an angel if I ran away.

SCOUT: You're just scared.

JIMMY: Are you still my friend?

SCOUT: Will you still help me with my dad?

JIMMY: Of course.

SCOUT: When?

EXT. SAD OLD WAREHOUSE. LATER.

Pan up the side of the building. JIMMY *is standing on the roof with his broken trumpet.* GABRIEL *appears next to him unexpectedly.*

JIMMY: I don't think things are going too well.

GABRIEL: Just be patient.

JIMMY: How can I be a guardian angel with this rubbish?
  GABRIEL *takes the trumpet and inspects it.*
GABRIEL: Nobody's forcing you to do this, Jimmy.
  GABRIEL *tries a note. It is broken and farts a coarse burp.*
  GABRIEL *gives it back to* JIMMY.
JIMMY: You're no help whatsoever.
  The warehouse is silhouetted in the afternoon sun. On the roof we see the outline of two figures: JIMMY *standing,* GABRIEL *on his rickety old bicycle.*

INT. CORRIDOR. HOSPITAL. AFTERNOON.
Slow-motion shot moving ethereally towards MUM *at the other end of a long hospital corridor.*

JIMMY (*V/O*): Dad's cancer is getting worse.
  MUM *is waiting outside a room.*
JIMMY (*V/O*): Cancer is like this little thing inside you that gets bigger and bigger . . .
  MUM *looks anxious.*
JIMMY (*V/O*): . . . kind of multiplying till you get too full . . .
  DAD *comes out of the* DOCTOR's *office and hugs* MUM. *The* DOCTOR *follows and gives* MUM *some bad news.*
JIMMY (*V/O*): . . . sometimes I feel there's a bigness inside of me. All sadness and littleness getting bigger and bigger . . .
  DAD *returns to the room to collect his coat. The* DOCTOR *draws* MUM *to one side – so* DAD *won't overhear. The* DOCTOR *explains something very serious to* MUM. MUM *turns away. The* DOCTOR *hugs* MUM.
JIMMY (*V/O*): . . . then it kind of changes and it's all the goodness in the world. And it's ticking like the clock on a bomb and it's tickling till I'm sick. And I'm bursting but . . .
  MUM *is crying. The* DOCTOR *squeezes her arm.*
JIMMY (*V/O*): . . . to everyone else it's invisible. But when the bigness bursts. It will burst kisses . . .
  DAD *comes out of the office in his jacket.* MUM *has stopped crying.*
JIMMY (*V/O*): . . . and everybody will see. And the kisses will

kiss your eyes like hummingbirds, little sweet kisses that
you can't tell are there . . .
MUM *and* DAD *shake hands with the* DOCTOR. *As they walk
away, towards us, the* DOCTOR *watches them sadly.*
JIMMY (*V/O*): . . . . sly kisses chasing you down the street.
Kisses on your lips and on your cheeks and your
nose . . .
The DOCTOR *calls out something.* MUM *and* DAD *turn. They
smile at the* DOCTOR. *No one smiles too much.*
JIMMY (*V/O*): . . . and no one will hate me any more 'cos I'm
an angel. They'll love the angels and the kisses and
everything.
MUM *and* DAD *walking towards the camera.* DAD *reaches for*
MUM*'s hand.*
JIMMY (*V/O*): And I will be flying around and everything will
be better. At least I think.
DAD *holds it tightly.*

INT. LIVING ROOM. SPUDS' HOUSE.
GRANDAD *in apron. The table is covered in food.* MUM *and* DAD
come in.

GRANDAD: Would you like something to eat?
MUM: You shouldn't have, Grandad.
GRANDAD *gives them both a slice of a cherry pie and pours them
coffee. Nobody eats anything.* JIMMY *enters.*
MUM: Come and have some of this lovely pie Grandad's
made.
JIMMY: I'm not hungry. I'm going to bed.
MUM: It isn't even six o'clock, Jimmy.
JIMMY: I know. Night night.
They all look solemnly at the pie.

INT. JIMMY'S BEDROOM.
JIMMY *is in bed. By his bedside are a gardening fork and trowel. He
sets his alarm and turns to go to sleep.*

EXT. BACKYARD. THE WEE HOURS.
JIMMY *is crawling on the ground.* SCOUT*'s face appears looking over the back wall.*

SCOUT: Jimmy.
JIMMY: I'll open the door.

>JIMMY *opens the door and* SCOUT *bustles in.* JIMMY *shuts the door.* SCOUT *bumps into the bin which makes a clatter. They freeze. Listen. Then, when the coast is clear, they continue to the side of the house where there is a small section of garden.*

JIMMY: Have you got it?
SCOUT: Here.

>SCOUT *takes a sock from his pocket.*

JIMMY: It's a sock.
SCOUT: I couldn't find a shoe.
JIMMY: Sssh.
SCOUT: What is it?
JIMMY: I thought I heard something.
SCOUT: Will it work with a sock?
JIMMY: I don't know. Couldn't you get a shoe?

>SCOUT *is about to answer.* JIMMY *stops his mouth while he checks the coast is clear.*

SCOUT: I'm sorry I was horrible the other day.
JIMMY: What about a hat or something?
SCOUT: It's all there was.

>JIMMY *passes a torch to* SCOUT.

JIMMY: You weren't horrible. But a sock.
SCOUT: Sorry.

>JIMMY *digs while* SCOUT *holds the torch.*

JIMMY: OK, put it in.
SCOUT: Don't you do a spell or something?
JIMMY: I'm an angel not a witch.
SCOUT: Are you still annoyed with me?
JIMMY: Shhh. If Dad hears you he'll go mental.

>*A light comes on.*

JIMMY: Shit. It's Mum.

>JIMMY *gives scout the trowel.*

>Just pretend you're weeding.

MUM: What are you doing out here?

JIMMY: Just some gardening, Mum.

MUM: It's four in the morning, Jimmy.

JIMMY: I'm just planting things.

MUM: What things?

JIMMY: Socks and that.

MUM: You're going to have to stop this, sweetheart.

JIMMY: I won't be long.

MUM: Come on. Don't be stupid.

JIMMY: It's not stupid. It's planting souls.

MUM: I really can't cope.

JIMMY: But you have to do it at night.

   MUM *spots* SCOUT.

MUM: What are you doing here?

JIMMY: It's his dad's sock.

MUM: Does your dad know about this?

JIMMY: He's dead.

MUM: What about your poor mother?

JIMMY: He's a Scout, Mum.

MUM: You'll have to go home now.

JIMMY: Why?

MUM: Because I say so.

JIMMY: Mum.

MUM: You'll wake your dad.

JIMMY: You're just jealous.

MUM: Jimmy, I am not jealous.

JIMMY: It's more than you can do.

MUM: What will the neighbours think, Jimmy? Inside. And give me that spade.

SCOUT: Bye.

   SCOUT *is left alone in the yard.*

INT. KITCHEN.

MUM: Sit down, Jimmy. There's something I need to talk to you about.

JIMMY: Is it because I woke you up?

MUM: No. It's about Dad.

JIMMY: Sorry I was digging so loud.

MUM: You have to try and understand.

JIMMY: What's the matter?

MUM: They're going to have to take him in, Jimmy.

JIMMY: Where?

MUM: To the hospital. The tumours are growing, you see.

JIMMY: Oh.

MUM: He won't be coming home.

JIMMY: Is he going there for ever?

MUM: Yes.

JIMMY: Are you going too?

MUM: Jimmy, he's going there to die.

JIMMY: That's why he's being so horrible, isn't it?

MUM: Just forgive him for me.

JIMMY: I'm trying my best.

MUM: I know.

JIMMY: But he won't die, Mum.

MUM: Jimmy, I think he will. They've stopped the treatment.

JIMMY: But . . .

MUM: I know it's hard.

JIMMY: But, Mum. Death doesn't exist.

MUM: Jimmy.

JIMMY: I'll make him better. That's what angels do.

MUM: You're not an angel, Jimmy.

JIMMY: I've been practising.

MUM: This isn't easy for me, Jimmy.

JIMMY: Mum. I saved a Boy Scout.

MUM: He's going to die and there's nothing anyone can do about it.

JIMMY: But the celestial powers.

MUM: Listen.

JIMMY: Believe me, Mum.

MUM: Jimmy.

JIMMY (*shouting*): No.

MUM: Sssh.

JIMMY: No, no, no.

   MUM *slaps* JIMMY *then hugs him tightly*.

MUM: I'm sorry.

JIMMY: You stupid idiot.

MUM: I didn't mean to.

JIMMY: I hate you.
MUM: Jimmy.
JIMMY: You smell of dog food.
MUM: Jimmy, I don't smell of dog food.
JIMMY: And cats' trays.
MUM: Jim . . .
JIMMY: And monkeys' bums and . . .
      MUM *starts to cry.*
JIMMY: . . . sheep's feet.
MUM: I'm sorry, Jimmy.
JIMMY: You don't really smell of sheep's feet.
MUM: You're going to have to help me, Jimmy. You're going
      to have to be very grown-up.
JIMMY: I'll try, Mum. Honest.
MUM: Give me a little cuddle before you go to bed.
JIMMY: Do I have to?
MUM: Yes, you do.
      MUM *hugs* JIMMY.

INT. JIMMY'S BEDROOM.
JIMMY *enters.* GRANDAD *is sitting on his bed.*

JIMMY: Are you crying again?
GRANDAD: No. Look.
    He gives a case to JIMMY.
JIMMY: What is it?
    JIMMY *opens it. An old silver trumpet glistens in the moonlight.*
GRANDAD: It belonged to old Dickie Curtis. He used to play
      for Harry Roy.
JIMMY: Who?
GRANDAD: Just practise it when no one's around. You hear?
JIMMY: You'll leave me one of your shoes, won't you,
      Grandad?
GRANDAD: Night night.

INT. MUM AND DAD'S ROOM. AFTERNOON.
DAD *is packing a bag with his pyjamas, etc. He seems very weak and*

frail. He puts the things carefully in the bag which is on his bed. He
seems short of breath and has to sit down without finishing. We see the
fear and fatigue in his face. JIMMY *comes into the room. He is carrying*
a toothbrush.

JIMMY: Dad.
  JIMMY *hands* DAD *the toothbrush.*

EXT. HOSPITAL. LATE AFTERNOON.
DAD *and* MUM *arrive at the hospital in an ambulance.*

JIMMY (*V/O*): Everything seems to be going from bad to
      worse.

INT. MUM AND DAD'S BEDROOM. NIGHT.
MUM *takes off her dressing gown and gets into bed alone.*

JIMMY (*V/O*): I've been practising like mad, but it's all
      useless . . .

INT. WARD 9.
DAD *is lying in bed.*

JIMMY (*V/O*): . . . like when you look at the stars . . .

INT. MUM AND DAD'S BEDROOM.
MUM *stares at the ceiling.*

JIMMY (*V/O*): . . . and they are a million years old . . .
      She can't get comfortable.
JIMMY (*V/O*): . . . and everything is dying and falling and you
      are tumbling . . .

EXT. SCHOOL PLAYING FIELD. MORNING.
Close-up of JIMMY *standing in the pouring rain in his football gear. He is soaked.*

JIMMY (*V/O*): . . . and there is no one to catch you . . .

EXT. GOAL MOUTH.
Rear view of JIMMY *standing in the goal mouth. Far in the distance we can see* CHARLTON *and the boys enjoying the match at the far end of the pitch.*

JIMMY (*V/O*): . . . and you are tiny and insignificant and if the history of the world was a beach, you are smaller than the smallest speck of sand dust and there are no wings to save you and you are all alone.
  The ball whistles past JIMMY'*s head right into the back of the goal.* JIMMY *has made no attempt to save it. He just stands impassively. We notice* GABRIEL *is standing next to the goalpost under a tattered umbrella.*

INT. METRO. EARLY AFTERNOON.
JIMMY *is sitting with* SCOUT. *They have a small case with them. They look nervously at each other.*

INT. HOSPITAL CORRIDOR.

JIMMY: Don't be scared, will you?
SCOUT: Does he look horrible?
JIMMY: Mum says not to mention it.
  JIMMY *and* SCOUT *look into Ward 9.*
JIMMY: If he throws a wobbler, just keep going. It's for his own good.
SCOUT: Are you sure this is a good idea?
JIMMY: Look. There he is.
SCOUT: He looks terrible.

JIMMY: He's asleep. Stay here till I give the signal.

They go in. JIMMY *gently touches* DAD*'s arm.*

JIMMY: Dad.

DAD: Hello.

JIMMY: Are you OK?

DAD: Smashing.

JIMMY: Good. Have you been out of bed today?

DAD: I took a walk down the corridor.

JIMMY: That's good.

DAD: I got tired though.

JIMMY: I bet you did.

DAD: Pass the mask.

> JIMMY *passes the oxygen mask.* DAD *breathes deeply.* JIMMY *kicks the bed in a bored manner.*

JIMMY: Can I try it?

DAD: It's only for if you're sick.

> *Beat.*

Stop kicking the bed.

JIMMY: How do you feel now?

DAD: Look Jimmy I'm not so good.

JIMMY: But you'll be all right won't you, Dad?

DAD: Well, they say that it's getting worse but there is a good chance that it'll not go into the other lung.

JIMMY: You look really old, Dad.

> DAD *coughs.*

JIMMY: How'd you feel now?

DAD: Not too hot.

JIMMY: I forgive you for smashing the trumpet.

DAD: I know I shouldn't have done what I did.

JIMMY: It's all right.

DAD: Only . . .

JIMMY: I know.

DAD: I love you, son.

JIMMY: Look who's here to see you.

> SCOUT *runs in with a trumpet and music stand.*

SCOUT: Hello, Mr Spud.

JIMMY: I know you think it's weird.

DAD: Jesus.

JIMMY: We have to try it. We've been doing it for weeks.

DAD: Jimmy, you're only eleven.

JIMMY: I'm his guardian angel.

DAD: I told you about him.

JIMMY: I'm an angel, Dad.

DAD: You're a deviant, Jimmy.

JIMMY: I'll save you. God will come and wipe the tears . . .

DAD: Everybody's looking.

> JIMMY *picks up the trumpet.* SCOUT *opens the music.*

DAD: I'm warning you.

JIMMY: It'll make you feel better.

> JIMMY *and* SCOUT *play a spiritual.* JIMMY *is a virtuoso.* SCOUT
> *sings like an angel. As their music soars they are embellished by a
> heavenly orchestra.* DAD *breaks into a coughing fit. The boys end
> beautifully, stunned with their playing.*

SCOUT: I think it made him worse.

JIMMY: Maybe it was too much for him.

DAD: Get out of here and don't come back.

SCOUT: I think we should go.

DAD (*to* SCOUT): And keep away from our Jimmy, you little
    bastard.

> JIMMY *grabs the trumpet, music stand and* SCOUT, *and runs out of
> the ward.*

> JIMMY *and* SCOUT *head down the street. At the end is a railway
> crossing. The lights are already beginning to flash as a warning of an
> impending train.* SCOUT *is carrying the music stand.*

SCOUT: You're supposed to be a guardian angel.

JIMMY: I thought it would be good.

SCOUT: You're crap at being an angel.

JIMMY: I couldn't help it.

SCOUT: You can't do anything.

JIMMY: I learnt the trumpet quick.

SCOUT: But that sock stuff was useless.

JIMMY: It was meant to be a shoe.

> JIMMY *and* SCOUT *reach the train tracks.*

SCOUT: Well, you made me look like a total divvy.

JIMMY: No, I never.

SCOUT: Your dad called me a bastard.

JIMMY: He didn't mean it.

> *The train approaches.* SCOUT *dashes across the line.*

SCOUT: I've had it. You aren't my guardian angel any more.
JIMMY: But I won't get accepted.
SCOUT: See. That's all you care about.
A train comes hurtling past. SCOUT *disappears behind it.* JIMMY *waits anxiously for the carriages to pass. When the train completely passes* SCOUT *is gone. Only the music stand is left.*
However, GABRIEL *is waiting on his bike. He cycles over to talk to* JIMMY.
GABRIEL: How's it going?

EXT. PROMENADE. WHITLEY.
JIMMY *and* GABRIEL *looking out to sea.*

JIMMY: I've tried everything I could to save him.
GABRIEL: I never said it would be easy.
JIMMY: But everything I do turns out useless.
GABRIEL: You just have to stick at it, Jimmy.
JIMMY: I don't want to stick at it. I want everything to stop.
GABRIEL: Look, keep at it. You'll see.

INT. LIVING ROOM. SPUDS' HOUSE.
MUM *and* GRANDAD *sit silently.* JIMMY *comes in looking very upset.*

MUM: How was your dad?
JIMMY turns and rushes upstairs without saying anything.

INT. CORRIDOR. HOSPITAL.
GRANDAD *walks up the corridor.*

INT. CHANGING ROOM. SCHOOL.
CHARLTON *looks at a note* JIMMY *has given him. He shakes his head in disgust.*

CHARLTON: That's it, Spud. Detention. tonight. For an hour.

INT. WARD 9. HOSPITAL.
GRANDAD *tries to get a chair from the stack in the corner, but it is impossible. A* YOUNG NURSE *helps him and places a chair next to* DAD*'s bed.*

   DAD *avoids* GRANDAD*'s gaze as he holds his hand. Then* DAD *looks him in the eye. Tears well up.*

DAD: Dad.
   They stare at each other.

INT. CHANGING ROOM. SCHOOL.
JIMMY *is standing in the changing room.*

CHARLTON: All right, Mr Spud. I think it's time we had a
      little chat. Don't you?
   JIMMY *looks at* CHARLTON.
CHARLTON: Look. It's just not on, Jimmy. You can't keep
      going on like this.
JIMMY: But you don't understand, sir.
CHARLTON: Don't tell me what I understand.
JIMMY: I'm sorry, sir. For the notes and everything. But . . .
CHARLTON: Jimmy. I know about your father.
   This dumbfounds JIMMY.
CHARLTON: I didn't bring you here to tell you off Jimmy.
      Look, when I was your age my dad got ill too. It wasn't
      his lungs. It was his pancreas. I know how I felt. I used
      to go and see him, and you just feel hopeless. Like
      there's nothing you can do. I remember sitting there
      and just thinking, I love you.
   CHARLTON *becomes choked.* JIMMY *doesn't know what to do.*
   CHARLTON *pulls himself together.*
CHARLTON: You see, I know how you feel, Jimmy.
JIMMY: You don't know anything about what I feel.
CHARLTON: You need to talk about it.
JIMMY: You don't know anything about me. I hate him, sir.
CHARLTON What?
JIMMY: I hate me dad. He's a bastard.

CHARLTON *goes to hold* JIMMY *but he pulls away.*
JIMMY: Get off. You're all bastards.
  JIMMY *runs out.*

EXT. SCHOOL PLAYING FIELD.
JIMMY *runs out of the changing room and across the field. He is crying
and we follow him closely. He runs and runs until he collapses
exhaustedly in the middle of the field.*

INT. JIMMY'S BEDROOM.
JIMMY *puts some socks and a jumper into his haversack.*

INT. KITCHEN.
JIMMY *is writing laboriously.*

JIMMY (*V/O*): Dear Mum, I have run away. I tried my best
    but it is rubbish. Sorry. Love, Jimmy Spud.
  JIMMY *picks up his bag and goes to leave. He hesitates and returns
  to the letter. He writes: 'P.S. I hope Dad gets better.'*

INT. FAT SAM'S. EVENING.
MUM *is frying fish.* SAM *tentatively hugs her.*

FAT SAM: I just want to say I'm sorry.
MUM: That's OK.
FAT SAM: And I was thinking. If you wanted to take him
    some fresh fillets. You know, just help yourself.
MUM: OK.
FAT SAM: It's the least I can do.
  JIMMY *stands at the other side of the road. On his back is the
  haversack. He looks sadly at* MUM *inside the shop. The swinging
  haddock that has been creaking in the breeze suddenly stops making a
  noise.*

INT. KITCHEN. SPUDS' HOUSE. LATER THAT EVENING.
GRANDAD *is sitting reading* JIMMY*'s letter.* MUM *comes in the back door. She sees* GRANDAD *looks worried.*

MUM: What's the matter?
   GRANDAD *passes her the letter. She reads it.* GRANDAD *gets up. He puts his hat on and picks up a small parcel wrapped in a plastic bag.*
GRANDAD: Don't worry, flower. He can't have gone far.
MUM: But, Ted . . .
GRANDAD: I'll be back shortly. It'll be all right.

INT. WARD 9.
DAD *is given an injection of morphine by a* NURSE. *He needs oxygen as his breathing is very poor.*

INT. CAB OF THE CRANE. LATE NIGHT.
JIMMY *is sitting with his trumpet looking out across Newcastle. He is perched looking out of the window like a forlorn bird.*

GRANDAD (*from below*): Jimmy.
JIMMY: Grandad?
   Suddenly, a head appears at the top of the access ladder at JIMMY*'s side.*
JIMMY: How did you know I'd be here?
GRANDAD: Christ, it's a long way up here.
JIMMY: What's that?
GRANDAD: I brought you a pie.
JIMMY: What about your back?
GRANDAD: Third prize in the meat draw. I put in a
   complaint to the committee.
   GRANDAD *winks at* JIMMY. *He perches on the ledge with* JIMMY, *puts the pie on a small cloth and starts to cut the pie into sections.*
GRANDAD: Are you all right, son?
JIMMY: Yes.
GRANDAD: Good.

JIMMY: Well, not really.

GRANDAD: Do you want some?

JIMMY: No.

GRANDAD: Delicious.

   Beat.

   Are you upset?

JIMMY: No.

GRANDAD: Why not?

JIMMY: I don't know.

GRANDAD: Look, you can see the Neptune Yard. They built the *Mauritania* down there.

JIMMY: I know.

GRANDAD: You haven't been to see your dad, have you?

JIMMY: No.

GRANDAD: They say he might not last through the weekend.

JIMMY: He hates me.

GRANDAD: He doesn't hate you.

JIMMY: He does.

GRANDAD: Jimmy.

JIMMY: If I had kids I wouldn't break their trumpet. I'd be pleased if they were musical.

GRANDAD: He didn't mean it. He's terrified.

JIMMY: If I had kids I'd encourage them to be angels.

GRANDAD: Look. Imagine how he feels. He's never going to see you again.

JIMMY: Is he really going to die?

GRANDAD: What happened to your friend?

JIMMY: He went away.

GRANDAD: Where?

JIMMY: Grandad. I'm crap at being an angel.

GRANDAD: You can only do your best, son.

JIMMY: But what if your best is rubbish? What if God is just a 'bastard'?

GRANDAD: Does it make any difference?

JIMMY: I don't know.

GRANDAD: If everything was perfect there'd be nothing for angels to do. You have to just love people for what they are, not what you want them to be.

JIMMY: But what if I am unnatural?

GRANDAD: How can you be unnatural. You're just you.

JIMMY: I don't know.

GRANDAD: All you have to do is go tell him you love him.

JIMMY: I can't, Grandad. All I wanted to do was save him.
It's useless.

GRANDAD: Nothing's useless, Jimmy. Anyway, individual
salvation's just bourgeois sophistry, son. Sometimes you
can't do everything, you just have to do what you can.

JIMMY: I think I'll stay here, Grandad.

GRANDAD: OK.

Beat.

I'll leave you the rest of the pie, Jimmy.

JIMMY: Grandad, thanks.

GRANDAD *packs away his things and makes towards the ladder.*

INT. CORRIDOR. HOSPITAL. VERY LATE.

JIMMY *creeps past the night attendant.*

The ward is in darkness. JIMMY *approaches* DAD *trying not to wake
him, but* DAD *stirs.*

DAD: Jimmy?

JIMMY: Dad.

DAD: It's practically midnight.

JIMMY: Sssh, Dad.

DAD: What are you doing here?

JIMMY: I had to see you.

DAD: Does your mum know?

JIMMY: Ssssh.

DAD: You shouldn't be here.

JIMMY: Don't say that.

DAD: This is all I need.

JIMMY: Dad.

DAD: What are you doing here?

JIMMY: Calm down. I came to tell you . . . nothing.

DAD: What are you doing, Jimmy?

JIMMY: I came to tell you – I still love you.

DAD: I just don't know what's gotten into you, son.

JIMMY: I came to make up. Are you all right?

DAD: All I want now is a bit of rest.
JIMMY: Do you want me to go?
DAD: No.
JIMMY: OK.
DAD: I can hardly breathe.
JIMMY: Do you want anything?
DAD: I want you to help me, Jimmy.
JIMMY: How?
DAD: I want to get it over with.
JIMMY: Dad.
DAD: Do you understand?
JIMMY: All I ever wanted was to save you.
DAD: Nobody can save me, Jimmy. It's humiliating.
JIMMY: Please, Dad.
DAD: I can't go through any more, Jimmy. It's agony.
JIMMY: I'm an angel, Dad.
DAD: Please.
JIMMY: But I came to help you.
DAD: The pillow.
JIMMY: No. Please, listen.
DAD: Put it on my face.
JIMMY: I'll never get accepted.
DAD: Please.
JIMMY: Dad, do you hate me?
DAD: No, I love you.

   DAD *pushes a pillow across the bed.*

JIMMY: I can't, I'm an angel.
DAD: Come on, Jimmy.
JIMMY: I can't. I love you, Dad.
DAD: If you love me, Jimmy.
JIMMY: Dad.

   JIMMY *takes the pillow and climbs on to the bed, tears are running down his cheek.* JIMMY *lays it gently on* DAD*'s face and pushes down.* DAD *jerks.* JIMMY *has to struggle to keep the pillow firm as* DAD*'s jerks get more violent.* JIMMY *starts to sob and he throws the pillow away.* DAD *is motionless.* JIMMY *shakes him gently.* DAD *still doesn't move.*

JIMMY: Wake up. Please, wake up.

   JIMMY *hits* DAD*'s chest.*

JIMMY: Dad. Dad. Please, Dad. No.

Suddenly, he is grabbed from behind. It is MUM.

MUM: Thank God you're here.

JIMMY: I was only trying –

MUM: It's all right.

JIMMY: Mum. He made me.

MUM: It's all right, Jimmy.

JIMMY: It's hopeless.

MUM: Jimmy.

JIMMY: I'll never be an angel.

JIMMY *breaks* MUM*'s grip and climbs on to the bed, shaking* DAD.

JIMMY: Wake up.

MUM: He's gone, sweetheart.

JIMMY: I'll bring him back.

MUM: Jimmy, you're not an angel any more.

JIMMY: I am.

MUM: There's nothing we can do.

JIMMY: Wake up.

MUM: Sssh.

JIMMY: It has to work.

MUM: Stop it.

JIMMY: *Hoc est corpus meum.*

MUM: Come on.

JIMMY: It's what you say. *Hoc est corpus meum.*

MUM: Honey.

JIMMY: Come on. *Hoc est corpus meum.*

MUM *grabs* JIMMY *and takes him off the bed.*

JIMMY: It's got to work.

MUM: You can't do everything you want to.

JIMMY: But I'm supposed to be an angel. *Hoc est . . .*

MUM: Shhhh.

JIMMY *breaks down.*

MUM: I love you, Jimmy Spud.

JIMMY *is devastated.* MUM *consoles* JIMMY. *A* NURSE *comes in and puts an arm round* MUM*'s shoulder. She gently leads them out of the ward. As* JIMMY *looks back, a ray of moonlight lights up* DAD*'s body.*

Close-up on DAD: *his eyes open in a startled expression.*

DAD: Bloody hell. I thought I was a gonner there.

JIMMY (*OOV*): Mam.
  Music soars.

EXT. WHITLEY BAY. A BEAUTIFUL DAY.
MUM *is holding* DAD's *hand.* GRANDAD *is looking out to sea.*
JIMMY *is perched on the railings.* MUM *takes out a camera and*
approaches a stranger to take a photo. MUM *prepares for the picture; she*
looks beautiful, years younger in a pretty dress. As the frame freezes into
a snapshot, JIMMY *appears to be floating several inches above the*
railings.

JIMMY (*V/O*): And I am light and all light and my body is
    rays . . .
  JIMMY's *POV:* MUM, DAD *and* GRANDAD *have their backs to*
  us. For the first time we really see the PHOTOGRAPHER. *It is*
  GABRIEL. GABRIEL *is beaming. The POV starts to float high*
  above the figures: we see everyone get smaller and smaller beneath us.
JIMMY (*V/O*): . . . and the rays are love and I am all love and
    I love who I want and I am bursting with kisses,
    hummingbird kisses on the lips of the sick and the lonely
    and the wretched and the mean and the kisses are me
    and I am the kisses and I am transformed as I transform
    you and I am love as I love you.
  Flying shot into the blinding brilliance of the sun.
JIMMY (*V/O*): All my body is rays.

Wittgenstein on Tyne

Wittgenstein on Tyne was originally performed at The Live Theatre, Newcastle-upon-Tyne as part of a cycle of new plays presented in two parts entitled *Twelve Tales Of Tyneside* on 16 May 1997. The cast was as follows:

Ludwig Wittgenstein	Donald McBride
Mrs Britton, *his landlandy*	Charlie Hardwick
Sandra, *her daughter*	Sharon Percy
Clark Cable, *a market gardener*	Joe Caffrey
Mr Braithwaite, *a local air-raid warden*	Trevor Fox

Directed by Max Roberts
Designed by Perry Hudson

Whistling in the dark. Beethoven.

A very tight spot snaps up on **Wittgenstein**'s *face. He is whistling.*

Wittgenstein   Ludwig Wittgenstein. Born Vienna, 1889.

He carries on whistling. He is enjoying himself.

The world's greatest living philosopher.

He carries on whistling.

Solved the major problems of philosophy. Twice. Professor of Philosophy, Cambridge University. Came to Newcastle, 1943. To work in the RVI. For the war effort. What is the use of sitting around thinking?

He whistles more Beethoven.

Prodigiously intelligent. Could whistle the whole of Beethoven. Very good, the whistling. Helps keep you relaxed, you know.

Continues whistling the Beethoven. Music swells under **Wittgenstein** *until it becomes loud and ecstatic. His head falls back as he is nearing orgasm and as the music reaches its climax an air-raid siren sounds. His face changes as the siren gets louder. He looks down anxiously at his crotch. We can't see anything except his face in the blackness.*

Suddenly a shaft of light illuminates him. He is receiving a blow job from a **Young Lad**. *A young girl,* **Sandra**, *comes running in. They both look anxiously at her and spring apart.* **Young Lad**'s *mouth is full and, not daring to swallow, he keeps his lips tightly closed.*

Mrs Britton, **Wittgenstein**'s *landlady, comes down the steps, following* **Sandra**.

Mrs Britton   Excuse me, Mr Wittgenstein, I hardly had time to put me teeth in.

Young Lad *still has his gob full and is looking the worse for wear.* **Sandra** *looks at the* **Young Lad** *suspiciously.*

Mrs Britton   I see you've got a nice young friend here.

Young Lad *still won't swallow.* **Sandra** *hands him a handkerchief. He spits in it discreetly, then wipes his mouth with his hand.*

Mrs Britton   Well, aren't you going to introduce us then?

Wittgenstein   This is Mr . . . Mr . . . ?

Young Lad   C-C-C-Cable.

He holds out his hand, then thoughtfully wipes it on his jacket.

C-C-Clark Cable.

Mrs Britton   Very pleased to meet you.

Sandra   Are you from the hospital too?

Young Lad   N-n-no, I just m-met Mr Witkinsteen and I was gi-giving him a b-b-b- –

Wittgenstein *looks in horror.*

Young Lad   B-bit of advice

Mrs Britton   Advice?

Young Lad   About his marrow.

Sandra   But Mr Wittgenstein hasn't got any marrows.

Mrs Britton   He hasn't even got an allotment.

Wittgenstein   We were discussing the matter theoretically. (*To* **Young Lad**.) Yes, very interesting. I expect you have to be going.

Mrs Britton   But there's an air raid, Mr Wittgenstein.

Wittgenstein   It's all right, the lad has got his bike and he only lives in Elswick.

Sandra   You can't go out now, you might be killed.

Mrs Britton   You're more than welcome here, son.

Wittgenstein   But . . .

Mrs Britton   Mr Wittgenstein.

She looks down at **Wittgenstein**'s *crotch. He stares at her.*

You have egg on your chin.

Wittgenstein   I beg your pardon.

Mrs Britton   You have egg on your chin.

Wittgenstein *checks his chin.* **Mrs Britton** *stares at his flies to indicate subtly where the problem lies, but this simply encourages everyone to stare at* **Wittgenstein**'s *flies – which are undone.*

Sandra   Your flies are undone.

Wittgenstein *realises and quickly rectifies the matter.*

Mrs Britton   Mr Wittgenstein, it's not like you. You're usually very fastidious. Now, Mr Cable. How long have you known Mr Wittgenstein?

An explosion. The door bursts open. In comes **Mr Braithwaite**.

Braithwaite   They've hit Peggy Rodger's. The place is a right state.

Sandra   Hello, Mr Braithwaite.

Braithwaite   Hello, Sandra.

Mrs Britton   This is Mr Wittgenstein, our lodger, and his nice young friend, Mr Cable. He's a market gardener or something.

Braithwaite   I beg your pardon?

Mrs Britton   A market gardener.

Braithwaite   Don't I know you?

Young Lad   I d-d-don't think so.

Braithwaite   You're the little bastard in the Dog and Parrot.

Mrs Britton   The Dog and Parrot?

Sandra   It's a queer bar.

Mrs Britton   What were you doing in an unusual bar, Mr Braithwaite? I understood you were teetotal.

Braithewaite   I was caught a bit short when I was passing through town. I stopped at the aforementioned hostelry not realising its provenance, and as I was relieving myself I was accosted by this gentleman.

Mrs Britton   Mr Cable! You attacked Mr Braithwaite? He fought in the Somme, you know.

Young Lad   I never attacked nobody.

Mrs Britton   What exactly did he do to you, Mr Braithwaite?

Young Lad   He made improper suggestions.

Mrs Britton   I'm not sure I understand.

Sandra   Mam.

Mrs Britton   Where is this place exactly?

Sandra   Down the end of Pilgrim Street.

Braithwaite   So, Mr Cable. What the hell are you doing in here?

Mrs Britton   Mr Cable came with Mr Wittgenstein. To talk about leeks.

Braithwaite   I don't believe you know the first thing about horticulture. Do you, lad?

He grabs **Young Lad**.

When would you normally pot a geranium? Eh?

Young Lad *looks blank.*

Braithwaite   You don't know, do you?

Young Lad   N-n-no.

Braithwaite   Exactly.

Sudden silence.

Mrs Britton   So what exactly were you both doing down here, Mr Wittgenstein?

Sandra   Mam.

Mrs Britton   Don't you Mam me.

Sandra   It's obvious.

Mrs Britton   What's obvious?

Sandra   He wanted a blow job.

Mrs Britton   Mr Wittgenstein, is it true you brought this young man down here to give him a job?

Sandra   Mam. Mr Cable was giving it to Mr Wittgenstein.

Mrs Britton   But Mr Wittgenstein is gainfully employed.

Sandra   A blow job isn't a job, Mam.

Mrs Britton   Well, what the hell is it?

Sandra   It means getting your knob sucked.

Mrs Britton   Where on earth did you hear of such a thing?

Sandra   Mr Braithwaite told me.

Mrs Britton   Mr Braithwaite, is this true?

Braithwaite   I may have mentioned it in passing.

Mrs Britton   I've never heard anything like this. Let me get this right. Mr Wittgenstein brought nice young Mr Cable down here for a sexual purpose?

Sandra   Yes.

Mrs Britton   Well, who were they going to have sex with?

Braithwaite   With each other.

Mrs Britton   But you're both men.

Braithwaite   They're a couple of turd burglars.

Wittgenstein   Sir, I resent your tone.

Braithwaite   Christ. Not a Kraut 'n'all.

Wittgenstein   I am not a Kraut.

Braithwaite   That's exactly what you are. A bleeding wurst swallower.

Wittgenstein   I am an Austrian. It was I who was annexed.

Mrs Britton   We'll have less of that sort of language, Mr Wittgenstein. I can't quite believe what I'm hearing. You brought poor Mr Cable down here simply to do this horrible act. Isn't it unhygienic?

Braithwaite   Poor Mr Cable! He was trying to do the same to me in the bloody Dog and Parrot.

Mrs Britton   You as well, Mr Braithwaite. What on earth is the world coming to?

Braithwaite   Let me assure you, madam, I declined the young gentleman's proposition in no uncertain terms.

Mrs Britton   But Mr Wittgenstein, I don't understand. You always pay your rent on time.

Braithwaite   It's disgusting.

Sandra   Actually, I think it's quite romantic.

Mrs Britton   Romantic.

Braithwaite   Quite romantic. It was hard-nosed buggery. There's our lads laying down their lives for King and country and you two are down here messing about like a pair of Greek bosuns.

Young Lad   Don't call me a b-bosun.

Braithwaite   I'll call you what I like. You Kraut gobbler.

Wittgenstein Will you stop inferring I am German?

Braithwaite Well, what are you then?

Mrs Britton He's a hospital porter.

Wittgenstein I am not a hospital porter.

Mrs Britton Yes you are.

Wittgenstein I am a technician.

Mrs Britton Well, that's news to me.

Braithwaite You don't look like a technician.

Mrs Britton Mr Braithwaite's a technician, aren't you?

Sandra And he has a club foot.

Mrs Britton Sandra, please.

Wittgenstein I *am* a technician. In the hospital.

Braithwaite I bet you're not a trained, though.

Wittgenstein No, I am not a trained technician. I am a trained philosopher.

Amazed silence.

Braithwaite A philosopher?

Wittgenstein Indeed.

Young Lad You n-never told me you were a philosopher.

Wittgenstein You never asked.

Braithwaite You're taking the piss.

Mrs Britton Language.

Wittgenstein On the contrary. I am indeed a trained philosopher.

Braithwaite (*sarcastically*) I bet you that's kept you in work.

Wittgenstein Sir, I held a chair in Cambridge.

Braithwaite   Exactly.

Sandra   He means he was Professor of Philosophy.

Mrs Britton   At Cambridge.

Braithwaite   A right clever shite.

Wittgenstein   Sir, I have an international reputation.

Mrs Britton   So what exactly is this philosophy of yours, Mr Wittgenstein?

Braithwaite   To go round shagging young boys in foreign countries?

Wittgenstein   No, sir, my philosophy is of a technical nature, questioning traditional notions of metaphysics as related to the epistemology of language.

Braithwaite   How many people believe in your philosophy, Mr Clever Clogs?

Wittgenstein   About two.

Sandra   Two?

Young Lad   It can't be much c-cop then.

Braithwaite   You be quiet.

Wittgenstein   Just because it is not fully understood does not make it erroneous. The ignorance of one man does not detract from the wisdom of another. Logic, I'm afraid, is undemocratic.

Braithwaite   Can you understand a word he's saying?

Sandra   He's saying, even if notions of truth and value are relative, the logical processes inherent in the language with which we make these judgements are absolute.

Mrs Britton   I've warned you, Sandra.

Braithwaite   Well, if you're so bloody clever, how come you're a hospital porter, eh?

Wittgenstein   I am not a hospital porter.

Braithwaite   Well, what the hell are you doing in Newcastle? Why aren't you off philosophising somewhere?

Wittgenstein   What is the point of philosophy in wartime? Surely you'd rather I worked shoulder to shoulder with people dignified by practical labour than sanctimoniously sitting round pontificating.

Braithwaite   What do you think you're doing now?

Wittgenstein   But I need to be with ordinary people. Not arid academics.

Mrs Britton   People like us?

Wittgenstein   Yes.

Braithwaite   Don't call me ordinary, pal, I've fought in the Somme.

Young Lad   I h-h-hope you're not t-t-trying to patronise us.

Wittgenstein   I'm not trying to patronise anybody.

Braithwaite   Who do you think you are? Coming over here, spouting philosophy and bumming our gardeners?

Wittgenstein   I don't think I'm anybody. Just because I am a philosopher, or a professor, or an aristocrat or an Austrian doesn't mean I'm any more important than any of you.

Young Lad   Aristocrat. You're telling me I've been s-s-shagging an aristocrat. Me dad'll kill us.

Mrs Britton   Surely not a socialist *and* an invert.

Wittgenstein   But that is the point. Just because I come from an aristocratic background doesn't mean I am an aristocrat.

Braithwaite   I don't know how else you become one.

Wittgenstein But I have given my entire fortune away. All I own is a deckchair and the complete works of Tolstoy. What does that make me? I am no longer an aristocrat. I am a philosopher.

Braithwaite Philosopher my arse. Listen, mate, you're a flipping bum bandit.

Wittgenstein But what does it mean to say I am nothing but this bum bandage? What do you mean ?

Braithwaite Exactly what I said. A shirtlifter.

Wittgenstein But, sir, what do you mean by 'meaning'?

Braithwaite What do you mean, what do I mean by meaning?

Wittgenstein Precisely that. What is the meaning of meaning?

Braithwaite Well, meaning is the meaning.

Wittgenstein If 'meaning is the meaning' you have said precisely nothing at all. A logical tautology.

Mrs Britton Hang on a minute.

Wittgenstein OK, a simple example. What, for instance, does 'five' mean?

Braithwaite Er. It's five things.

Wittgenstein Five things are five things. I put it to you again what is 'five', sir?

Braithwaite Five is five.

Wittgenstein But what does it mean? Define it.

Braithwaite *is blank.*

Sandra It's between 'four' and 'six'.

Wittgenstein Excellent. Five derives its meaning through being between 'four' and 'six'. But what is four and six?

Mrs Britton   Not much these days.

Wittgenstein   Four is after three and before five. And et cetera ad infinitum. Do you see?

Braithwaite   You've lost me, pal.

Wittgenstein   What is a table?

Young Lad   S-something to put things on.

Wittgenstein   But if I sit on it? Is it a chair? A table is a table because it isn't a chair. It only has 'meaning' because we can put it in its place in our linguistic system.

Sandra   So it's just a way of describing things. There is no real 'meaning'.

Young Lad   Eh?

Sandra   Like in a dictionary. If you look up one word to find out what it means, it only gives you another word. So you look up those words and they only refer you to other words and so you go round in circles.

Wittgenstein   Precisely. You see there is no 'meaning', only a linguistic description. A language game. There is no essence. I ask you what is an Austrian? You say not an American. Not a German. This is good. But then I ask you what *is* an Austrian. And you say . . . ?

Young Lad   S-s-someone from Austria.

Wittgenstein   But what *is* this person?

Braithwaite   A bloody arsehole.

Mrs Britton   Mr Braithwaite!

Wittgenstein   What is this person? A Jew? A communist? A speaker of German? A homosexual? Who exactly are you talking about? What exactly does this person mean? You cannot define a person. A person does not mean anything. The whole idea of 'meaning' is totally redundant.

Braithwaite   I don't know what this has got to do with anything.

Sandra   I do.

Mrs Britton   Shut up, Sandra.

Sandra   It's got to do with everything.

Wittgenstein   You are desperate to give things a meaning. Some reductive fixed meaning, so you can define them. And once you can define them, you can control them. And once you can control them, you can put them in boxes and bury them in the ground. But the only way to do this is to fix a meaning where logically there isn't one. What is a book? It just is. What is the sun? It just is. What is God? What is life? What is you? What is I? It just is. Sir, I am a German speaker. I am a Jew. I am a poof. But let me tell you all is not what it seems. I am not a German or a Jew or a poof. I am only me.

Mrs Britton   Could you run through that again?

Braithwaite   You come over here dipping your wick and now you're lecturing us with your highfalutin' ideas about the meaninglessness of the meaning of meaning. I should kick your arse right back to Baden-Munich.

Sandra   There's nothing wrong with his ideas.

Braithwaite   Nothing wrong with his ideas!?

Sandra   I quite like them.

Mrs Britton   Sandra, love, it's people with ideas that have got us to the mess we're in today.

Braithwaite   It's all right for you rich bastards, but I've never had the opportunity to sit around thinking.

Sandra   What about when you're on the allotment?

Braithwaite   I'm too busy gardening.

Sandra   Even in the potting shed?

Mrs Britton   But, Mr Wittgenstein, if there isn't any meaning, this is terrible.

Braithwaite   What about God?

Wittgenstein   Recognising the limits of our own patterns of thinking is the only way to truly contemplate the unknown and the unknowable. Philosophy is the truest form of spiritual contemplation. But it is not about answers, it is about questions. Questioning our very prejudice.

Young Lad   If there isn't any answers, what about s-s-science, then? There's plenty of answers in science.

Wittgenstein   Science has no answers. What is the answer to life? The only answer science can give is 'death'. Yesterday I walked past a bookshop. In one window were the books of Freud and Einstein; in the other pictures of Schubert and Beethoven. And I saw where we have come in one hundred years. Is the universe any more profound because of Mr Einstein? Are our minds any more fathomable because of Mr Freud? All these sciences: linguistics, economics, sociologies. They ask how big, how small, how many. We all become numbers. And when we are numbers we can be erased. This is science. But listen to Beethoven and there are no answers. There are no simple equations. Mr Beethoven is asking what makes us human. What we have lost is a world not where there are endless answers and solutions, but where there are mysteries. This is what I have learnt. The first lesson of all philosophy is inimical to science. It is that we know nothing. Philosophy is a religion of disbelief. All about us is a mystery we cannot begin to encompass, thus the only logical thing to do is to ask what is human about ourselves. We have reached the stage that it is easier to destroy the whole world than to discover oneself. And this is science. This is the so-called answer. Even as we speak they are making bombs to blow up entire cities and we sit and argue about where I put my penis. I wonder what we have become. I wonder what we have become.

Mrs Britton   I think you are over-analysing things, Mr Wittgenstein.

Sandra   How can you over-analyse something?

Mrs Britton   When you haven't got time for anything else.

Braithwaite   It seems he's got plenty of time to go buggering about in air-raid shelters.

Wittgenstein   People are dropping bombs on us.

Braithwaite   But it just isn't British.

Wittgenstein   Then you must be unfamiliar with the English public school system.

Braithwaite   Don't start being smart with me. At least I'm not a Kraut.

Wittgenstein   What is this 'British' with its brambly hedgerows and warm beers and pillar boxes and Oxo cubes and pound cakes and dog-eared parsons and village greens and interminable Sundays. It is a nation of mindless sentimentality. Passionless prejudice, terrified of sex, of ideas, of strangers, of living. This is the only modern European nation that has not had a revolution, not because there is no poverty, inequality or injustice, but because of your sure bloody complacency. You let your bosses keep you ignorant and your peers make you feel proud of it. Thinking has nothing to do with poverty. A poor man can think just as clearly as a rich man. Sainthood has always been predicated on it. No, you make yourselves poor because your lives are unexamined. Because all your nostalgia has made you sick. And that's why I hate your Blitz spirit, your happy-go-lucky working-class humour, and your shepherd's pies, and your sooty terraces, and knockabouts of a Sunday. Because it is an unthinking excuse for your lack of real endeavour. This is what I hate in Britain. And this is why I hate every last one of you cheeky cheery Geordie fools.

Young Lad   L-listen, I just gave you a blow job.

Sandra   I'm not complacent.

Braithwaite   That's it. I've had enough.

He takes his stick.

What will it mean if I smash your ruddy heads together?

Wittgenstein   It won't mean anything. You club-footed cretin.

Braithwaite *takes a swing at* **Wittgenstein**. *He misses but clunks* **Young Lad** *on the head. He is felled.*

Mrs Britton   Stop it at once.

Sandra (*trying to stop* **Mr Braithwaite***'s assault*)   You never complained when I gave *you* a blow job.

Everybody stops.

Mrs Britton   You did what?

Sandra   He said it was a lollipop.

Young Lad   See, you h-hypocritical bastard.

He dies.

Mrs Britton (*reprimanding* **Young Lad**)   Hey! (*To* **Sandra**.) I don't believe this.

Sandra   I got his coupons.

Mrs Britton   But, Sandra, you're only thirteen.

Sandra   But, Mam, after all, he fought in the Somme.

Young Lad   How c-c-come he fought in the Somme if he had a club foot, eh?

He dies again.
Everyone looks at **Braithwaite**.

Braithwaite   I never actually said I 'fought' in the Somme.

Mrs Britton   I bet you never left Shieldfield.

Mrs Britton *takes a swipe at* **Braithwaite** *with a kettle. She kills him.*

Sandra   I think you've killed Mr Braithwaite, Mam.

Mrs Britton *falls to the ground in grief.* **Wittgenstein** *stares at the carnage around him.*

Wittgenstein   Let's try and be philosophical about this.

Sandra   What's that meant to mean?

Wittgenstein   I'm fucked if I know. That is what I am trying to tell you.

The sound of all clear.

Sandra   That's the all-clear.

Wittgenstein   All-clear?

The faint sound of a doodlebug. Getting louder.

Wittgenstein   Well, I guess I'll see you at breakfast.

The sound of a huge explosion. White light blinds the audience.

Music: Beethoven.

Blackout.

Genie

Genie was first performed at Live Theatre Newcastle-upon-Tyne on 30 March 1999 as part of a Paines Plough and Live Theatre co-produciton entitled *Black On White Shorts*. The cast was as follows:

Genie   Angela Lonsdale
Susan   Tracy Gillman

Directed by Jessica Dromgoole
Designed by Dominie Hooper

Characters

Genie, *a teenager – who was locked in a room for most of her life.*
Susan, *a linguist – who wasn't.*

Setting

The stage is bare but for the few required props for each scene. There is a television downstage left – as near to the audience as possible. The TV shows clips from *The Brady Bunch* when it is not showing the title of each scene, e.g., 'Suspension of Disbelief'.

Prologue

Susan *at a blackboard.*

Susan   The first thing you have to understand is that she was kept in a bedroom from birth until the age of twelve. We called her Genie. The question was whether she could in fact acquire language. Genie. Like out of a lamp. Innocent, magical. She was just like a genie. And in a way we came to her, to ask questions. To solve some questions.

Scene One: Blind Faith

Music: 'I Would Rather Be Blind' by Rod Steward and the Faces.

Genie, *in a loose floral dress, blindfolded by an airline sleeping mask, is tied to a tiny toy chair. She is like Lewis Carroll's Alice. The stage is in darkness. A shaft of light appears downstage.* **Genie** *manoeuvres her chair towards it. As she gets closer, an apple on a string drops into the lightshaft. As* **Genie** *tries to catch a bite of the apple with her mouth, the shaft of light goes out.*

Another shaft of light appears in a different part of the stage and she moves awkwardly towards it. Again an apple drops down into the light but this time a sign appears on the string holding it, simply stating: 'APPLE'. **Genie** *laboriously gets there and starts trying to bite it (her arms still tied to the chair).*

The scene ends when **Genie** *manages successfully to bite out a mouthful.*

Scene Two: Suspension of Disbelief

Genie *in a chair. As the speech continues she gets up and on each line comes further forward in her strange rabbit walk. She is trying very hard.* **Susan** *is watching from upstage.*

Genie   Not . . . Stop . . . blue . . .
. . . fishnis . . . stop . . .
I . . . not . . . I . . .

. . . am . . . I . . . big . . .
am . . . so . . . bignot . . .
I . . . blue . . . am . . . so . . .
. . . blue . . . fishbig . . .
I . . . am . . . fish . . .
in . . . big . . . blue . . .
. . . sea . . . see?

Genie *purses her lips like a haddock and briefly scuttles like a rabbit-fish.*

Scene Three: Transformational Grammar

Genie *throws open her desk and it explodes into a child's party. There is a cake and seemingly a thousand balloons filled with helium that pop out.*

Genie *is somewhat hidden.* **Susan** *talks from the side through a microphone again.*

Susan   Genie. Would you like a piece of pie?

Genie   Thank you very much.

Susan   Genie. Would you a piece of pie like?

Genie   Thank you very much.

Susan   Would Genie like you pie of piece?

Genie   Thank you very much indeed.

Susan   Pie piece. You would like of, Genie?

Genie   Thank you –

Susan (*cutting her off*)   You, piece of would pie, like Genie?
Genie. Pie would like of piece of Genie. Genie.
Pie would like a piece of Genie.

Genie *looks mildly confused. She quickly rabbit-walks downstage.*

Scene Four: Chomsky

Genie *is sat in her chair again. She is in a twilight. There is a quiet barking somewhere behind her. It is presumably* **Susan** – *but we can't see for sure. The barking becomes steadily louder throughout* **Genie**'s *speech. She is deadly serious.*

Genie   I room was . . . Potty sat-sat-sat- . . .
or holefor . . . not sat . . . doo-doo piss . . .
for not pot . . . for . . . time . . .
speaknot . . . shitpot . . . so . . . for . . .
time . . . wotnot . . . I . . . blue . . . and . . .
. . . that . . . wot . . . My . . . oh, my . . . sore
. . . budda . . . bred . . . and I big . . .
. . . holefor . . . (*squeals*) . . . not sat . . .
stopit . . . shitpot . . . Sssssh . . .

She is silent and listens to the barking.

Potty sat-sat-sat. Phew! . . . By . . .
on . . . for . . . it . . . six . . . move . . . six . . . six . . . six . . .
Potty-wot . . . pot-pot . . . lose six . . .
. . . bunny rot . . . daddie-wot . . .
. . . not . . . stop . . . wot . . .
. . . not . . . please . . . dogstop . . .
sssh . . . woof . . . liptop . . . stopnot . . .
Ooooh . . . dadstop . . . shitpiss . . . dogwot
. . . please . . . daddie . . . not . . . bark . . .
. . . like . . . a . . . dog . . . please.

Scene Five: Jeopardy

Genie *is sitting at an old-fashioned school desk.* **Susan** *is asking her questions through an amplified microphone.*

Susan   Just relax. Are you sitting comfortably? Then we'll begin.

There is a vast ticking of a cosmic clock. **Genie**'s *face appears on the TV screen.*

Susan   General knowledge. Who was the first President of the United States of America?

Genie   George Washington the First.

Susan   Where did Judas Iscariot kiss Jesus Christ?

Genie   Er?

Susan   I'm going to have to hurry you.

Genie   On the nose?

Susan   Gethsemane. Arithmetic. If it takes four men four hours to dig a hole four feet by four feet. How long will it take two men to dig the same hole, two by two?

Genie   One . . . hour . . . fifty minutes.

Susan   Theology. Does God exist?

Genie   Erm.

Susan   I'm going to have to hurry you on this one.

Genie   Yes. No. Pass.

Susan   Relativity. Which is lighter: a pound of feathers or a pound of lead?

Genie   Pound of lead.

Susan   Which is better: to have loved and lost or never to have loved at all?

Genie   To love at all.

Susan   Which famous author, on entering the United States of America, said: I have nothing to declare except my genius?

Genie   Oscar Wilde.

Susan   Who put the bop in the bop-showop-de-bop?

Genie   Pass.

Susan   Is the redemption of the proletariat in Marx through the transformative power of labour merely teleological mystification or does it have real claims to a materialist theology?

Genie   Er, yes.

Susan   If I spat in your face, would you turn the other cheek?

Genie *obviously doesn't know.*

Susan   Genealogy. Which came first the chicken or the egg?

Genie   The egg.

Susan   The chicken.
Eschatology. Does the contradiction in monotheistic systems of thought between agency and determination pose a problem for the notion of a redemptive afterlife?

Genie   Pass.

Susan   If you had all the money in the world, what would you do?

Genie *is confused.*

Susan   If you had one wish what would it be?

Genie   Oh!?!

Susan   You are shipwrecked on a desert island: which ten records would you choose to have with you? In descending order of preference.

Genie   Crazy Horses. Crazy Horses.

Susan   I'm going to have to hurry you.

Genie   That one by David Soul.

The buzzer goes.

Susan   Sorry, time's up . . . Genie, you did very well.

Scene Six: Pascal

Genie *has two tape recorders. Each has a transcript by it. She tapes each voice on the relevant tape recorder, imitating **Susan**'s voice for one and a man's voice for the other.* **Susan** *operates the record buttons for* **Genie**.

One   It's remarkable. Using language to articulate prelinguistic experience.

Two   Sure, it's a breakthrough, but . . .

One   'But' . . . that's typical.

Two   Just hear me out.

One   Why? I know damn well what you're going to say.

Two   What does it prove?

One   I know it doesn't prove anything. I know proof is a logical process not an experiential one, but . . .

Two   But . . .

One   God . . .

Two   You know your whole idea of scientific method. Faith in objectivity. It's nonsense. Where has grand theory got you? She may have done it anyway; she might be too dumb to ever do it. It all proves nothing.

One   Look, I don't know. Of course I'm uncertain, that's why I'm a scientist. Sceptical faith. I mean, suppose God doesn't want us to know He exists. He could do that, He's God, isn't He? I say who knows, but isn't it better to hedge your bets. You don't have to be deluded, just logical. Absence doesn't necessarily mean something's not there. It's Pascal.

Two   It's horseshit.

Scene Seven: Spinoza

Genie *rewinds the tapes and they play back in a hideous cacophony. She goes to a spot upstage as* **Susan** *gradually turns the tapes down and plays the piano.*

Genie   Thank you, God, for giving me the beautiful dawn.

Thank you, God, for giving . . . me the gift of speech.

Thank you, God, for giving me the power of science to help me please.

Thank you, God. For Kandy Korn, and plastic bottles, and plastic buttons, and plastic eggs, and plastic dogs, and plastic dolls and such like.

Thank you, God, for all the human beings that have helped me.

Thank you for the consititutional right of free speech.

Thank you, God, for the little doggies that piss up the side of trees.

Thank you, God, for Donny Osmond and Richard Nixon and the government mental health care programme.

Thank you, God, for being you and smiling down on us every day. And for cheering us up when we are blue. And saving all the dead souls even when it wasn't their fault. And for making the sky and the sea and the ocean and all the little fishes in it. Thank you.

Two's Company

Two's Company was first performed on 30 November 2000 at the Live Theatre Newcastle as part of *NE1* a production of twelve new one-perspn plays. The cast was as follows:

Karaoke Master   Joe Caffrey

Directed by Jeremy Herrin
Designed by Perry Hudson
NE1 Editorial direction by Max Roberts and Lee Hall

Karaoke Master   It's quite good doing these karaokes. I mean, it makes for a good excuse. I mean, it's been a lifesaver, to tell you the truth. Not that it would have to be a karaoke necessarily. I mean, it could be a disco, or even a travelling salesman. Anything that gets you out the house. It's not that I want to lie. I mean, I don't lie. Not really. You don't have to actually lie all the time. It's just, you know. Karaoke – could be anywhere. It's come in useful.

But, you know, I'm not a bad man. I mean, not in the sense I'd do anyone any real harm. Not intentionally. I mean, fair enough, I have been known to sign on when I've been pulling in a couple a hundred a week, now and again. And I have been known to charge a bit more than was strictly agreed for the odd office party when they're all too pissed to remember what day it was. I mean, I have to make ends meet, don't I? But it's not what you'd really call 'bad'. It's not bloody paedophilia, for Christsake. No. I'm not a bad man. I'm not a violent man. I wouldn't steal things. I've never murdered anybody. OK, I've got me faults. I snore. I fart in bed. Et cetera, et cetera. But if anybody was going to criticise, I think the most they could say about me was that I loved too much. Loved too much. Is that a sin, is it?

It was an ordinary Tuesday night really. I'd got home early, Tom was off school with the flu and I had sausages and beans and Sheila had bought a nice Victoria sponge to have with a cup of coffee but I said that I'd had a big lunch at the Little Chef down near Billingham on me way back from me 'regular gig' down in Catterick, the 'regular gig' where I have to stay over, so she put it in the fridge. Now to be quite honest I think it's a bad idea putting cakes in the fridge as they always end up tasting of raw onions. You know that weird metallic taste when you take them out the next day. Any rate, it got uz out of the Victoria sponge. So, I was just going to get away early when Sarah came in screaming the place down. She'd been at Guides and came back in a right paddy. Apparently she'd had a right bollocking off Brown Owl for some reason. And to be quite honest I divvint blame her, Sarah's been going round with a face like a butcher's arse for months now, but I was fucked if I was going to get drawn into a tribunal about the rights and wrongs of fucking Brown Owl, so I just gave some money to shut her up and got out sharpish.

Now the advantage of Sheila thinking I'm driving all the way to Carlisle to do a bloody karaoke is I get a little bit of respect for my hard work. A sort of implicit acknowledgement that I'm doing something worthy. I mean, if I'm prepared to drive all that way just to keep things going well, you get that healthy distance, there's no questions asked. That's the great thing about Sheila really. She hates the karaoke. She couldn't shoot coal. And to be quite honest she hasn't a clue how much I'm really earning. And anyway, she doesn't do too bad herself not since she got the new job at the estate agent's. I mean, I met her when I worked down the yards of course. I think she came to the karaoke about three times and that was it. Any rate, it was about then she got up the stick and so that was the end of that anyway. Stroke of luck really. I suppose if she'd been an addict or something I would never have met Karen. Or I would have met Karen, but maybes I wouldn't've ended up marrying her. But such is life, eh. Anyway, I say I'll see her in the morning. Regular as clockwork. And I'm out of there and straight over to Newbiggin Hall.

Anyway, on account of the authoritarian nature of the Girl Guide movement and the petulance of twelve-year-olds I was a bit late when I arrived and me tea was in the oven. Sausages again but this time with a nice onion gravy. I tell you one thing about Karen, she makes decent gravy. Admittedly, she's let herself go over the years. I'm not being judgemental. I'm no oil painting myself. But at least I keep meself in shape. Which is no mean feat with all these dinners. I suppose if I was stuck in that bloody flat with a toddler I might be the same. But she's a nice woman, Karen. She's a caring woman. It's not obvious when you meet her, you think, oh aye, all tits and front teeth. But once you get to know her – you know there's more to somebody than meets the eye.

So I wolfed down the sausages while we discussed various matters such as the gas bill, little Toby's jumpsuit, the technical limitations of the Sunderland defence, the price of eggs and Victoria Beckham's new haircut. Then we went straight to bed. Bang. Hello. How's your father and head down for a bit of kip.

It's not that I particular enjoy the sex. There's nowt wrong with uz, like. And I mean, I'm not one to look a gift horse in the mouth, so to speak. But after five and a half sausages, two lots of gas bills, and the forty-five-minute drive up from the coast, carnal pleasures are a lot less appealing than a bit of shut-eye, to tell you the truth. But when I'm there, that's what I do. Straight to bed, at the earliest opportunity. I worry, you know, it's not normal, is it? She's bound to think something's up. Normally, you'd finish your sausages, open a bottle of wine and watch a bit of telly, eat some crisps, et cetera, et cetera. But somehow I feel a fraud – eating crisps. It's not right, is it – just watching telly – it would seem an insult to Sheila. In fact, it would be a sort of insult to them both. Not to mention the kids. That's the whole point – it's an insult in general, I don't know, to life, to God, isn't it? It's an insult if you don't make the most of every waking moment. And also we're sort of more equal in bed, when we're lying there. Somehow what she doesn't know about in bed isn't as bad as what she doesn't know about in the sitting room. It's funny that. But you know what I mean, don't you?

I've only once gotten their names mixed up. And that only happened because I was knackered. I'd pretended I was doing a night shift to Sheila when really I'd been at Karen's and somehow that week it all got out of hand, and by Thursday I'd not really slept for three days. Not with doing enough jobs to bring the rent in. I tell you it's not easy paying for two households. So anyway I was in the full throes of passion with Sheila, I mean Karen. And all of a

sudden I couldn't take it any more and I started drifting off
in the middle of the job, and I sort of lapsed off for a second
and I as I came I could hear myself going: 'Sheila, Sheila.'
And then I realised what was going on. It was like someone
had thrown a bucket of cold water on uz. And there I was
looking at Karen. And her eyes were closed and she didn't
say nothing. And I just carried on. And there she was, just
oblivious to everything. And I'll never know if she heard or
not.

And maybe that's the point. It's not what you think, not
what goes on up here that counts. Maybe it doesn't matter
whether she knows or not. What matters is what she does.
And to all intents and purposes, we have a normal marriage.
Admittedly she must think I work some funny shifts, like.
But what matters is that we love each other. Same for Sheila
– what matters is that we love each other. That's all.

So back to the night of the six sausages: so we were in bed
just lying there and by now it was after eleven. And we lay
there in the dark, not talking. Just breathing. And we both
smoked my fags. It wasn't sad, it was just like we had
nothing to say to each other. And what I really wanted to do
was go to sleep. But somehow it wasn't right. Somehow
what was important was just being there, quiet. And after a
bit I got up and went to the toilet, and as I came back I
looked in on the bairn and there he was fast asleep. His little
mouth wide open, like a little spuggy waiting for his mam.
And I stood there at the door stark bollock naked just
looking at the little thing breathing. And then I realised
something weird, I realised for the first time in ages, for the
first time since I brought him home from the hospital, I
suddenly felt like a dad. That's when I realised I never was
with him alone. How could I be? With all the kids, I was
always with them, with Karen or Sheila. It was different
when Sarah and Tom were little, before I met Karen and
that. But for years now, I only ever saw them with their
mam. And I'd never seen Toby that way. I'd never really
seen him as mine. Even though I was there when he was

born, even though I'd changed his nappies and fed him food, et cetera, et cetera, et cetera. I never felt like he was really mine. He was Karen's, wasn't he? I mean, he was really an accident. But there in the dark I really felt connected. I really felt like he was mine. There he was, a little miracle of life, there in the dark. And of all the things I have done. Fair enough, I should never have married Sheila, and almost certainly I should never have married Karen. And I should give up smoking and I should have explained things years ago. But in all the things that you do or you might do, there's probably nothing that compares with that, is there? There's nothing really that compares with making a life. Out of nothing. That is a completely weird thing. One minute there's nothing, the next minute there's everything for that person. You've made the whole universe change with that little person. It's a Mystery, isn't it? The more you think about it, the more mysterious it becomes. Sometimes you look at it and you go, Oh, well, it's just the facts of biology, it's just the normal course of life. But if you stop and think about it. It's like taking a drug. It's like vertigo or something. When you try and ask what happens. Nobody can explain it, can they? They maybe can explain the facts. Eggs and spunk and fertilisation and that. But they can't explain what it's really about, can they? Not when you look at those little faces and they're in their little cot. It's not really an *explanation*, is it? What living is, what death is. What it means that one day you just won't be here. And I looked at him sleeping not an idea is his head, not an idea of the world or death or anything. And you think one day he'll be some old bastard looking death in the eye, when I'm long gone. And there's nobody can tell you what that means.

Karen came in and touched my arm and I physically jumped. For a moment there I had forgotten that Karen even existed. Well, I suppose I must have known in the back of my mind, but for a moment she was irrelevant to what I thought of Toby. Mind you, I never wanted to call him Toby. To be quite honest, I think it'll be a curse, but it was

Dad's name and with him dying young and that, and the fact that after all she was going to be doing the donkey work, I thought it was one of those little battles you have to concede. I don't suppose it's that bad. Not as bad as Enid. That's what it would have been if it was a girl. It was a toss-up between that and Eileen, thank fuck he was boy.

As I say, you might think Karen's all tits and front teeth, but there's more to her than meets the eye.

Anyway, I looked at her. She was standing there in the amber light that came from the street lamp outside. And I thought she wasn't in such bad nick actually. Not considering that she doesn't get out much. And suddenly I thought, Hey, I hope she's not playing away while I'm busting balls doing this karaoke and fiddling the housing benefit. And then I thought you bastard. How the hell's she going to play away? Where the fuck does she go? Nowhere. Not since little Toby. It's not her fault. She's not a bad person. In fact, she is a good person. She is a caring person. And she stared at me. And took my hand. And I was naked too. And there we all were. Standing in the bairn's room like a proper family. And then I saw that she was crying.

And she said that there was someone else, wasn't there. And I said don't be stupid. I told her that I loved her. Which is true. And she kept saying, Have you met someone. And I was reassuring her. I hadn't met anybody. Who the fuck would I meet? I haven't got time to fart never mind 'meet' anybody, not with two wives, three kids and a budgerigar. Which is absolutely true, although she didn't know it. And I think she believed me. You never know, do you? But I think she believed me, because she wanted to believe me. And it wasn't like I wasn't a devoted father. It was just I wasn't devoted all the time, or I mean I was devoted all the time, but I wasn't actually there in person very much. Which I'll admit is a bit of a handicap. But I mean, when I am there, I'm as nice as ninepence. And to some ways of thinking this is a much better thing than being there more often but being a complete pain in the arse.

The thing is, of course, being completely driven by guilt all of the time, I'm vigilant to every opportunity where I can make up for having two wives and that. I mean, if you have an 'affair' that's because somehow you are dissatisfied with life. And when you're dissatisfied no matter what you do to conceal it, it always comes out, doesn't it? That's psychology, that. That you can't really hide anything at all. That what you really are is this weird uncontrollable thing inside you. And everything else is just a veneer. That everything else – what you do, what you say, how you act, what you think – all of this is just on the surface and who you really are is underneath. That's psychology, that. You can't control what's underneath. But that is when you're unhappy with your lot. And they can tell. They look at you and nothing you can do can make what you really feel inside go away. You're an open book. And they can read off the facts no bother.

Whereas if you're a bigamist – I hate that word. Bigamist. It's so . . . old-fashioned. Whereas if you're a bigamist, probably you're not 'dissatisfied' with one relationship. As a matter of fact, psychologically, you enjoy one relationship so much you want another one, as well as the first one. It's like the opposite of having an affair. It's like the opposite of everything. It's not like life is a contrast between one thing and another. Life can be all sorts of things at the same time. It can be happy, sad, moving, boring. All sorts of things. All at the same time. It's not that I stopped loving Sheila when I met Karen. It's not like I stopped loving Tom or Sarah when Toby was born. It's not that I loved Toby less than them because he was called Toby. Life's not like that.

I'm not saying bigamy would suit everybody, mind you. You have to be fit as lop to get away with this game. But it's not a bad way of life. I'm not a bad man. I'm not even a dishonest man. The trouble is I never wanted to hurt anybody.

Just one little fib, that's all it takes. 'You are single, aren't you?' Thinks. Well, it's only a one-night stand. Yes. You just say yes because you don't want to hurt her feelings. You don't want to ruin the situation. Then the next time, it's worse. If you tell her now you really will ruin the day. And it goes on and on. The trouble with me is I'm too nice. The trouble with me is I just don't want to hurt anyone's feelings. And nobody's feelings are hurt. As long as I keep to me special rota. As long as I keep everything in order everybody's happy. Nobody's any the wiser.

And we went back into the bedroom. And she seemed to be happier. She was sitting on the bed smoking. And I was thinking about Tom and his flu, and Sarah and the Girl Guides. You know, seeing little Toby, in a weird way it made me feel even closer to Tommy and Sar. And then she asked me: 'You haven't got any children, you know, from a previous relationship, have you?' And I looked at her, and I couldn't think of what to say, so I said: 'No, what gave you that impression?' And she said: 'Nothing. Just something you said.' And I thought, Fuck, what the fuck have I said? So I said: 'What did I say?' 'You just once said you thought children when they were born, they were born good but the world corrupts them.' That was it?! That's what I had said. 'Is that it? What made you think that meant I've got other children?' 'The way you said it.'

a) It is unlikely that I ever said such a thing. b) It is unlikely that I said it in a way that would make somebody assume that I said it because I was already married and had two kids. So I just said: 'No, of course I haven't got kids already.'

And Karen just looked.

Was that a bad thing to have said?

I don't know. I wanted to say, Yes, I have got two kids, one's a miserable little sod, but I love her, and the other one's got flu. And I've got a wife and I love her. And we met in the Stage Door in 1984 and we split up for a year in 1987. And I have you and little Toby and what's wrong with that? What's wrong with loving you all? All right it isn't normal. All right I have to tell a few white lies now and again. But it's better than being alone and miserable.

And Karen just looked.

And I knew she knew.

And I had seen that look before. I had seen Sheila look at me before. That look. Like you're looking right through a broken heart.

I love you. You know that, don't you?

And she just looked, which meant she did.

'Come back to bed,' she said.

And I looked her straight in the eye. And I knew I had to say something.

'Howway, lover,' she said.

And I went back to bed. And just lay there.

I'm not a bad man. Honest.

I just lay there. My heart was pounding. In the darkness.

And Karen just lay there too. And quietly she went to sleep.

I'm not a bad man.

And finally after a while I drifted off too.

Really, I'm not a bad man.

Am I?

Well, there you go. Next up tonight is . . .

Child of Our Time:
Children of the Rain

Children of the Rain was broadcast on Radio 4 on 3 July 2000. It was compiled from fictional material and interviews with children in the North of England.

The cast members were: Ben Tibber, Sita Patel, Samantha Valentine and Alex Whilbey.

The production was directed by Kate Rowland.

The rain, a distant siren.
Kids running into school. (Newcastle)
Register. (Newcastle)

Gradually the intro to 'Wonderful World' by Sam Cooke creeps in . . .
as the singing starts, the class dies down . . .

Girl   Ermmmmmm . . .

Voices   'I don't know'

Sita   *Child of Our Time* – the final instalment – *Children of the Rain.*

Quizmaster   How many children do you think are in the world?

Girl   Er . . . dunno.

Quizmaster   How many children do you think are in the world?

Boy   I knaa, I knaa, I knaa . . . I know this one. Oh, I forgot.

Quizmaster   How many children do you think are in the world?

Voices   Two and a half billion.

Quizmaster   How many children do you think there are in Britain?

Voices   Quite a few.

Quizmaster   How many children do you think are in the world?

Voices   Billions.

Quizmaster   What is the capital of Korea?

Girl   Don't know.

Quizmaster   What is the capital of Finland?

Boy   Sweden.

Quizmaster   What is the capital of Brazil?

Boy   Sunderland.

Quizmaster   Say what you think. There are no correct answers. How many guns do you think there are in the world?

Voices   Not sure but there should be less.

Quizmaster   How many guns do you think there are in the world?

Voices   Too many./Hundreds./A million million million./Two million./Infinity.

Quizmaster   How many children do you think there are in the world?

Boy   Twenty-three and a third.

Quizmaster   How much does a polio vaccination cost?

Voices   Fifty-nine pounds./Twenty-five pounds./Seven pounds./Sixty pounds.

Quizmaster   How much does each nuclear warhead cost Britain each year?

Voices   A billion pounds.

Quizmaster   How much does a polio vaccination cost?

Voices   Seven pounds fifty.

Quizmaster   How much does a Dreamcast cost?

Voices   Two hundred pounds.

Quizmaster   How much does a Dreamcast cost?

Voices   Four hundred and ninety-nine pounds and ninety-nine . . .

Quizmaster   How much does a Dreamcast cost?

Voices   One hundred and ninety-nine pounds and ninety-nine p./A hundred and fifty from Charlie's.

Quizmaster   Who is the Secretary-General of the UN?

Voices   Robin Cook./Alan Shearer./A person.

Quizmaster   Who is the Secretary-General of the UN?

Boy   The Pope. David Beckham.

Quizmaster   Who is the Secretary-General of the UN?

Voices   Colonel Gadaffi?/I don't knaa what the UN is . . .

Quizmaster   What makes you scared?

Voices   Spiders and snakes and things like that on the
telly. If I see a spider . . . well, I don't mind little spiders
but a really big spider, I just hate them, all the legs
everywhere . . .

Quizmaster   Who is the Secretary-General of the UN?

Boy   Kofi Annan. A nice cup of coffee.

The school bell rings.

*Sound of rain from a sound-effects recording bleeds into the intro to
'Hand Me Down My Silver Trumpet'.*

Sita (*stark and bright*)   Every year one hundred and seventy-
seven thousand, thousand trillion sperm are ejaculated
during sex in Great Britain alone.

Last year five hundred thousand children were born in
Great Britain.
There are two-point-five billion children in the world.
There are twelve million children in the UK.
Twenty-two thousand children in Great Britain are blind.
There are a hundred and ten thousand convicted child sex
offenders in the UK today.
Kofi Annan is the Secretary-General of the United Nations.

Quizmaster   There are no correct answers.

The intro for Bing Crosby starts.

Sita   The capital of Korea is Seoul.
The capital of Finland is Oslo.

A decent lachrymose chunk of Bing.

As the chords fade . . .

Sita   The average British child has seen thirty-seven thousand killings on TV by the age of thirteen.

Quizmaster   What makes you frightened?

Voices   Lookin' into the sky at night-time, everything is so far away you feel dead little.

Peas, cos I feel they're gonna jump off the plate.

Quizmaster   What makes you frightened?

Voices   When your mum and dad are arguing and you . . . like . . . really, you're thinking, 'Oh, are they going to split up?' Like, you get really, you start crying and then they start crying and it just makes matters worse.

Quizmaster   What makes you frightened?

Girl   Er . . . I dunno.

Voices   When you hear about all the wars .. and that Britain's getting involved . . . Something could happen over here.

People being killed, like, just around the corner from where you live . . . and in the nearby park, people being raped and killed.

Thinking about what could happen to us in the future. Cos we don't know for sure and it's just uncertain.

When they're saying things like the sun's going to burn out and Earth is going to disappear.

I've got a rabbit that's outside and if I forget to go and feed it and I have to go out at eleven o'clock or something.

Quizmaster   What makes you frightened?

Voices   When it's thundering and lightning, I get
frightened then, in case there's going to be . . . the light's
going to go out or something like that. It's just, like, if there's
no TV or radio or you don't know what's happening.

The dark makes me frightened cos you can't see where
you're going.

Eric Satie piano music.

Sita   One hundred and seventy-five million children under
the age of five are malnourished.
There are four guns for every child in Texas.
A quarter of all deaths are the deaths of children.
There are a hundred and forty-four nuclear warheads
belonging to the UK. They cost a lot of money.
Only sixteen per cent of the children in the world with TB
are getting adequate treatment.
Thirty-five thousand children are on a register of children in
danger.

Piano music fades.

Quizmaster   What makes you angry?

Voices   When the Leeds and Galatasaray fans were
fighting and the Galatasaray fans who murdered the Leeds
fan went into the courtroom and they were just . . . and all
his family were saying we're proud of you . . . and I thought
it's not right. And when I see on the news the House of
Commons and I was thinking why do these people run our
country because it's just like a circus, it's not how it should
be because all they are doing is trying to get at each other,
the different parties are not bothered as much about what is
getting done . . . they're saying, 'Oh, we can do this, you
can't.'

Quizmaster   What makes you angry?

Voices   Money, because the world revolves around
money. That's how the world is, it's money now. Nobody
does nothing for nothing. You have to pay them money.

The world revolves around money, there wouldn't be guns without money. Wouldn't be violence without money. Money's involved in everything.

Quizmaster   What makes you angry?

Girl   Don't know.

Quizmaster   What do you really hate?

Voices   German./Maths./Victoria Beckham. (*Sharp intake of breath.*)

Quizmaster   What do you think is evil?

Voices   The Devil, I suppose.

Quizmaster   What do you think is evil?

Voices   Nonces and rapists . . . paedophiles . . . murderers.

I think it's being bad inside a person because if you're evil I think it's your soul and what's inside you, not what comes out because that's violence. But evil is there.

Quizmaster   What is the most violent thing you have witnessed?

Voices   My uncle got hit, but that was partly my fault because we were playing Preston so that was a really big match and we won and I was outside singing and then this man came up to my uncle and said 'Tell your daughter to shut up or I'll hit ya,' and he just hit my uncle, he just got hit in the face.

Sita   Over the last decade two million children have been killed in armed conflict.

Quizmaster   What is the most violent thing you have witnessed? There are no right or wrong answers.

Voices   It was when I was walking home after school, there were these two lads fighting and then this other lad grabbed the baseball bat and hit him across the face with it and it hit him on his head or something like that, and his eye was all cut open, there was blood all over his face.

Quizmaster   What is the most violent thing you have witnessed?

Voices   The most violent thing I have ever witnessed is me dad hitting me mam about seven year ago. It's all been rosy since then.

Sita   Over the last decade six million children have been seriously injured in armed conflicts.

Voices   I've seen fights at school, but I've seen much more worse on telly.

Quizmaster   What is the most violent thing you have ever heard about or seen on the telly?

Voices   On *Cops*, the American one where they die violently . . . in the room . . . cos there was a conjunction [*sic*] on him . . . and they had just dropped the conjunction on that day and he never knew about it and he went into the house and he shot the woman, and he shot the baby, in the cot . . . the baby was only about six months and you seen it lying in the cot . . . with all the blood and everything . . . that was horrible.

Sita   Every year sixteen thousand people are murdered by guns in the USA.

Voices   I think on telly, it was about a couple of months ago. It wasn't that violent but it was racist. . . Stephen Lawrence . . . the thing, it was on telly . . . and you saw it, when he was getting beaten up . . . it wasn't that violent but it made you think 'racist' and then when you see . . . what else did they do to him? They stabbed him and then . . . they ran after his friend and then his friend was trying to take him in and he had all blood everywhere . . . and *Saving Private Ryan*. I've got that on video, I don't know why, and that's like legs being blown off, the heads, the eyes in the sockets . . . and that's awful.

Quizmaster   What do you think is evil?

Voices   People, like, calling you names, bawling at you for no reason at all. They just do it to look good in front of their friends.

Eric Satie piano music.

People, who hurt people. Even if they do realise or don't realise, but they just don't say sorry or anything afterwards . . .

Evil, it's like without conscience . . .

Sita   One-point-two billion people in the world live in poverty including six million children.

Living in poverty means living off less than one dollar a day.
Two million girls in Africa have undergone genital mutilation.
Last year, one-point-nine million children died of diarrhoea.
Malaria kills a child every forty seconds.
Over the last decade two million children have been killed in armed conflict.
The capital of Oslo is Seoul.

Intro to 'Hand Me Down My Silver Trumpet'.

Rain, which carries over **Quizmaster** . . .

Quizmaster   Does God exist?

Girl   Err . . .

Quizmaster   There is no right or wrong answer. Does God exist?

Girl   Errrrr . . . I don't know.

Quizmaster   Remember, there are no correct answers. Does God exist?

Voices   Yes.

Yes.

I believe that if you think He exists then He will do. But if you believe that He doesn't exist then He won't.

I'm not sure, cos no one's ever come back with evidence that He does.

What is the point of us being here if there is no God. You have to have someone there to create us, evolution and all the science things . . . well, where does the science come from then?

Bang into the singing of 'Hand Me Down My Silver Trumpet'.

Quizmaster   What do you think love is?

Voices   It's hard to describe because you can love your brother but not like him but, like, you love your friends because you like them, so it's really hard to describe. It can be really liking something but, like, you love your family but you don't necessarily like them so it's really hard. It's like being close to somebody or something . . . being around them.

Quizmaster   Remember, there are no correct answers.

Voices   Well, there's unrequited love, that's not a mutual feeling between each other . . . but I think love is a strong emotion about someone, that you just feel and when they get hurt, you are hurting too because you care about them.

Quizmaster   Does God exist?

Boy   Aye, I seen him down the chip shop on Friday.

Quizmaster   What was he wearing?

Boy   I forgot.

Quizmaster   What was he wearing?

Boy   A mink coat.

Quizmaster   What makes you angry?

Voices   People who are collecting the third world debts, they don't need the money at all but it's an awful lot of money for the people who are having to pay them so why they just can't forget about it, I just don't know.

Quizmaster   What makes you sad?

Voices   When me father died.

Quizmaster   There are no correct answers.

Eric Satie piano music.

Voices   One of the times when I was most sad . . . I was only young at the time . . . we went on holiday to Scotland and it was like the best holiday I have ever had. It was great and everything . . . um . . . and then we had to go at the end and I was really upset cos I didn't want to go and it was this big house we were staying in and I just wanted to stay there.

I don't know how to put this really . . . but when someone really close . . . who's always been, like, athletic or really strong and that's getting really weak, getting really ill and there is nothing you can do about it. You know it's going to go on for ages. You know they're not going to die quickly, but they are dying, and there is nothing anyone can do about it.

And, like, when one of your best friends turns against you all of a sudden and then everyone else turns against you and you can't do anything. You try and be nice but they just don't want to know. They're just all the time at you, all the time. Cos they say you're better than them at something.

When you're watching on the third world countries . . . all the children starving and they've done nothing wrong and it's the same as, like, war. People have been forced to fight that don't want to and it isn't actually them that want the land or the extra money or anything like that.

I love dogs and animals and when I see adverts of them, the RSPCA adverts, it makes me really sad.

When someone famous like Jill Dando gets killed, you can't understand why because they are really nice but then someone goes and kills them . . . you just can't believe it.

Music continues and fades into rain.

Quizmaster   What makes you sad?

Girl   Errmmm. I don't know. When someone calls you something for no reason and that. You know, when they like say things. That's about it really . . .

Quizmaster   Would you say you were a happy person?

Girl   Ermm . . . Not really, no . . .

Quizmaster   Would you say you were an unhappy person?

Girl   No.

Quizmaster   What kind of person would you say you were?

Girl   I don't know. Sort of, normal.

Quizmaster   What things make you happy?

Girl   Well, the telly, sometimes . . . and I quite like playing out. But it gets a bit boring as well, so . . .

Quizmaster   What makes you bored?

Voices   Silence . . . bores me. Can never sleep at night . . . / Staying in the house, can't stay in the house. / Aye, that's terrible. / Every day . . .

Just homework.

Silence, I like to hear people's voices.

Geography, makes me really really bored. I just hate the subject.

Yeah, me too.

When somebody goes on about something and they keep on repeating themselves and repeating it and they don't let the situation down, they just keep going on about it, it makes you really bored.

When I get to my grandma and grandpa's, every time I go, they get the family tree out and boring things like that and I don't want to hurt their feelings and say that I don't want to look through it but it's very boring.

Rain.

Quizmaster   What things make you happy?

Voices   I'm just happy when I'm not bored.

Quizmaster   What things make you happy?

Boy   Shagging lasses.

Quizmaster   Do you think you're funny?

Boy   You're the one asking the questions.

Quizmaster   Why are you so defensive?

Boy   I'm not defensive.

Quizmaster   Do you consider yourself to be ignorant?

Boy   No. I'm not ignorant. I don't have to answer these questions you know.

Quizmaster   There is no right or wrong answer. What is the average wage in Sierra Leone?

Sita   The average wage in Sierra Leone is one hundred pounds per year. The average wage in Brazil is two thousand, five hundred dollars a year.

Quizmaster   What is the average wage in Brazil?

Voices   A hundred and twenty-five pounds . . . ten pounds . . . two pence . . . three pounds . . .

Quizmaster   What is the average wage in Sierra Leone?

Voices   I don't know where that is . . . two pounds . . . two pound fifty . . .

Quizmaster   Where is Sierra Leone?

Voices   Africa./Kosovo./In a third world place./Is it not near Indonesia?/I like that word . . ./It's in Africa./Is it?/Isn't it where that big war's going on . . . ?

Quizmaster   Who is the President of the USA?

Voices (*whole class together*)   Tony Blair.

Quizmaster   Who was John Stuart Mill?

Voices   A mill owner./A writer./An evil dictator in Croatia.

Quizmaster   Who was John Stuart Mill?

Voices   A basketball player./A traveller./An inventor . . . an inventor, he sounds like an inventor./What's his name?

Quizmaster   Who was John Stuart Mill?

Voices   A – book – writer?/Just have a guess.

Quizmaster   Who was Louis Pasteur?

Voices   Did he make pasta?/A painter./He made pasteurised stuff . . . milk./He made . . . mould . . . something to do with mould . . . he found mould!/No that was –/He made cheese.

Pasteur gazing at mould.

Quizmaster   Who was Louis Pasteur?

Voices   An artist./He made pasta./He invented the vaccination of . . . he invented some kind of vaccination./ The vaccination of typhoid./Impressionist./Invented anaesthetic./He invented the machine that pasteurises milk.

Quizmaster   Who are the Sami?

Voices   Is it the Chinese mafia? Is it the Cuban mafia?

Quizmaster   There are no right or wrong answers.

Voices   Is it the short word for sandwich?

Quizmaster   What is your favourite food?

Voices   Chilli./Curry./Curry./Haggis and sweet and sour noodles Hong Kong-style./Indian or lamb with mint sauce.

Quizmaster   What is the most important thing ever invented?

Voices   The toilet./Vaccinations./Well, it wasn't invented . . . it was discovered – electricity.

Quizmaster   What is the most important thing ever invented?

Voices   Electric underpants./Guns./The printer.

Quizmaster   Who are your heroes?

Voices   Malcolm X./Muhammad Ali./Superman./The inventor of Pokémon./Alan Shearer./Tina Turner./ Engelbert Humperdinck.

Rain fades up over next section.

Quizmaster   What was the Vietnam War about?

Voices   Errmm . . . Forrest Gump was in it . . ./ Vietnam./Something to do with the American army./ Something to do with Brazil./Something to do with bombs./And America!/Nuclear, atomic bombs . . ./Was it Japan?/Ban the bomb-type thing!/America won.

Quizmaster   What sort of differences do you think there are between your life and the life of a child in Sierra Leone?

Girl   I don't know.

Quizmaster   What sort of differences do you think there are between your life and the life of a child in Sierra Leone?

Girl   Well, there's that war on. And they've got no shoes . . . And you might get kidnapped . . . I dunno. Oh, and some of them get mutilated and that. Like the girl on the telly. They get mutilated . . . and they don't have much money.

Quizmaster   What do you think are the differences between your life and the life of a child in Finland?

Girl   Dunno. Cold? Weather?

Eric Satie piano music fades up.

Quizmaster   Who are your heroes?

Girl   I dunno.

Rain fades.

Sita   John Stuart Mill was a writer and a philosopher.
At the age of seven Orson Welles knew *King Lear* off by heart.
In 1801, at the age of seven, Andrew Bunning of Cheshire was hanged for stealing a spoon.
Until 1875, the age of consent was twelve.
At the age of thirteen, Lady Margaret Beaufort gave birth to King Henry VII.
At the age of three, John Stuart Mill started learning Greek. By seven he had read all of Plato's dialogues. At eight, he started to learn Latin. By twelve, he had digested Ovid, Horace, Livy, Aristotle, most of the classical comedies, geometry, algebra, differential calculus, written a history of Rome, an abridgement of the universal history of the classical world and a history of Holland, and composed several verses in Greek. At thirteen he made a comprehensive survey of all hitherto existing political economy.

Rain fades up.

Quizmaster   Why don't you say anything in class?

Music stops.

Girl   I dunno. I just don't.

Quizmaster   Do you think it's because you live in a children's home?

Girl   No, I don't know.

Quizmaster   Do you think you are lonely?

Girl (*pause*)   No. I mean, there's loads of people I know. And I can have me one-to-one. And there's Emma. I mean, sometimes she pisses . . . sorry, sorry . . . sometimes she makes me mad and that, say if I go round to her house and we've arranged to meet and then I go round to her house and when I get there she's not in and it's a complete waste of time . . . then I get mad because that's just taking advantage of us . . . it's not fair. What was the question again?

Quizmaster   Do you like living here?

Girl   I think I'm happier here than I would be in a foster home. I mean, I've been to about five and none of them were any good for us. I mean, in the last one I had to go to bed at nine o'clock. It's just plain ridiculous, that. I know this kid, right, he's only eight and he, called David Bowman, he doesn't have to go to bed until eleven. And he has me stuck there and that. I hated them, I really did, they try to be nice to us but . . . I mean, I'm nearly fourteen now. I'm happier here than I was in a foster home. Definitely yes.

Eric Satie piano music.

Quizmaster   What would you like to be when you grow up?

Girl   I dunno. I haven't really thought about it. (*Pause.*) Maybe a nursery nurse.

Quizmaster   Who are your heroes?

Voices   Nelson Mandela because he stopped the apartheid./John Logie Baird./Marie Curie./Princess Diana.

Sita   The Spice Girls have sold thirty-six million albums worldwide.

Quizmaster   What do you think of the Spice Girls?

Voices   They are really rubbish but they're quite good to laugh at./I feel sorry for them really, cos, like, they're a bit sad, aren't they?/I think that was a big publicity stunt./I can't stand the way Sporty Spice breathes when she sings.

Quizmaster   Remember there are no correct answers.

Voices   I think they spice up my life so I like them.

Music: Sam Cooke, 'Wonderful World'.

Sita   The average pocket money in the UK is two pounds and five p.
A quarter of fifteen-year-olds are regular smokers.
The average child in the UK drinks two hundred litres of Coke a year.

Music: Sam Cooke, 'Wonderful World'.

Sita   Over one hundred children have been killed by NATO bombings in the last two years.
A hundred and twenty-five million children in the world work full-time. Over two hundred and fifty million children work part-time.
Thirteen million children have lost at least one parent to AIDS.
Last year two million children died because they did not have access to safe water.

Rain.

Sita   Horatio Nelson joined the navy aged twelve.

Quizmaster   Who invented the telephone?

Girl   Err . . .

Quizmaster   What do you think your future has in store?

Girl   I never really think, like, about the future. I mean, how can you think of your future. I mean . . . um . . . I dunno.

Quizmaster   What do you think are the biggest problems facing children today?

Girl   Dunno. Well, there's bullying and that. Or like when somebody accuses you. Or say you've said something when they know you've never said 'owt.

Quizmaster   Those are the biggest problems?

Girl   I dunno. (*Pause.*) You know it isn't easy being in a home like this. I mean, sometimes I just sit here and wonder why this has happened to me. I mean, they don't know what it's like, do they? They don't know what it's like to have to sit in your room twenty-four/seven. They don't know what it's like to be here. All I want is a normal home, with a normal family. All I want is a normal house. People who'll be nice to us and that. You don't know what it's like to live here in this poo hole. You don't know what it's like. I've got this sister, right, and she's down in Middlesbrough and I only see her, right, what, like five times a year. Five times a year. That's me sister. That's not right. It's not right to be here. It's horrible. People don't know how horrible it actually is. It's not right, is it? All I want is somebody to love us. That's all I want.

Quizmaster   Do you wish you were in a normal family?

Girl   No. I just said that. I just said it as a joke, you know. It's what you say. I quite like it here. It's better than being stuck in some horrible foster home.

Quizmaster   Do you ever keep in touch with any of your foster parents?

Girl   Not really, no. I mean, the last ones. They were wanting to adopt us and everything, but . . . well, they were just mental, really. The bloke used to go round with sandals on and that. They used to come here when I first came, and said I could go back whenever I wanted to, but why would I want to go to that poo hole. Well, I suppose they were quite kind. Sent us sixty pounds for me birthday . . . I think . . . I think it was sixty pounds. Maybe it was Christmas. Anyway. That's the last I heard from them.

Quizmaster Did you thank them?

Girl I can't remember. Maybe's I did. I probably forgot.

Quizmaster Did you thank them for the sixty pounds?

Girl No.

Quizmaster What do you want for your future?

Girl Dunno. A big house. Maybe Emma could live there if she behaves herself. I don't really know about the future. I just take one day at a time.

Quizmaster You said that already.

Girl Did I? Do you think I'm boring?

Eric Satie music cross-fades with rain.

Quizmaster What do you think is the most important thing ever invented?

Boy The bog brush.

Quizmaster What makes you angry?

Voices When people are racist towards my dad.

When people are racist and they're horrible to other people just because they're different.

I hate racism, I hate fighting in the world and I hate everything that's wrong in the world.

If me mam makes us tidy up me bedroom or makes us eat any of the vegetables I don't like. When people are racist or sexist or you know . . .

I get angry at my mam when she does reverse psychology on us. That really works.

I was doing the Hitler project and I saw all the stuff about the Holocaust . . . that makes us really angry . . . like killing all the Jews and all that.

And putting them in the shower and then putting the gas in and they'd just choke.

Sita   Seventy per cent of deaths among adults are due to behaviour they started as children, including smoking, drinking and sexually transmitted diseases.

Quizmaster   Would you say you were a boring person?

Girl   Me?

Intro to 'Hand Me Down My Silver Trumpet'.

It stops as if someone's dragged the needle off the record player and Marvin Gaye starts up:
'Live life for the children' etc.

Sita   Macauley Culkin earned more than thirteen million dollars for *Home Alone 2*.
A hundred and thirty million children have no access to primary education.
The world's richest two hundred and twenty-five people own forty-seven per cent of the world's wealth. That is equal to the combined wealth of the poorest two-point-five billion.

Quizmaster   What would you do if you were rich?

Voices   Give some of it to my family. Give some of it to charity. Buy a huge, huge villa, buy some cars, buy everything that I didn't have before and probably like put some away for investment, like, if I had children or something like that.

Sita   The three richest people in the world have more wealth between them than the combined wealth of the forty-eight poorest countries of the world. The top fifteen richest people have more personal wealth than the total GDP of the whole of South-East Asia.

Quizmaster   What would you do if you were rich?

Voices   I'd give it to the NHS and people who need the money, and just, charity, and then I'd go and spend a bit on myself, obviously.

Sita   The top thirty-two richest people in the world have more wealth than the whole of China, which has a population of one-point-two billion. Thirty-two people. One-point-two billion. Think about this.

Eric Satie piano music.

The estimated cost needed to achieve universal access to basic social services for all the people in the world (that is, basic health care, reproductive care for women, adequate food, adequate safe water and sanitation) is about forty billion dollars a year. Or four per cent of the combined wealth of the richest two hundred and twenty-five people in the world. The interest rate in the United Kingdom is six per cent.

Quizmaster   If you had all the money in the world, what one thing would you buy?

Voices   Ibiza./What's Ibiza?/A country./Ah, I thought you said 'a betha'./I'd buy everything in the world./A little plant in a plant pot./Anything I wanted./A nice Ferrari.

Sita   Forty billion dollars would provide food, health care and sanitation for everyone in the world. Eleven billion is spent on ice cream in Europe every year. Seventeen billion is spent on pet food in Europe and America. Thirty-five billion is spent on corporate entertainment in Japan alone. One hundred and five billion is spent on alcoholic drinks in Europe every year. Four hundred billion is spent on narcotics. And seven hundred and eighty billion is spent on the military every year.

Quizmaster   If you had all the money in the world. What one thing would you buy?

Voices   I'd help out all the third world countries and get rid of, like, all the homeless people and give them homes and help them.

Sita   It would cost six billion to give every child on earth a basic education. Eight billion a year is spent on cosmetics in the United States alone.

Voices   I'd stop all wars. I'd make no such thing as poverty and I'd be a bit selfish and I'd, erm . . . make sure Blackpool got promoted to Division Two and just kept on going up and got loads of money.

Sita   Over twenty-five million children sleep on the streets. One hundred and seventy-five million children under the age of five are malnourished.

Voices   I'd give teachers more money because if you think about it doctors and nurses are taught by teachers and also so I can afford to go on holiday because my dad's a teacher.

Sita   There are twelve million children in Great Britain. Three million children spend Christmas in a home where nobody has a job.

Music stops.

Quizmaster   If you had all the money in the world what one thing would you buy?

Voices   Happiness.

Quizmaster   What do you think your ideal future would entail?

Rain.

Boy   Shag lasses, have loads of money, have a yacht and play for England. Oh yeah, and help the third world and all the starving children and that.

Quizmaster   Are you proud of yourself?

Boy   I said I'd help the third world and that, didn't I? And aye, I'd help all the babies with AIDS and cripples that couldn't cross the road and that. And if there were people taking the piss out of spakkas and that I'd get a gun and shoot their heads off and then I would make a big bowl of porridge and feed all the starving children of Africa.

Quizmaster   There are no right or wrong answers.

Sita   The average life expectancy in the USA, UK and Finland was roughly seventy for the year 2000. In Sierra Leone it was twenty-five and ten months. In Brazil it was fifty-nine. In Bangladesh it was fifty.

Quizmaster   What do you think your ideal future would entail?

Voices   After I'd been to university, I suppose become a millionaire . . . getting loads of money and, like, having nice – not having to worry about things, not having to worry if you'll be able to pay for your shopping or things like that.

Quizmaster   If you had three wishes, what would they be?

Voices   Stop violence. Get rid of guns and stop all . . . well, to help like all the third world countries and get rid of all the homeless people and give them homes and help them.

Quizmaster   If you had three wishes what would they be?

Voices   Peace, happiness and money.

Quizmaster   What?

Voices   Peace and no discrimination with anyone . . . equality and just a feeling of security.

Quizmaster   What do you think your future holds?

Voices   My future will hold very many good things but there are weaknesses in human beings and like I said before,

I was scared, and I am scared of . . . but I think . . . the
future excites me too.

Rain.

Quizmaster   What do you want to be when you grow
up?

Girl   I dunno. I haven't really thought about it.

Quizmaster   What visions do you have for your future?

Girl   I dunno. Just take one day at a time, don't I?

Quizmaster   What do you think your future holds?

Voices   Settle down, find somebody that loves you for
who you are, and to have children and have a lovely family
and have a lovely life with a nice house and be secure for
when you're older and you have no worries about family or
anything.

Quizmaster   There are no right or wrong answers.

*Music: Crosby, Stills & Nash, 'Teach Your Children Well', fades up
over next speech.*

Sita   There are four guns for every child in Texas.
There are two-point-five billion children in the world.
There are twelve million children in the UK.

Music fades under next section, cross-fading with rain.

Sita   The capital of Finland is Helsinki.
Seventy-five billion Cokes are drunk in America every year.
Seventy-eight per cent of all school leavers have one or
more A levels.
A quarter of all deaths are the deaths of children.
A hundred and thirty million children have no access to
primary education.
Girls in Britain are eleven times more likely to commit a
crime than fifty years ago.
Over forty per cent of the world's population are under
eighteen.

It is not known how many guns there are in the world. Four-point-one children are born every second. That's over eleven thousand during the course of this programme.

Rain.

Child of Our Time:
Child of the Snow

Child of the Snow was broadcast on Radio 4 on 5 June 2000 as part of the *Child of Our Time* series. It was based on a research trip to Finland, 250 miles inside the Arctic circle. The cast was as follows:

Matti   Ben Tibber

Directed by Kate Rowland

Drumbeat.

Matti's Story

Drumbeat.
Yoik.

What is the sound of this?

The sound of snow.

Seanas.

Drumbeat.

What is the sound of this?

The sound of slushier snow.
Drumbeat.

Skarta. What is the sound of this?

Hard, icy snow.

Sarti. There are a hundred and fifty words for snow.
Sarti is when a layer of frozen snow acts as a sheet of ice
before other layers form on top. Very bad for grazing. What
is the sound of this?

The sound of snow.

The sound of snow. Minus thirty.

Drumbeat.

OK. What is the sound of this?

Yoik.

That is yoik.
What is yoik?

More yoik.

Yoik is this singing what people do.
This is yoik with beat.

Yoik with beat.

Which is more modern. And very popular abroad as it has tradition and synthesisers. Yoik is supposed to be singing that makes you pure. Personally, I prefer Robbie Williams. Which is really Minna's record. Minna – who is my sister – actually prefers the Spice Girls. There's no accounting for taste.

What is this?
'How many people are in the average Sami household?'
It's the first part of the famous Sami joke.
The end of the famous Sami joke:
'n + 1, where n equals the average number in a Sami household.'
'Eh?' people ask.
'Yes,' is the reply. 'n + one anthropologist.' Which is true, I think.

What is the sound of this?

A reindeer.

My reindeer. Shitpants.

Drumbeat.
Blast of yoik.
Drumbeating into sound of Sibelius.

I remember, it was the day when Nils Persen disappeared. It was wintertime – at the time when there is no light at all. At about December, when we've done the reindeer separation, and it starts getting really cold, the lights go out for about eleven weeks. Well, when I say they go out. You can still see some things, like the moon, and maybe a bit at midday when the sky is more blue. But it is one endless night really, like the summer is one long day with a dip in it each nightfall. But as the sun still blazes, so the dark is pitch at winter. And Nils Persen, one of the reindeer men who drink beer in the bar of the Hotel Inari, had been in the bar of the Hotel Inari for three days. And they all had been drinking beer and every day the reindeer men would come out from the bar for an hour and ride around on their snowmobiles for a while in the car park and then go in for more. Or sometimes they'd fight with knives or something, but no one ever got killed or anything, my dad says it's because they're too drunk, anyway I suppose the reindeer men without children have got to have something to do. And on they drank and on the third day, Nils Persen ordered a bottle of aquavit, and drank it down in one. Aquavit is the fire of life. It is a drink filled with herbs and wormwood. And he stumbled outside to get some air. And everybody stumbled out with him and they rode round on their snowmobiles until it was time to go in. But then Nils said that he had had enough. That he was going home. That he was going to go home across the lake, on his snowmobile. And everybody said that he shouldn't do it. That he was far too fat. And he had drunk the aquavit. And that he should come inside for some breakfast. But Nils Persen said he was going home across the lake. And they said, 'The ice.' But he said, 'Bugger the ice,' he was going home the short way lake or no lake. And all the reindeer men tried to stop him but when he fell off twice they just put him back on and went inside for a few more days. And then off went Nils Persen.

And in the dark bar where the men sang yoiks and the fire was blazing, they could hear the buzz of Nils Persen's snowmobile as it droned off like a fly in the darkness, and the men sang on and dreamt of summer, then there was the crack and it shook the whole night, and the buzzing stopped, and the men stopped singing. And they all rushed out and peered into the darkness. And someone said to go on to the ice, but then everyone said no, not when there'd been a crack. And they peered out over the lake. And everything was darkness. And someone got a light and they crept out bit by bit across the lake and peered into the darkness. But there was nothing. There was no snowmobile, no crack, no hole in the ice, no Nils Persen, nothing that anyone could see. Just endless dark. And they knew even if they all went out they'd not find him. He was gone in a black hole in the black. For ever.

And after a few weeks, there was still no sign of Nils Persen.
And when the light came back, when it was safe to go into
the ice, across the lake to find poor Nils Persen, they could
find nothing. Only the endless perfect ice. No cracks, only
thick seanas and crisp dry snow. And deep and buried for
ever was Nils Persen, frozen with the fishes – full of aquavit.
And it was in that night that I first heard the Kalevala sing. I
mean, I heard a bit at school, but it was then I heard it sing.
Mam sang it out to keep us from being bored. To keep away
the dark. She said it was as ancient as the lake, as ancient as
the yoik. But on the Internet it said it was written up much
later by this bloke a hundred and fifty years ago. But it came
from older stories. And that night I heard it sing. Even
though I didn't even know Nils Persen. And didn't even
know that he would be the first person I knew that died.
Even if I didn't really know him. I knew who he was. And
Mam sang us these old tales. And I didn't know anything.
About the EEC. Or the reindeer men in the Hotel Inari. Or
poor old Nils Persen. But I heard the sound of where I came
from.

Drumbeat.

I have a good mind to start the singing and tell the story of
our past. As the words melt in my mouth and stream out
through my teeth, they unfurl like a tine of fire, and my little
sister, we will start singing and we will all sing together
about the lands of the North and we will sing the beginning
for everyone to hear, the young children growing and the
old men as they die and the song will bind us together – the
song will keep us warm – and I will lilt a light into the
world . . .

Or something like that.

And I will snap the tales out of the cold and scoop the songs
from the frost and wind the whole story into a ball and I will
take home the coil and I will light the lilt into the world.

Honestly. It really is like that. All of it.

And in the beginning there was nothing, just the girl made of air and she lay down across the sky and raised her knee for rest, and down came a bird, and said, 'I will build my dwelling on this wind, I will live on the billows and set down on her knee.' And there it built its nest and laid two golden eggs, snug as the air girl lay asleep, then one hatched one day, and the tickling bird woke the sleepy air girl and down fell the nest with the last egg, down into the firmament and as it fell it cracked, and the bottom half fell and became Mother Earth, and the top part fell and became the heavens above and the yolk flew out and became the sun for it was golden, and the white of the egg flew up and it became the moon, and whatever it was in the egg that was mottled flew up and was the stars and whatever in the egg was black became the clouds of the sky. And still the air girl swam, and still the sun shone, and cold the new moon gleamed, and behind her swam the slack water of the night sky.

And this is how we were made. Although it's a bit controversial and that, with the big bang, Christianity and the EEC. And it is generally considered that the world was not made out of eggshells or lazy air ladies and that – but it was made out of nothing – in a big explosion – which is much more likely when you think about it. I suppose a lot of things are different now with the big bang and the EEC and everything. History is different. But I suppose back then, in the beginning, there was only future or there was more future than past, where as now, there's probably more past than future. Well, as far as we know. I mean, if you can't agree on the past, how can you agree on the future?

Not that I remember before the EEC. But Dad says it's different now.

For example, Dad never used to be tested. And you can't catch a reindeer by the horns as that is 'cruelty to animals'. Although you are allowed to have battery farms of chickens. And you are not allowed to shoot bears. Which is also cruelty to animals, except I think bears are 'cruelty to animals' in themselves especially when they kill reindeers.

Shitpants's brother George was killed by a bear, we went out one morning and there he was lying and his neck was bitten – almost through. The bear hadn't eaten George, not properly, it had just killed him. For fun probably. It's not that a reindeer is much of a threat to a bear, especially not George or Shitpants.

You are only allowed to kill bears if they are trying to kill you. That's why bear stew is so expensive now. Because the EEC have banned you from killing bears. But if you do kill a bear, in self-defence, then the best thing you can do is sell it to these blokes that make it into a stew and then you can sell it to the tourists, for a fortune. I'm not saying people should just go out and kill bears for no reason or anything. Just that if a bear eats all your reindeer how can you survive? Do you know that when a bear hibernates it plugs up its bottom with wax – and in the spring it pops out like a cork. They're quite weird bears – going to sleep all winter long.

But to be quite honest, who'd actually know? You know if you shot a bear. Here. Miles from anywhere. As long as you kept it quiet who'd find out? That's what Dad says. It's not like you're going to report it to the EEC. And get arrested. Not that I have killed a bear. I have never killed anything. Except a few fish, and some birds and reindeer. But I only killed the reindeer because it had fallen down a cliff. And anyway, even if you did kill a bear and wanted to report it, where would you report it to? There aren't any police in Inari. There aren't any police for two hundred miles. And there aren't any offices for the EEC, either.

We don't need any police. Because there isn't any crime.

Which is good.

If you lived in a city or something there'd be drugs and crime. And pollution. And people begging on the streets and sirens and loud music. And here there is nothing.
No sirens.
No crime.

OK, once in a while there might be a bear or something. But the air is clear and clean.

Drumbeat.

What is the sound of that?

Drumbeat.

That is the sound of a Sami drum. It's what shamans used to beat. They'd beat the drum so they could sing to the dead. Not that anyone sings to the dead any more. There are some people that sing to tourists. And Mari Boine, she plays a drum and that. But that's more like jazz. Here's a bit of Mari Boine.

Mari Boine.

Mari Boine is a Sami. With beat. There haven't been shamans for hundreds of years. Not since it was banned. It was banned to be a shaman. And to be quite honest I'm not surprised. My nanna said that shamans believed people were created because this woman had it off with a bear. Absolutely ridiculous. Then everybody converted to Christianity. Not that I go to church mind. Only on a wedding or something. And then it was banned to speak in Sami. For ages and ages. Grandma used to have to do it in private apparently. This was before the EEC.

Once it was banned to speak in Sami and now they teach you in school. And some people say what's the point of speaking Sami. But Mam says, 'You try describing a three-year-old female reindeer with her antlers sticking straight up in the air in a two-syllable word in any other language.'

Which is true.

In Finnish it would be 'bladhdibladhdi bladhdi bladh baldhbladh'.

In Sami it is 'oik'.

Mind you, there are lots of words which aren't very useful now.

Such as 'Jabmuidaibmu'. Which means 'the land of the upside down'.

Well, there's not much call for that. Not any more.

That's where dead people go. Jabmuidaibmu. Everything is back to front. Whereas everyone knows you go to heaven. Or just rot, or something. I mean, it's a nice idea. Everybody going about the wrong way up. But it's not very realistic. Put it this way, I don't think Jabmuidaibmu is a part of the EEC.

I suppose we have quite a lot of governments, really. First there is the EEC, then there is the Finnish government, and then there is the Sami parliament. Which goes across quite a few countries. Norway and Sweden and that. I don't quite know what they do or anything. Mam was a member – she got voted on from Inari. But I don't know what she did there. I'm not sure she knew. But, you see, it's not like we are free to just do what we want. Just because there are no police or anything. There are loads of governments. I love it here.

And I suppose everybody is governed really. By the stars or the gods, or the weather or the parliament, and what have you. Wherever you are, you are connected. You are never really on your own. Even in the middle of the forest. Even if you were completely lost. You would still be connected. On your mobile phone. Or to nature. Or to something else. You are never alone. You are always connected.

What is the sound of this?

Spice Girls. Sporty Spice.

That is Sporty Spice. What is the sound of this?

Ginger Spice takes the lead.

Ginger Spice.

Posh Spice.

And this is Posh Spice.

Minna was very upset about the Spice Girls. In fact she cried when Ginger Spice left. Although even she hated *SpiceWorld* – the movie. She likes *Titanic* – the movie – the Spice Girls, books about horses and fly-fishing. She started to get into lassoing and stuff but now she just prefers fishing. She either wants to become an astronaut and go to the moon to see the beautiful moon flowers – hello! – or be a reindeer woman like Mam. What else does she like? Donald Duck. We both like Donald Duck. Erm . . . playing with Shitpants and Flowernose. Flowernose is Minna's favourite. They both live outside. Not all the reindeer go with the herds. By the way, Shitpants isn't called Shitpants, really. He's actually called Panicpants. But that's what we call him. And then there was George before the bear ate him, and Tim. Tim is Minna's as well.

One day Tim had gone missing for a bit. And then Dad got this phone call all the way from Ivalo and it was this woman and Tim was outside her cabin eating her flowers, so Dad had to go all the way to Ivalo to fetch him. Then the next day the woman rang again and said that Tim was back again and had eaten all of her potatoes. So Dad had to go all the way back. The very next day.

Tim is a glutton for potatoes.

Mostly reindeers eat moss.

Drumbeat.

What is the sound of this?

Silence.

Listen again. What is the sound of this?

Silence.

Can you hear it?

Silence.

It's the sound of snow falling.
What is the sound of this?

Silence.

That is the weather turning.
And this . . .

Silence, then an animal cry.

. . . is just silence. Hear the silence. You see. There is never just nothing.

Silence.

When I was born there was an explosion. Not here. But far away. I was born on the twenty-sixth of April 1986. And at twenty past one in the afternoon. As Mam had me in Inari. More than a thousand miles away there was an explosion in a factory, in Russia. In this factory they made electricity out of nuclear fuel. And they were testing the machine – the reactor – for its safety but it didn't cool down properly and it went off. And it went off and blew a hole in the wall – and a fire started and all the nuclear fuel started to catch fire – and the whole roof of the place, called Chernobyl, caught fire.

This thing that man had made was out of control. Just one little mistake had made this huge catastrophe – and without the roof and everything all the radiation driftened up into the air. Three hundred times worse than at Hiroshima. And the fire was out of control. And got hotter and hotter and so they sent helicopters to drop water on the fiery mass but the water evaporated even before it would hit. The fire was so hot the steam broke up and just became separate elements. Just oxygen and hydrogen and made the fire worse. And it was so hot that the stones around it melted. The iron melted too. Everything around it melted and fell into the fire and made it hotter and hotter. And soon it was 2,500 degrees and no one could go near it. But what was worse was what they couldn't see.

And this went on for days. And the only way to stop the fire was to freeze the ground underneath it to slow it down. And so they injected the ground with frozen gas till it was minus one hundred. And for days the fire raged and the men fought it knowing now that they would die. But finally the freezing cold slowed the reaction down just long enough to bury it with sand, and then surround it with concrete that they sprayed over, till finally it was caught, and they had buried it, even though deep inside it was still burning.

I'm not saying it exploded because I was born.

It was just a coincidence. It is just a fact.

Deep in the heart of Russia, further than anyone from Inari has ever been, was a fire, and from the fire was a cloud. And from the first explosion it rose two kilometres in the air, and from the fire as it burned it filled a plume wider than the lake, a tower of poison that no one could see and the winds blew and so that's how it happened.

And that was Chernobyl. Which in Russian means wormwood. Which means a bitter plant. A bitter plant that they put in drinks. Bitter drinks of fire.

It wasn't the cloud that mattered. It was the rain. The gentle summer rain. When they measured the grass it was so poisoned they had to dig it up and burn it. The whole ground was laid with radiation. And in other places they had to pour away all the milk from all the cows that had eaten grass. But it wasn't until much later that they tested the reindeer. And in September when they tested them it was twelve times what it should be, then in October they tested it and in some reindeer it was a hundred times what it should be. And they told everyone to stop eating reindeer. But nobody bothered. They said they should kill all the reindeer. But no one bothered doing that either. And in the end they just said we should be careful, as it would maybe be ten years for it to get back to normal and even by the time I was thirty-six there would still be radiation in the plants around me from the day I was born.

From an explosion a thousand miles away.
That no one could see. Or hear.

And for a while the government bought up all the reindeer meat and fed it to minks and stuff. It wasn't like it would kill you automatically if you ate it. It was just a precaution. It's not like we were going to die like the firemen or the kids from the town of Chernobyl. It was just a precaution. And that's why they test Dad. And the other reindeer men. They test them for the radiation. Which fell like invisible snow.

But the reindeer didn't die.

And we kept on with the farming. Like the Sami have done for ten thousand years et cetera. And we have survived. After all, we've been herding reindeer two thousand times longer than they've been making nuclear electricity, and four thousand times longer than the EEC. So we weren't going to stop for a bit of radiation. But they say they will test Dad until he's an old man. I don't know. Maybe they'll test me too.

Minna has a pen pal in Russia now. She is called Minna too. I call her Minna Two. She often sends letters and stuff but hardly ever calls as they don't have any money in Russia. Minna Two is the great-granddaughter of Grandma's second cousin. She is going to be a reindeer person. Here is a letter that she wrote to Minna One.

'Dear Minna,
Thank you for the Donald Duck magazines. I have been playing with Pushkin my reindeer today. He ate all the potatoes in Mrs Gudanov's garden. At school we did maths, and music. I am learning the violin and we had liver casserole. Some of the normal people don't have any money and Gretta in my class ate a rat that her mother cooked. Tomorrow I am going swimming.
Yours sincerely,
Minna.
PS Can you send me more Donald Ducks.
PPS How is George?
PPPS Who are the Spice Girls?'

Minna Two is a Sami too. Funnily enough none of their reindeer were affected.

We weren't allowed to talk to Minna's family for forty years apparently. This was to do with communism. But we can talk to them now. But as you can see – they don't have much to say.

And so life goes on.

Long live Donald Duck!

Drumbeat.

What is this?

A reindeer.

That is Shitpants. What is this?

A lasso.

That is Shitpants being lassoed.

Some shimmering Sibelius bleeds under the start of the next speech then fades . . .

It takes a long time to become a reindeer man. You can't learn it in college or anything like that. We do environmental science at school and stuff but reindeer husbandry is only chapter twenty-seven. Being a reindeer man is not something you study. It's something you do. It can take, maybe ten, twenty years. Maybe you never stop learning. I got my first one when I was one. That was Flowernose. We all have reindeer. And that's when I got my own sign. The sign is what you cut into the ear of the reindeer. Just a little sign. It hurts no more than if you caught your ear on a tree or a bush. But then I know it's mine. If it gets lost or when it runs with the herd. And my sign is mine for ever. And even when you're one or two you help look after the reindeer as best you can. No one person can look after all their reindeer. You just do what you can, and because everyone has a go all the reindeer are looked after. And I got my first knife when I was two. I carry this round everywhere. So I can cut wood, or if a polecat came or something I could protect myself. Or if I need to cut something. And I will carry this knife until I die. I mean, I might get other knives as well, but this one will be special.

You see, reindeers have to move to stay alive. You can't keep a farm of reindeer in a field. Not that there are any fields. They would just die of starvation. They would eat all the moss in a couple of weeks. And even if you fed them grass or something they would end up with diseases. They have to roam. Each year they go maybe a thousand miles. Through the forests, over the plains. Sometimes right to the sea as far north as you can go. Right to the sea. They get to the sea and turn round and come home. Some get lost. Some are sick or hurt. They might be attacked. And so the reindeer men have to help them. And in the winter, if the ice freezes and they can't cut through the snow to the moss underneath, you have to take them food. If you left everything to nature we'd starve, you'd end up with all your reindeer dead. In the summer when the grass is long, you have to cut it and dry it and keep it for the winter. And in the winter you have to find the reindeer out in the forest. And keep them all alive. Everything we do is for the reindeer.

And there are no roads in the forest where the reindeer go. (Gran only got a road to her house in 1986.) Sometimes you can go by snowmobile. But sometimes you have to go on skis. Out into the forest in the black of winter sometimes for weeks at a time. And there are no maps to teach you. You can't learn where you're going. You have to have the map in your head. It's not something you can see, everything around you is the map, it's not on any piece of paper. The world is the map, every tree and stone and bush, that is the map of the world. Reindeers don't need a map, animals don't need a map and they find their way back after hundred of miles.

And you don't just look after your own. The work of the reindeer is everyone's work. And if the weather turns you

have to go back out even if you've just come home. And so
everyone works for everyone else. This isn't communism or
anything like that. It is just common sense. And we are all
quite well off. Quite 'jabalas' – which means rich, in our
way. We have the Internet and mobile phones and Donald
Ducks et cetera. But we don't spend much. There is nothing
to spend it on. In Sami, 'jabalas' doesn't just mean having
lots of things, or money, it means having knowledge. And at
the end of the year we have the separation. Before the long
winter descends, we collect all the reindeer and each one is
caught and each is divided by the mark on its ear. And the
ones we'll take are taken. And the ones that we let back are
let back. And everyone has their own reindeer to sell, to eat,
to skin for our boots or a drum or whatever. And then
they're let go until the next year; all the work is everyone's
work and the reindeers are free.

The reindeer is a very versatile animal. You can have
reindeer stew, smoked reindeer, reindeer soup, reindeer pie,
reindeer with dumplings, dried reindeer. You can make
shoes out of the skin. You can make tools out of the bones.
You can use the antlers to give to tourists. You can have
reindeer kebabs. Make a drum. You can have roast reindeer
with potatoes. Et cetera.

That's what's funny really. We can't live without the
reindeer, and the reindeer can't live without us. And so it
takes years to learn this. To learn the map of this world.
And sometimes when it is minus forty outside, and it has
been black for the longest time. I sometimes wonder what
it's like to be in a city. But then I know I would be bored.
What is there to do in a city? In your house, with the
pollution, and the drugs, and criminals who will rape you,
and everybody living on top of each other, and if you want
to go swimming you have to pay. Everybody in a city seems
bored. There's nothing to do in a city, except go to work or
go home. But there is always something to do here. In this
fresh air. Every day is full of things to do. And sometimes
you have no choice, and sometimes you have every choice

in the world. I could go swimming, or lassoing or fishing or picking berries or I could go on the Internet or anything. I could do anything.

In the Kalevala. When the sun and moon were formed, the great poet of the North sang his song until the sun stole up from behind the horizon and squatted on the peak of a pine. Then Louhi, the foul-toothed hag, leapt to the tip of the tree and caught the moon and the sun in her hands and brought them to the dark end of the northern lands. And she hid the moon from gleaming in the darkness of a rock and stopped the sun from shining in a mountain of steel and deep they shone, and when no light would escape, she stole the fire from the cabins and from every room a flame and darkness fell on all the land. And there was an endless dark night.

And the Old Man of the skies, watcher of heavens, looked into the pitch and saw no sun or moon. No light in this world and crept along the rim of a cloud, but could see no sun or moon. And seeing that the light of the world had been buried he struck his great sword on his vast fingernail. And it cracked a spark into the high heavens. And so he hid the spark in a golden purse and gave it to the air girl to lull it, to blow it into a new sun and a new moon. And she lulled the fire and wagged the fine flame, and she wagged and lulled till the lids of heaven shone with the fire in her hands, but then she slipped and dropped the saving spark of the heavens and down it fell into the darkness of this world.

And so the great poet set off to find the flame. And sailed the black seas till he came to land and he met an old woman and enquired where he might find the flame that dropped from the sky. And the old woman said that flame had done harsh deeds, that red ball had fell through level heaven and had cleaved the sky and fallen on Thor's cabin where it broke the breasts of his daughters, split the sons' knees and it burnt the child in his cradle, and as the child went to Death, the mother, to save others in this dark world, dropped the last spark into the lake where it boiled the waters and it foamed the elements of water to the brim of the pines, it was just now a spark but it grew as hotter than any fire in the world, and in the chaos of the water a bluish whitefish approached the broken flame and swallowed down the tine of fire to save the world from its destruction. But the pain was immense, and the little blue whitefish, when its woe was too wretched, called to be eaten, so the world would be saved. And then a trout ate the whitefish, till its pain could no longer be borne, and so a pike ate the trout and saving the world swam out into the black. And men lived in darkness as the fish suffered, became grizzled and swam. And so did the great poet decide to catch the beast and sowed a hemp to make a net.

And so he scooped the oceans for the pike. They caught roach and tiddlers and perch and ruffes and bass and bream. But not the pike. And in the vast dark, so they went on fishing for fire. And they sang to the wave-wife, the watery mistress, to give up her goods, and in desperation they beat the water till it gave up all the fish that were in it and there was the grizzled pike. 'Do I dare touch it without mitts of stone?' said the poet. 'Without tongs of iron can I break out the fire?' But on his words from out of the sky came a sword and split the pike, and in the pike was the trout, and in the trout was the blue whitefish and in the whitefish was a red ball, a tine of fire, and it raged up into flame again to scorch the tips of the trees, but the poet took the cold of the North, with the slush of plains and the ice of Lapland he froze back the flame, he froze the ground where it lay and placed it tight in a pot and took it himself to every hearth in the North, and so they got back their fire, and so the craftsmen went back to forging a new sun and moon. And the old hag turned into a dove and flew away.

Sibelius: 'Ekko the Fire God' – inspired by this story.

This was the story-song of the long night. The frozen fire. And deep in the lake was poor Nils Persen, froze upside down as a block of ice. Wormwood in his stomach. And this is just a short version of what I remember. About man and fire, in that ancient darkness.

Anyway, what has it to do with anything?

In the Bible it mentions wormwood. Did you know that? In the book of Revelations.

'And the third angel sounded, and there fell a great star from heaven, burning as it were a lamp, and it fell upon the third part of the rivers, and upon the fountains of waters; and the name of the star is Wormwood; and the third part of the waters became wormwood; and many men died of the waters, because they were made bitter.'

Weird, eh?

Drumbeat.
Silence.
Robbie Williams' 'Angels'.
Silence.

That was Robbie.

Silence.

Last summer we went fishing with Mam. We went in the car to the North to Kelmolk. A hundred kilometres. And it was a day when the sun did not go out. We went to Kelmolk and went in a boat and all afternoon we rowed across the lake. And across the lake, we put on our rucksacks and we walked over the hill for eight kilometres. And then we stopped and we fished and we didn't catch anything at all. And we walked on. And when we were tired we slept in the grass covered in mosquito repellant. We slept and looked up at the bright night sky. And the next day we fished again. In the big northern lake. And I fished and Mam fished. Then suddenly I felt a pull. And I shouted, 'Mam, Mam. There's a fish.' But I couldn't get it up. And then Minna ran down to the bank with the net to pull it up. And then she fell in. But she grabbed the fish and we pulled it out. And its skin was every colour in the world, shining a rainbow in my hands, flipping like a muscle, like the sheen of light. And then I carried on. And Mam carried on. And then Mam caught a fish and it got away. And in the night we slept open

to the heavens as bright as day. And the next day Mam
caught three fish and I caught two. And we walked back
over the hill. And all afternoon we rowed across the lake. In
the summer sun. And we drove back a hundred kilometres.
And I slept in the car when Mam drove. And we cooked the
fish in breadcrumbs for when Dad came home.

Long silence.
Yoik.

I'm not sure. Maybe there are a thousand people who live
north of us. A thousand people. Thirty thousand reindeer. A
million fishes. Who knows. But I think it is about right. I
mean, if more people came that would be fine. But I think at
the moment it's just about right. I love it here.

This is the sound of the world.

The sound of the world.

And there isn't anything in it, that I am not a part of. And
there isn't anything in it, that's not a part of me.

More sound of the world.

I do still get scared in the dark. And if I do sometimes I get
into Minna's bed. Or sometimes I play Robbie Williams. Or
sometimes I just think.

Nothing bad has happened to me. I have my reindeers. I
won three awards at the Inari Lasso Festival. Even when
Grandma died it wasn't so bad. She had been ill so long.
And I didn't really know Nils Persen. The worst thing I
think would be not to become a reindeer man. But there's
always forestry. I could do that. Nothing is bad here. Maybe
the mosquitos.

Things that I like:
Lassoing, fishing, Donald Duck, Shitpants, picking
cloudberries, reindeer racing, swimming. Err.

Things I don't like:
Liver casserole, sausage soup, liver steaks, Ginger Spice,
pollution, drugs, the dark. Mosquitos.

Batman. I don't like Batman.

Drumbeat.
Yoik.

It's hard to know what to say. If I've said enough. Maybe
I've said too much.

What is the sound of this?

Long silence . . .

*. . . long enough for us to be really listening, to be disconcerted . . . as
long as we can bear . . . before it is broken by the . . . credits . . .*